POWER IN STONE

POWER IN STONE

Cities as Symbols of Empire

GEOFFREY PARKER

REAKTION BOOKS

For Julie and Martin

Published by
Reaktion Books Ltd
33 Great Sutton Street
London EC1V 0DX, UK

www.reaktionbooks.co.uk

First published 2014
Copyright © Geoffrey Parker 2014

Printed and bound in Great Britain
by TJ International, Padstow, Cornwall

A catalogue record for this book is available from the British Library

ISBN 978 1 78023 286 7

Contents

Note on Spelling

Historically the spellings of non-English names accord with the way in which these names have normally been pronounced in English. Thus Roma has become Rome, Lisboa has become Lisbon and Bruxelles has become Brussels. This convention has remained largely unchanged over the years.

However, in those parts of the world with entirely different systems of writing and spelling there have been some problems. Very often the form of name used in English has borne little relationship to the actual name and the way it may be written. Thus the names of such Chinese capital cities historically known as Peking, Nanking and Chungking do not correspond with the Chinese pronunciation and the way in which they are written in the Chinese script. In the late twentieth century the adoption of a new transliteration by the Chinese has come to be accepted as being the standard form. As a result the names of these three Chinese capitals are now transliterated as Beijing, Nanjing and Chongqing using the spellings specified by the Chinese themselves. Sometimes this can cause confusion as the new spelling may not correspond at all with the usual western pronunciation. Many new and unfamiliar spellings, such as Qin for Chin and Qing for Ching, have had to be accepted but they can cause confusion among those who find the new transliteration difficult to cope with.

In the case of India, many of the place names, such as Bombay and Calcutta, were originally given by European colonialists and these spellings were in use until quite recently. Major changes did not come about until the early twenty-first century and these have not always come to be widely used. While Bombay is now generally written as Mumbai, names such as Chenai (Madras) and Bharuch (Baroda) have proved less easy for Europeans to accept.

In the case of the spelling of Mongolian names, the fashion for Chinese transliteration has spread to what was for many centuries a Chinese province but which has since the Second World War been an independent country. However, the Chinese transliteration has not been followed here because the older spelling has continued to be widely used both in Mongolia and elsewhere. Thus the spelling Karakorum has been used in preference to Qaraqorum. However, the Mongolians themselves have transliterated names such as Ulan Bator as Ulaan Baatar and this has been followed here.

Some names have a historical use which may have literary and other associations. After the play by Christopher Marlowe the name of the fourteenth-century central Asian conqueror came to be known as Tamburlaine. This was an Elizabethan Anglicization of Timur or Temur Lenk, meaning Timur the Lame. Today the most usual English spelling is Tamerlane, although other transliterations may still be found.

In a similar manner the thirteenth-century Mongol khan and emperor became known as Kubla Khan after the poem by Coleridge. Qubilai Khan, the Chinese transliteration of his name, is accepted here since, although a Mongolian, he was the founder of the Chinese Yuan dynasty.

Overall, the author has aimed to use what is judged to be the most generally accepted and acceptable spellings. In the case of European spellings using the Latin script, the usual English conventions have been followed. Elsewhere while note has been taken of new spellings, and in many cases these have been adopted, in other cases those judged to be most easily understood and accepted by an English-speaking reader have continued to be used.

Prologue: Symbols of Power

'Look on my Works': Ozymandias, King of Kings

I met a traveller from an antique land
Who said: Two vast and trunkless legs of stone
Stand in the desert . . . Near them on the sand,
Half sunk, a shattered visage lies, whose frown,
And wrinkled lip, and sneer of cold command,
Tell that its sculptor well those passions read
Which yet survive, stamped on these lifeless things,
The hand that mocked them, and the heart that fed;
And on the pedestal these words appear:
'My name is Ozymandias, king of kings:
Look on my works, ye Mighty, and despair!'
Nothing beside remains. Round the decay
Of that colossal wreck, boundless and bare
The lone and level sands stretch far away.

'Ozymandias' was written in 1818 and it was seemingly inspired by a visit which Percy Bysshe Shelley made to the British Museum to see the colossal statue of Ramesses II which had been brought there from Egypt a few years previously. This statue certainly astounded all who saw it with the sense of power which emanated from it. It told early nineteenth-century Britons of a great kingdom which had flourished when Britain had still been in the Stone Age.

Ramesses reigned from 1279 to 1213 BC, ruling over a powerful and prosperous kingdom. He was not backward in claiming his share of the credit for this and he left a legacy in which he was the central character and largely the instigator of all that was achieved during this

The statue of Pharaoh Ramesses II in the British Museum.

'Golden Age' of ancient Egypt. He clearly intended that the knowledge of his achievements should be widely known both to his own people and to future generations. An important feature of this self-aggrandizement was his new capital, Pi-Ramesses Aa-nakhtu – meaning the House of Ramesses II – but his most monumental display of power lay elsewhere. He had huge statues of himself placed widely throughout his domains, most significant among which was the vast complex at Thebes known today as the Ramesseum. This complex included a temple, a palace, a treasury and other buildings as well as large numbers of statues. Everything was designed to demonstrate the greatness of the pharaoh and it was here that the statue was found in the early nineteenth century. Originally discovered by Napoleon's Egyptian expedition of 1798–1801, it was the British, one of the principal victors in the Napoleonic wars, who eventually had it removed to their own capital city.

With the Ramesseum the pharaoh sought to display himself as the supreme ruler, but it had another function and this was to present in stone the essentials of successful kingship. Paramount among these was that the king should be at all times visible to his subjects and this Ramesses sought to do through the multiplication of statues of himself throughout his kingdom. There was also the necessity for the king to have divine blessing for his endeavours, and this was ensured by the fact that in ancient Egypt the pharaoh was himself divine. A pronouncement in stone by Ramesses was, 'Listen . . . for I am Râ, lord of heaven, come to earth.' Braudel points out that this divinity was translated into the size and dignity of the monarch as he would have appeared in his statues.[1] It was also essential that he behave as a strong ruler and have success against his foreign enemies. Ensuring prosperity was necessary too, in case of revolt by disaffected subjects, but that had to be a more long-term policy objective. In the words of Neil MacGregor, the director of the British Museum, 'The whole of the Ramesseum conveyed a consistent message of imperturbable success.'[2]

MacGregor considers that Shelley's poem was actually less a meditation on imperial grandeur than on the transience of earthly power. However, it is surely both because the poet stresses that the statue conveys powerfully the grandeur of earthly power which preceded its fall. During the time of this grandeur Egypt was one of the great civilizations of the world and its influence was widely felt. Despite the transience expressed in the conclusion – 'The lone and level sands stretch far away' – ancient Egypt had a profound effect on the whole story of humanity. This was the true legacy of Ramesses II and of the whole of Egyptian history, and the colossal statue in the desert is to be seen as a symbol of this as well as the desolate remains of a vanished empire.

Just as Ramesses emphasized the necessity for kings to be visible, such visibility was intended to convey something specific and this also was accomplished through the medium of stone. 'The frown' and the 'sneer of cold command', as Shelley put it, were intended, in the poet's imagination, to be displays of power.[3] The citizens of the budding British

Empire were certainly astounded and amazed by the sense of power conveyed by this ancient statue. It may have been a power which had by then long vanished, but it had clearly been dominant in the world of its time. And 3,000 years later, early nineteenth-century Britain was about to enter a similar position of dominance but on a far larger world scene. At the end of the same century in which Shelley wrote 'Ozymandias', Rudyard Kipling expressed similar sentiments about the British Empire which was by then about to enter its own period of decline.[4]

The Ramesseum, then, was a kind of textbook for the achievement and retention of power. In many ways, it can be seen as being a kind of stone version of Machiavelli's *Il Principe*, instructions forged in stone for would-be imperialists. It is not clear who might subsequently have read these stones because the remains were found deep in the sands of Egypt by later empire builders, but the principles continued to be followed by subsequent power-seekers. The demonstration of overwhelming power, success against enemies and the achievement of prosperity have all been inherent in subsequent imperial ventures. Until the twentieth century at least, divine approval and guidance have also been vital prerequisites and these have been built into the display of power in stone. Most significant of all, perhaps, has been the visibility of the ruler and of the regime in order to demonstrate its close association with the symbols being displayed.

The transposition to stone of a whole imperial edifice has been found throughout the ages to be an effective way both of overawing the populace and intimidating opponents. It can take the form of statues, pictures, temples, palaces and grand edifices of many sorts. Of course, these must also be linked with other elements in the Ramesseum text-book, most notably effective government, heroic achievements and divine support. All combine to produce the necessary justification for the wielding of power. It is in the city as the centre of power that all these things can most effectively be brought together and combined into a powerful statement. It is there also that the power which is displayed can be wielded to greatest advantage.

Power and Domination: Empires and their Symbols

The idea of empire goes far back into human history and is closely associated with the parallel idea of power and the impulse to control and to dominate. Such organized control can first be observed in the cities of the early civilizations originating in the valleys of the Nile,

Tigris-Euphrates and Indus. The word 'civilization' derives from the Latin *civitas* – city – and the beginnings of civilization are closely linked with the first cities. Stated in the most general terms, civilization can be defined as the culture of cities.[5] There has clearly been a close relationship between the development of humanity, the process of civilizing and the existence of cities.

In the first instance cities came into existence as specialized centres where trade and manufacture could most effectively take place. They were the hubs of the new and more complicated economy which emerged out of the earlier agricultural and pastoral societies. They rapidly accrued other functions and for these, ever more specialist workers were required. Builders were needed for construction and, with increasing sophistication, architects and artists for the design and adornment of churches, temples, castles and the grand palaces of the rich and powerful. This in turn called for the provision of a guaranteed food supply for the increasing numbers who were not actively engaged in producing it. The creation of cities was thus possible only after the development of more intensive food production and this necessitated the domestication of farm animals and the growing of food crops.

Another urban function which appeared early on was the political one, that of the government of the city and of its surrounding region. This required the existence of a state powerful enough to maintain control within the city and to defend it from any external dangers. A class of leaders – kings and princes – arose and their power was associated with that of the cities. They began to build strongholds from which to exercise this power and to ensure their own safety from other would-be leaders who might seek to remove or replace them. The prime external function of these early wielders of power was the defence of their city and its surrounding lands from which came the essential supplies of food and raw materials. As a result of this the whole operation began to assume a wider territorial dimension. Particular cities were chosen as centres for the exercise of power and this was the origin of the 'capital' city from which power was exerted over ever-larger territories. To ensure law and order in the city, leaders required enforcers which necessitated various forms of policing. For the defence of their territory, and eventually for its extension, rulers recruited professional armed forces.

It was out of such enlargement of the territory controlled that the idea of empire was born. More and more territory was added to the emerging system both for the purpose of ensuring its security and in order to increase its wealth-producing capacity. Usually this entailed adding areas and populations which initially at least may have had little in common with the original state. This stage of development may have been accomplished by the dominance of one particular city over others but more usually, and especially in Asia, it was accomplished by an external force which was not initially associated with any one particular city. Such force generally emanated from those pastoral societies which continued to exist in areas more suitable for animal herding than for agriculture. The aggressiveness of such rural populations was motivated by a variety of factors, most commonly centring on the improvement of life and conditions. Their naturally nomadic existence, which often led to confrontation between tribes, adapted them both to rapid movement and to the use of weaponry. They were thus well able to attack and subjugate urban societies which, in spite of their wealth, were often quite unable to defend themselves against the onslaught of such powerful invaders.

Throughout human history there have been many types of empire. These can be classified into three types: continental, marginal and maritime. In this classification, the nature of the empire is dependent largely on the geographical conditions in which the imperial process takes place. The terminology used here is derived from the historical geographer Halford Mackinder, who saw the evolution of political systems as closely related to the location and geographical potential of the areas in which they were located.[6]

The continental empires originated particularly with the peoples of central Asia. These nomadic pastoral societies centred on the steppes, the temperate grasslands of Eurasia, which extend across the continent from the Far East to the Ukraine. From there the pastoral nomadic peoples gradually spread out into the surrounding regions. This spread was caused by many factors, important among which appear to have been population pressures and climate change, both necessitating the search for better grasslands and a more reliable food supply. These societies came to view the sedentary agriculturalists and city-dwellers around the margins of Eurasia with much interest, eventually invading these lands with the aim of being able to have the kind of life which the inhabitants of the cities were perceived to enjoy. An early example of such an aggressive nomadic people were the Assyrians who, in Byron's poem, 'The Destruction of Sennacherib', 'came down like a wolf on the fold', overrunning large areas of the Middle East and establishing a powerful imperial state during the early centuries of the first millennium BC. These were then followed by other similar peoples such as the Medes.

The first great empires, then, were established by these 'imperial nomads' of central Asia, flourishing in both the Asiatic heartland and in the marginal lands around it. Trading contacts between the marginal lands of west and east took place intermittently over the centuries but often the dangers in central Asia made such trade difficult or even impossible. This eventually motivated the nations of the maritime fringes, in particular those of Europe, to seek safer and more reliable routes to the east, leading to the development of sea routes and the beginning of a new form of empire. From the sixteenth century, maritime imperialism produced the dominant form of empire, and by the nineteenth century these empires, based mainly in Western Europe, covered much of the globe. The great exception to this was the enormous Russian Empire, which was highly continental and was viewed by some analysts as being a kind of successor state to that of the Mongols.[3] Its rivalry with the leading maritime empire of the time, the British, led Mackinder to contend that the continental–maritime rivalry was the basic phenomenon of universal history, a contention which has come to be much discussed.

With the approach of the end of maritime imperialism in the middle of the twentieth century, a form of neo-imperialism replaced it. This centred particularly on the United States of America, which was able to build up immense hard and soft power, constituting in effect a non-territorial form of imperialism. It was certainly not empire in the old sense but it represented the projection of power over vast areas, giving the USA the same kind of ascendancy that the old maritime empires held in their heyday. The rivalry between Britain and Russia was now replaced by that between the USA and the Soviet Union. The Cold War between the two continued for most of the second half of the twentieth century. It was not until the twenty-first century that the situation changed radically but, as will be seen, the idea of empire was by no means at an end.

From the outset of the urge to achieve domination over lands and peoples, the symbols for the display of power have always been in evidence. These have been the tangible expressions of the might and magnificence of those who wielded it. It is in cities that such symbols have been brought together most effectively for the purpose of impressing all those who behold them. The principal objective of this was to influence the behaviour of those who beheld it towards a state which possessed such formidable power. While the buildings and their adornments spoke far louder than words, a number of the wielders of power also expressed their meaning and significance. Timur Lenk proclaimed, 'Let he who doubts our power look upon our buildings.'[7]

The main purpose of this book is to examine cities which have been built as symbols of empire and so have been used to display 'power in stone'. While such cities share many common characteristics, there are also many differences among them. Much depends on the nature of the power being wielded and what those who wield it wish to convey. A selection of cities will be examined in terms of what they reveal about power and the way in which they have not only represented it but also contributed to its achievement and maintenance. The cities chosen have been the centres of those great states which have in one way or another been dominating forces in the world of their time. While there have been powerful imperial states in other parts of the world, notably in South America and parts of Africa, it is those of Eurasia which have had the greatest effect on the world as a whole and these will be the main ones to be examined.

The first great power of this type was Persia, and its ceremonial capital Persa, the Greek Persepolis, was the first city to be built specifically for the purpose of displaying power and ensuring that the subject peoples and others were very much aware of it. It was the first capital of a ruler who could assert, with little fear of contradiction, 'Look on my works, ye mighty, and despair.'

Persepolis and the Persian Empire

Persepolis is one of the very earliest examples of a purpose-built imperial city. Here city, throne and power were fused together in a massive display of the magnificence of the Persian Empire which stretched across the ancient world from the interior of Asia to the shores of the Mediterranean.

The Persians were a nomadic people of Aryan stock who had moved southwards from Central Asia to the Iranian plateau around the end of the second millennium BC. Here they came into contact with a far more advanced people, the Medes, and for a time became their vassals. However, relations deteriorated when the Medes became fearful of the growing power of the Persians and decided that it was time to bring them to heel. The Medes invaded Fars, the Persian homeland in the Zagros mountains, but they were defeated at Pasargadae, south of the Zagros mountains, in 550 BC. The Persian king, Cyrus II, pressed home his advantage and attacked Ecbatana, the Median capital. There was little resistance; the Medes' empire collapsed and Cyrus became master of an ever-larger territory. By the middle of the sixth century BC, Cyrus can be considered as having become the world's first true emperor ruling over a huge landmass with a great diversity of peoples. The Persians took over the empire of the Medes and in so doing inherited much of their civilization, including their political organization and the concept of kingship. It was around this time that Cyrus assumed the title of ShahanShah – in ancient Persian 'Khshayathiyanam Khshayathiya' – meaning 'King of Kings' or 'Great King'. The Medes always retained a special position in the Persian Empire and in some ways, as has been wryly observed, the Mede empire did not so much come to an end as undergo a change in management. In many statues and bas-reliefs, the Medes are often depicted as being virtual co-rulers of the empire.

Cyrus proved himself to be a good and wise ruler and invariably treated his new subjects with great care. He allowed them to keep their religions and often their political systems as well. Cultural attributes such as language and customs were not interfered with. He is especially remembered with respect and affection in the Bible for having ended the Babylonian captivity of the Israelites and for allowing them to return to their homeland. He even provided assistance for the rebuilding of the Temple in Jerusalem. In this way, the new empire began as a model for future empires but this was, unfortunately, not followed up by Cyrus's successors. Nevertheless, Cyrus's dynasty, the Achaemenids, continued to rule the enormous Persian Empire for over 200 years.

Cyrus and his successors realized that the Persian dominance over a large part of the known world of the time required some justification and this was provided by religion. The religion of the Achaemenids was Zoroastrianism, a monotheistic faith that had originated in Persia probably in the seventh century BC. It is believed to have been established by the prophet Zoroaster – or Zarathustra – and it centred on the worship of Ahuramazda, the 'Wise One', who was invoked to protect the dynasty. Ahuramazda is usually represented as a winged disc known as the Faravahr, which is the sign of divine glory. The god has also sometimes been represented as a human figure. The Zoroastrian religion involved what has often been thought of as fire worship. In fact it was nothing of the kind and the constantly burning flame in the Zoroastrian temples was there to represent purity and goodness. Ceremonies associated with the eternal flame were central to the rituals of the religion. The whole world was seen as a place of conflict between the good spirit, Spenta Mainyu, and the evil spirit, Angra Mainyu. The rise and success of the Achaemenid dynasty was always closely associated with this religion and its kings were believed to hold their office directly from Ahuramazda. Zoroastrianism always retained a central role in the Persian Empire and in its symbolism. Its importance is seen very clearly in the temples and the inscriptions, in stone and precious metals, which have been found throughout Fars. One of the earliest of these is the gold tablet of King Ariaramnes, an indirect ancestor of Cyrus II, which is known to have been used by Cyrus. It reads as follows:

Ariaramnes, the great King, the King of kings, the King in Persia, Teispes the King and grandson of Achaemenes. Ariaramnes the King says : this country Persia, which I hold, which is possessed of good horses, good men, on me the great God Ahuramazda bestowed [it]. By the favour of Ahuramazda I am the King [in] this country Ariamnes the King says : may Ahuramazda bear me aid.[1]

It is believed by some historians that Cyrus may have found this tablet and transferred it to his own palace so as to be associated with both Ahuramazda and with his illustrious ancestor.

Early on Cyrus realized the importance of establishing a capital city from which the empire would be ruled and, following his victories in the west, he returned to the Persian homeland of Fars and there embarked on the building of a great palace at Pasargadae. Called in old Persian Pasragarda, meaning 'camp of the Persians', this had been an early gathering point for the nomadic Persian tribes. Later it was the site of the great victory over the Medes and so held a position of considerable importance for the Persians. It was seen as being where the Persian Empire had originated and so it rapidly gained the aura of being a sacred place. This was chosen to become Cyrus's de facto capital for the rest of his reign.

With the death of Cyrus in 528 there was a struggle for the succession and after the short reign of his son Cambyses II, during which the empire continued to grow in size, the throne passed to another branch of the dynasty and Darius I ascended the throne as Great King. While Cyrus had established his capital at Pasargadae, Darius, at first uneasy on his throne, decided that a new purpose-built capital was necessary as a clear demonstration of his own power. The new capital was intended to be a symbol of his own reign and so would distance him from his illustrious predecessor. However, Pasargadae was chosen as the site for the splendid white limestone tomb of Cyrus, built to reinforce its position as the most sacred place for the Persians. Darius chose a site some 50 kilometres to the southwest for his new capital Parsa, which was to become known to the Greeks as Persepolis. It was to be Darius's greatest building project and the most important symbol of his power.

The city is located on the plain of the Marv-e Dasht, surrounded by high mountains. There appear to have been many reasons for the choice of this particular site for the project, a number of them relating to Persian history and mythology. The tales of the early Persian kings were collected by the great Persian epic poet, Ferdusi, in the Shahnameh, the Epic of the Kings,[2] and the area around Persepolis was believed to have had associations with the mythical early kings of Persia. The most important of these was Jamshid, and Persepolis came to be familiarly known as Takht-e Jamshid, 'The Throne of Jamshid'. The area is also

The Tomb of Cyrus the Great at Pasargadae.

traditionally the home of Rustum, the great Persian hero best known in English through Matthew Arnold's poem 'Sohrab and Rustum'. The importance of the sun, and possibly sun worship, can also be seen in the fact that the eastern entrance of the city has been aligned in accordance with the point at which the sun rises over the plain on the summer solstice.

As is usually the case, besides these mythical origins, there were also more practical reasons for the selection of the site. The city is located deep in the Zagros mountains at a height of 1,500 m. This would have made it a cooler place for the court to reside than the low-lying land of Mesopotamia where Susa, the city where the day to day running of the empire actually took place, was located. The Persians, who had come from the north, would certainly have preferred this climate and the landscape which surrounded the city would also have been far more congenial to them. The site is also in the valley of the Kor river which would have provided a water supply for the population. As the population grew, ample water could also have been brought down from the surrounding mountains using the intricate system of underground watercourses, the canats, which the Persians had invented. The Kor followed a structural depression in the Zagros which is aligned from northwest to southeast, facilitating communication with Susa and other major centres of the empire. The great axis of communication of the empire was the 'Royal Road' which connected Sardis with Susa and was later extended eastwards to Persepolis itself. Finally the importance of the geology cannot be underestimated. The local limestone was easy to work and proved to be an ideal material for the great buildings and monuments of the city. Thus a powerful combination of mythological, historical and geographical factors combined to produce what must have been judged at the time to be the most appropriate site for the location of Darius's imperial capital.

Work on Persepolis commenced around 520 BC. The city was built on an immense platform which rises some 15 m above the surrounding land. Besides providing stability for the foundations, this would have made the city visible from a greater distance and enhanced its effect on all those who approached it. It was intended above all to be a demonstration of the power of the ShahanShah and of the empire over which he ruled. The main entrance to the city was a flight of steps shallow enough to allow for horses. The whole city was clearly designed with ceremonial purposes very much in mind. Its architecture was derived from that of the conquered peoples, in particular the Assyrians and Babylonians, but it possessed a greater sophistication than either. The brutal ostentation of the Assyrians was softened by the Persian architects.[3] At the top of the steps the Gate of All Nations leads into the Apadana, the great hall where many ceremonies of state took place. Another unfinished gate on the same side of the platform leads to the Hall of the Hundred Columns. This was also used for ceremonial purposes. In both of these halls at various times state business would have been conducted and the Great King would have received the homage of his subjects. There was also another massive building on the platform housing the state treasury. As Persepolis was the place where tribute was received, the stored wealth of the dynasty had to be safeguarded. The decoration of the Apadana centred on the twin bull capitals surmounting the pillars which are also to be found elsewhere in the palace.

Among the most telling carvings are those along the wall of the monumental staircase leading up to the Gate of All Nations. Here bas-reliefs depict the subject peoples climbing the steps and bearing the annual tribute for the Great King. In many cases it is possible to make out from their dress and appearance, and from the gifts they are bearing, the lands from which they came. This is confirmed by the inscriptions found in and around the city. While on the gold tablet of Ariaramnes there was great emphasis on Persia and its virtues, by the time of Darius it was rule over the vast imperial possessions which was being justified. Such an inscription in Persepolis reads:

Persepolis: Bas-relief of Darius the Great at the head of the Great Stairway.

I am Darius, the Great King, the King of kings, the King of countries, which [are] many , the son of Hystaspes, an Achaemenian.

Darius the King says: by the favour of Ahuramazda these [are] the countries, which I acquired, with this Persian people, which had fear of me [and] bore me tribute – Elam, Media – Babylonia – Arabia – Assyria – Egypt – Armenia – Cappadocia – Sardis – the Ionians, those of the mainland, and those of the sea – Sagartia – Parthia – Drangiana-Bactria – Sogdiana – Choriasmia – Sattagydia – Arachosia – India – Gandara – the Scythians – Maka.[4]

On the bas-reliefs the Elamites bring a snarling lioness, the Bactrians a two-humped camel, the Egyptians a bull and the Ethiopians elephant tusks. The Indians have axes and a donkey. The Armenians are shown holding a horse and a large vase and the Assyrians a bull and spears. Undoubtedly many of these things would have been symbolic and the real tribute would be of gold and other precious metals destined for the treasury.

The Medes are also depicted on the bas-reliefs. Although also subjects of the Persians, they were always accorded a privileged position and were respected as the people who had made possible the great achievements of the Persians. The Persian relationship to the Medes was similar to that of the Romans to the Greeks; they were the civilizers and mentors of the imperial people. On the grand staircase, while the Medes had the honour of leading the procession, they are also shown in the role of officials conducting the ceremony.

Halfway up the grand staircase, on the wall behind the guards, was the Faravahr, the winged sun disc and symbol of Ahuramazda. Forbis considered this staircase to be 'perhaps the most engrossing socio-historical documentary ever put into stone' and 'a hand-chiselled filmstrip of obeisance to the emperor'.[5]

The two doorjambs of the Gate of All Nations at the top of the stairway are faced with the figures of the winged bull, bearded and crowned. Over the gate is another bas-relief of the winged god Ahuramazda. The level of the Apadana audience chamber was raised above that of the rest of the platform. There Ahuramazda is also protecting the Throne of the Great King. It was in this hall that Darius and his successors would have received the homage of the representatives of the subject peoples and the tribute which they brought.

Bas-reliefs on the Great Stairway at Persepolis showing subject peoples of the Persian Empire bearing gifts to the Great King.

It is not possible adequately to understand any great Persian building project without including the gardens surrounding the buildings.
These were always of great importance as they were both places of
relaxation and demonstrations of wealth and power. The Persian word
for garden, *paradiso*, actually means an enclosed space and this has given
rise to the word 'paradise'. This also later became associated with a
whole complex of buildings and gardens. It therefore represented an
integrated townscape proclaiming both the splendour and the power of
the Great King. This holistic Persian concept was later taken up by the
other peoples who were influenced by them.

The building work at Persepolis begun by Darius was later
continued by his son and grandson, Xerxes and Artaxerxes. The whole
area around the capital became part of an extended sacred region for
the Persians but Pasargadae retained its special position as the site of
the tomb of Cyrus the Great and so of veneration for the founder of
the imperial dynasty. The two were close enough to be linked both as
twin symbols of the Empire and as justifications for its existence. It
was in Pasargadae rather than Persepolis that the elaborate
coronation ceremonies of the Great Kings were conducted. However,
other royal tombs were located in Persepolis or nearby. The tombs of
the successors of Darius I, including Artaxerxes II and III, are on the
hill immediately overlooking the city. Some 10 kilometres to the north
of Persepolis is Naqsh-i Rustam where the tombs of Darius and other
successors were carved out of the rock face. On the tomb of Darius
there is again an inscription justifying the world dominance of Persia.
It includes the following :

> Darius the King says: Ahuramazda, when he saw the earth
> disturbed, after that bestowed it on me; made me king. I am the
> King . . . Ahuramazda bore me aid until I did what has to be done
> . . . Me may Ahuramazda preserve from harm, and my house and
> this country . . . I am the friend of right. I am not the friend of wrong
> . . . He who does harm, he according to the harm so I punish.[6]

This constitutes one of the first clear statements of imperialism. Thus
within this small area the Great Kings were crowned, buried and the
record of their achievements was recorded in the rock.

Hicks saw Persepolis as having been 'a gigantic living monument
– a conspicuous demonstration of the Persians' rise from rude nomads
to world masters, a colossally immodest salute to their own glory'.[7] It was

The Tomb of
Darius the Great
at Naqsh-i Rustam
near Pasargadae.

certainly perhaps the most ambitious building project ever undertaken
up to that time.

The Greeks were the only significant people the Persians failed to
add to their empire. Their cause was championed by the Macedonians,
whose aristocracy was highly Hellenized, and this military people were
to be the downfall of the Persian Empire. In 335 BC Alexander of Macedon
(Alexander the Great) attacked the Persians and defeated them. The
last Achaemenid king, Darius III was killed by his bodyguards and in
331 Alexander was himself proclaimed 'King of Kings'. He reached
Persepolis in 330 BC and, as a demonstration of his victory and his
contempt for the Persians, set it on fire. The city was reduced to ruins and
was never used as a capital again. It had been the symbol of an empire
that was always alien to the Greeks and Alexander had other plans for
his new empire. He endeavoured to Hellenize the conquered lands and
planted cities, modelled on the Greek *polis*, across them. These cities,
among them many 'Alexandrias', were key to the process of Hellenization.[8]

The Persian King Shapur I accepting the surrender of the Roman emperor Valerian; rock relief near Naqsh-i Rustam.

Immediately to the east of Persepolis he established the *polis* of Gulashkerd, which was one of many in the historic Persian lands. Alexander intended the capital of his new empire to be at or near to Babylon, but he died there in 323 at the age of 36, well before his empire could be consolidated. Greek cities were established as far east as Afghanistan and Central Asia but Hellenization was patchy and many of these cities soon lost their Greek identity, merging into their oriental surroundings. Alexander's only real legacy in this respect was Alexandria in Egypt which, although a splendid city that for a time became the centre of the Greek world, was never the centre of an empire.[9]

After the Hellenistic period and a Parthian interlude, the Persians resumed their imperial power and the Sassanian dynasty was established in AD 224. The first king of this second Persian Empire was Ardashir I, himself from Fars, a fact he used to claim legitimacy for his dynasty as successor to the Achaemenid. His own successor was Shapur I, who resumed the style 'ShahanShah' and adding the title 'of Iran and non-Iran'. Although the capital of this new empire was Ecbatana on the route to Mesopotamia, the 'sacred lands' around Pasargadae and Persepolis retained their significance. Here are found the tombs of the Sassanian kings and rock carvings of events in Persian history dating from this period.

The main external confrontation of this second Persian Empire was with the Romans who were by this time bent on extending their power eastwards from the Mediterranean into the Middle East. The Persian-Roman confrontation was to last for many centuries and dominated the foreign policies of both empires. One of the most noteworthy of the carvings at Naqsh-i Rustam dating from this period depicts the triumph of the Persians over the Romans. Shapur I, on horseback, is seen receiving the surrender of the Roman emperor Valerian who had been captured in battle in AD 260. The humbled emperor is on his knees before the ShahanShah. While this second Persian Empire did not have the triumphant success of the first, it certainly proved a match for Rome.

The Persepolis capital region continued to retain its significance until the fall of the Persian Empire to the forces of Islam in 651. Nine years earlier the Arabs had swept through the ruins of the old capital and many of the carvings with human figures were defaced. They were deemed to be un-Islamic as was the old Zoroastrian religion. Persepolis soon disappeared beneath the dust and sand of the semi-desert and the main centres of Islamic power were located elsewhere.

While Persepolis remained a legendary capital, evidence of its existence was lost in the sand for many centuries. It was rediscovered by travellers in the eighteenth century and excavated by archaeologists in modern times. In the 1970s it was to have one more moment of quasi-imperial glory when Reza Shah Pahlavi used it as the backdrop for a great – and final – celebration of his country's dynastic heritage.

2

'Three Romes': City-state, *Imperium* and Christian Capital

The concept of the 'Three Romes' was formulated by the monk Filofei (Philotheus) of Pskov, who wrote an epistle on the subject to Grand Prince Vasili III of Moscow (1505–33). In this the monk made the following assertion:

> The First Rome fell because of the Apollinarian heresy,[1] the second Rome, Constantinople, was captured and pillaged by the infidel Turks, but a new Third Rome has sprung up in thy sovereign kingdom. Thou art the sole king of all the Christians in the world.

Filofei then concluded his epistle with an apocalyptic statement: 'Two Romes have fallen, but the Third Rome, Moscow, will stand, a fourth is not to be.'[2]

The 'Romes' about which Filofei was talking were, of course, the three successive centres of European power during its long conflict with the Asiatic empires. It was the Greeks who first made the distinction between 'Europe', by which they meant the Hellenic world, and 'Asia', the eastern lands which since the sixth century BC had been dominated by the huge and menacing empire of Persia. The Great Kings Darius and Xerxes had both attempted to subjugate the Greeks but neither of them had been successful, and this proved in the end to be the Achaemenid dynasty's greatest failure. The second Persian Empire, that of the Sassanians, found itself very soon up against the Romans, the powerful successors to the Greeks and heirs to Hellenic civilization. Like the Greeks, a Mediterranean people, the Romans were ambitious to dominate the Middle East, and by the second century AD the eastern frontier of the Roman Empire had reached the Euphrates. From the outset, the new Persian Empire was forced to look westwards to confront this danger to their historic hegemony over Mesopotamia. For much of their existence these two empires were in conflict with one another, a conflict which very often led to open warfare.

While Persepolis and its surroundings remained sacred space to the Sassanians, as a result of this threat from the west they moved their capital and principal base of operations to Ctsesiphon in Mesopotamia. This city was just north of Babylon and on the other side of the Tigris from Seleucia, the colony established by the Hellenistic Seleucid kings. Its choice reflects the western orientation of the empire and its preoccupation with the conflict with Rome. It was thus in, Vaughan Cornish's terminology, a 'forward capital' – a capital close to the endangered frontier, designed to mobilize the resources of the state to remove the threat and secure the vulnerable frontier regions.[3]

Rome had begun life as a city-state, much like those of Greece, but it soon diverged from the classical city-state model and was successful in achieving a position of dominance over Italia, the name at that time given to the Italian peninsula south of the Rubicon river. The Italian *urbs* had never been quite the same as the Greek *polis* and in any case the situation in the Italian peninsula was very different from that of Greece.[4] It was this difference which enabled Rome to achieve a dominating position of a kind in Italia which Athens had attempted but never achieved in Greece. Using this as a springboard, and defeating Carthage (its main rival in the western Mediterranean), by the first century BC Rome had secured control over almost the whole of the inland sea. As a result, this became *Mare Nostrum*, 'our sea', and it soon resumed the role it had fulfilled in the time of the Greeks and Phoenicians as a great routeway for maritime trade. However, this time it was not divided and the main beneficiary from the trade was Rome. The major trade routes of the Mediterranean now converged on Portus, the port of Rome, and the supply of the growing metropolis with its increasing needs became its most important function. All roads, by land and sea, soon led to Rome.

Rome had evolved from a city-state into an empire and so, unlike Persepolis, it was not one of those cities built for this specific purpose. The 'Seven Hills' of Rome each display different facets of the city and the successive stages in its evolution. The oldest was the Palatine Hill, retaining its vestiges of the old city-state, while the adjacent Capitoline Hill was the location of the Capitol from which the consuls and senators governed Rome and its possessions. As Edward Gibbon puts it, 'The hill of the Capitol was the head of the Roman Empire, the citadel of the earth, the terror of kings.'[5] Besides this, as the site of the all-important temple of Jove (Jupiter) it was also a sacred place. In between the hills was the Forum, and many other principal state buildings and temples to the gods of this polytheistic empire were located around this. At its centre was the *Lapis Niger*, the black stone which was by tradition the tomb of Romulus, the legendary founder of the city. Nearby also was the Coliseum which was the foremost place of mass entertainment, much of it involving gladiatorial combats. Grand as they were, these buildings had been constructed over a period of time and gave the impression of being thrown together in a jumble rather than set out to produce an impressive ensemble at the heart of the empire.

Although Rome was far from being a city built as a symbol of empire, it is scarcely possible to pass over it when dealing with the subject of imperial cities. As has been observed, the basic concept of empire as understood in the western world derives from Rome and most of the terminology of empire and imperialism used in the west is of Latin origin. The city of Rome, the *urbs romana*, was transformed within a century into the *Imperium Romanum*. Initially this *imperium* signified the authority granted by the senate to officials of the Roman state for the performance of specific tasks in its name. During the period of the Roman Republic, *imperium* could be exercised only outside Italia itself, and under the strict supervision of the senate, but this all changed when Julius Caesar began the transformation of a limited and specific *imperium* into total authority throughout the domains of Rome. In 49 BC he led his army across the Rubicon river, the northern boundary of Italia, and by this act defied the power of the senate in Rome. This precipitated a political crisis during which Caesar was assassinated. After the civil war which followed, Octavian, Caesar's designated heir, was in 27 BC accorded the title of *Princeps* and the right of unlimited *imperium* was bestowed on him. This was the *imperium maius* and from then on its holder styled himself *Imperator*. Octavian took the imperial name 'Augustus' and began the process by which emperors asserted their power more and more and justified this by claiming divinity. The religious and political authority of Rome had become fused into one.

In this way the last vestiges of the city-state were removed and Rome was transformed into a vast and tightly controlled territorial state. The Mediterranean world dominated by Rome had become in many ways very similar to Persia, which had been so reviled by the Greeks for its authoritarianism and lack of freedom. This was part of what the Greeks called 'Asiatic' and which they condemned for the total absence of those features they considered 'European'. These they considered essential to the civilized life.

Many new cities were built in the Roman Empire but these *civitates* were closely bound up with overall Roman rule and never possessed the independence and freedom that was a principal feature of the Greek *polis*. They were little more than municipal towns with Roman magistrates as their governors. At the same time Rome itself was being transformed with grand buildings but it soon grew so enormous and unsanitary that it was not a place in which the emperors wished to spend much time.

In many ways Rome's continuing strength was less as a city than as an idea. This arose from the internal peace existing within the empire and the protection it afforded, initially in the Hellenic world but subsequently northwards into Europe and eastwards to the Middle East. 'Civis Romanus sum' became a guarantee of safety throughout the vast territories of the empire. Such was the power of this idea that by the third century it had become virtually impossible for those living within its boundaries to conceive of a world without Rome as its unifier and protector. It was widely believed that 'quando cadet Roma, cadet et mundi' (when Rome falls, the universe will fall with it). In other words the stability of everything was increasingly seen as being dependent on the existence of the great city itself.

From early in its history, the Roman Empire had been faced with two major problems, one outside and the other inside its boundaries. Outside were its enemies who coveted the territory it had occupied and pacified. Initially, the most dangerous of these were the Persians in the east and the barbarians in the north. Inside the Empire the problem was the arrival of a new religious sect, Christianity, the origins of which were almost coincidental with those of the Roman Empire itself. It was a Middle Eastern religion and from the outset it presented a totally different model of life from that of Rome. While the Romans, like the Greeks, were polytheistic, the new religion was monotheistic and had evolved a system of beliefs quite different from those of Rome. Unlike the Achaemenids who had been tolerant and even supportive of the many religions practised by their subject peoples, the Romans encouraged and even expected their subjects to worship their gods. Since the emperor himself claimed divinity, the fusion of the political and religious meant that the worship of the Roman gods was seen as being a basic requirement of loyalty to the Empire.

These external and internal conflicts plagued the Roman Empire for the greater part of its existence. The singular antipathy to Christianity had its origins in Rome's relations with the Jews who had from the outset been very reluctant to accept its hegemony. The fact that relations were so bad may have contributed to the savage persecution of the Christians which followed. This included the use of Christians as victims in the bloody entertainments that took place in the Coliseum, involving gladi-ators and lions. Such persecutions continued until the fourth century AD but, despite this, Christianity continued to make inroads throughout the Empire and its inexorable advance was noted in the highest imperial circles.

In 303 the emperor Diocletian staged what was to be the last per-secution of Christians. Three years later Constantine was proclaimed Caesar in York.[6] He had a very different attitude to Christianity from that of his predecessors, realizing that it would be more sensible to come to terms with Christians rather than persecuting them. Ten years later Constantine defeated his rival Maxentius at the battle of the Milvian Bridge. According to the legend, before the battle he had seen the vision of a cross in the sky above the battlefield bearing the words 'In hoc signo vinces'.[7] If his victory was the work of the Christian God, then it certainly seemed propitious to have this God on the side of Rome rather than against her. The following year all persecution came to an end and in 314 the Edict of Milan gave official toleration to Christians. After some 300 years, Christianity had attained the same legal status as paganism. This acceptance of the Christian God was the most profound ideological change ever to take place in the Roman Empire. It also heralded the most fundamental geopolitical change ever to take place and this was the definitive transfer of the centre of power away from Rome.

By the third century Rome was already losing its significance as the heart of the Empire. By then the real centre of government was where the emperor happened to be at any particular time, and this had often been with the army in the frontier zones. A line of important cities close to the most vulnerable frontiers stretched southeastwards across Europe and into the Middle East. These were the main bases of military operations and they included Colonia Claudia Ara Agrippinensium (Cologne), Mediolanum (Milan), Sirmium (Sremska Mitrovica), Sardica (Sofia), Nicomedia (Izmit) and Antioch (Antakaya). It was among these cities that the real military and political power of the Empire lay and for a time they came to possess the joint role of 'forward capitals' in the sense understood by Vaughan Cornish. Diocletian himself rarely visited Rome. He is said to have come to the capital in his official capacity only once and that was in 302 for his formal Triumph. This was the last such great imperial ceremony ever held in Rome. It is significant that Diocletian was also the first emperor to move his official capital eastwards and for this he chose Nicomedia on the extended frontier line. This city was on the eastern shore of the Propontis (Sea of Marmara) and so was actually in Asia Minor. As the city of Rome itself became more and more irrelevant, the Empire became increasingly focused on the eastern threat.

Constantine likewise did not make Rome his capital. To him Rome was not only badly located for the running of the Empire but was too full of associations with paganism. He immediately determined to embark on the building of a new city and for this he chose a site close to Nicomedia but on the European shore of the Propontis. It was named after the emperor himself and its official designation was 'Constantinople, New Rome'. From the outset it was seen as a second Rome. To Constantine the city was the new 'Christian capital' of the Roman Empire, as opposed to Rome which had been the old pagan one. It was dedicated to the Blessed Virgin much in the way that pagan cities had their own patron gods or goddesses. He maintained that the choice of site was inspired by divine intervention. In the words of Emil Ludwig, 'According to legend the Emperor began to lay the foundations of his city in Scutari on the far shore. But eagles snatched the surveying lines, carrying them across the Sea of Marmara and dropping them in Europe.'[8] However, just to be sure, Constantine is said to have consulted the Delphic oracle as well.

There were also sound geographical and geopolitical reasons for moving the capital to the east. The place chosen was the site of the old Greek city of Byzantium which had an important commercial role in the Hellenic world. It was a port with excellent maritime communications between the Black Sea and the Aegean and was also on the land route to the east across the Balkans into Asia Minor. While this sea route across the Black Sea led to Colchis, the land of the Golden Fleece, there was another maritime route northwards to the mouth of the Dnieper river and this connected with the great river route via the Dnieper and the Volkhov to the Baltic Sea. This route was later followed by the men of Rus', the first Russians, who travelled along it from their Scandinavian homeland and founded the first Russian cities. Along this 'Route from the Varangians to the Greeks' came not only trade with the capital of the Empire but a host of other Greek influences, political, cultural and religious.

In this way, the new capital was well located both with a trading system which had existed over the centuries and one which would gain importance in the centuries to come. Its site also confirmed that eastern orientation which had long underlain Rome's foreign policy. From the outset, the Roman Empire had justified itself as being the protector of the Hellenic world and now, at the beginning of the fourth century, it was moving its centre of power into that world and so becoming more a part of it than ever before. In addition to this, the Greek lands were among the richest parts of the Empire, with valuable commodities like precious stones and spices carried there from the east on the trade routes. The centre of political power was now also moving into the centre of economic power.

Finally there were, of course, specific military reasons for the move. The greatest external dangers to the Empire came from the east. The Persians had been the age-old enemy of the Greeks and by this time the Sassanians ruled over the most powerful state with which Rome had to contend. Most of the emperors had fought, and some had died, in the eastern campaigns. It was the object of the Romans to defeat this old enemy conclusively and so to secure a dominant position in the Middle East. Another factor reinforced the military reasons for the move and this was the appearance of a further external danger – the barbarians, who had begun moving westwards and by the fourth century had reached the frontiers of the Empire. It was also a reason for the increasing importance of the great line of cities from Colonia to Antioch and it is significant that Constantine, like his predecessor Diocletian, chose to build his new capital on this line. This particular external danger to the Empire was most in evidence in the eastern frontier regions where the barbarians had begun to move southwards towards the Danube. The site chosen for the new capital was thus very suitable to deal with the threats on both the Danubian and the eastern – Mesopotamian – frontiers.

Besides its strategic position, the site of the new city was spectacular. It was maritime, lying between the Sea of Marmara and the Black Sea. It also had its own protected harbour, the Golden Horn, which allowed the sea to stretch well into the heart of the city. The city was built with great care and splendour. Very little of the old Greek city remained except for the Acropolis which was one of the few earlier buildings to be incorporated into the new city. The Roman city centred on the Forum Augusteum and close to this was the imperial residence facing the sea. This was subsequently joined by a number of other residences built by later emperors. To the west of the Acropolis was the Hippodrome; other forums, including the Forum of Constantine, were also located nearby. Although designated by Constantine, as 'the Christian Capital', many signs of the old paganism continued to survive. Initially, at least, the new Christian empire was tolerant of other religious beliefs and was disinclined to abandon its pagan past completely. The glory of Rome itself was certainly not to be completely forgotten in the new capital. The Hippodrome incorporated the temples of Castor and Pollux and on one side of it was the tripod belonging to the Delphian Apollo, on which stood an image of the deity. Indeed, paganism persisted to such an extent that nearly half a century after Constantine, the emperor Julian was motivated to bring back the old religion. By that time the hold of Christianity was such that his attempt proved unsuccessful. Nevertheless, paganism was never far below the surface of the early Christian empire.

What is most significant about Constantinople is the fusion of Greek and Roman which can be seen in both religion and architecture. The Greek names 'Byzantium' and 'Byzantine' were used from early on and eventually, following the fall of the western empire to the barbarians, the name Byzantine Empire came to be generally adopted.

That the city built by Constantine and embellished by his successors was indeed a new Christian capital was evidenced by the large number of churches and other religious buildings which it contained. At its centre was the greatest Christian church of all, the cathedral known as Hagia Sofia in Greek and Santa Sophia in Latin. Although it can now be seen as the epicentre around which the city's life revolved, it was actually built well after the reign of Constantine, during that of the dynamic sixth-century emperor Justinian who is best remembered for having made one last attempt to reclaim the western regions of the empire from the barbarians.

Hagia Sofia was the largest Christian church ever to have been built up to that time and was designated as the mother church of Christianity in both the city and the Empire. It was built between 533 and 537 and its architects claimed that its design derived not from them but from 'the celestial inspiration of the Emperor'. It is indeed considered the supreme example of the Byzantine church form and was clearly intended as a demonstration of the power and splendour of the Eastern Roman Empire. Gloag commented that 'the arch principle employed with mathematical precision and intellectual felicity . . . gave to the interior of Justinian's church that vivacious interplay of ascending and expanding curves. The masterpiece was never repeated.' Overall the result, wrote Gloag, was to produce 'a grave richness of effect . . . the light descending from above, light pouring through innumerable arched windows, [which] gives new and exotic values to form and colour'.[9] No other building encapsulates so well both the splendour of the new Christian empire and its theocratic character. From then on most of the great ceremonies of state of the eastern empire took place there and it gained a significance far greater than that of any of the secular buildings in the city.

The interior of Hagia Sofia.

The basileus – emperor – was and remained closely bound up with the Christian Church, which came increasingly to have the role of principal justification for the existence of the state. The basileus and the patriarch, respectively heads of state and Church, took on the role of its joint leaders. In the words of Browning, the emperors 'saw the Empire as a unique political entity, the heir of the Roman Empire of pagan times, with its pretensions to universality. They also saw it as a unique theological entity, a part of God's grand design for the salvation of mankind.'[10] This fact is emphasized in icons in Hagia Sofia and elsewhere that depict emperor and patriarch together with Christ.

At the end of the fourth century the emperor Theodosius divided the increasingly unwieldy Empire into two distinct parts for purposes of administration. On his death in 395 this division became a permanent one along what came to be known as the 'Theodosian line'. Justinian's attempt to bring back the western empire was a complete failure as by then the barbarians were firmly in control of the western half. Yet the eastern empire was to last for another 1,000 years. Its longevity compared to the western empire was remarkable. It owed much to the wealth of its territories and its possession of a readily defensible core area centring on the Aegean Sea. Constantinople, although a latecomer, rapidly became pre-eminent among the line of frontier cities stretching from Colonia to Asia Minor. Indeed, it was transformed into what in the Middle Ages came to be regarded throughout Europe as the greatest city in the world. While it was a forward capital, it was also well located as both a political, economic and military centre of power.

Unlike Rome, which had been abandoned early on, Constantinople was to remain the centre of both political and religious authority until its fall. The nature of the Byzantine Empire is clearly seen in a mosaic depicting the emperor Justinian presenting a model of Hagia Sofia to the Virgin. It is also evident in a marble sculpture nearby depicting the emperor in a triumphant pose mounted on a horse. According to Browning this emperor could be either Justinian or his predecessor Anastasius. Below him are subjects bearing tribute and above him is the figure of Christ bearing the Cross. The comparison with the tribute bearers in Persepolis, bringing their tribute to the Great King protected by Ahuramazda, makes very clear the similarity between the two empires by this time. Their religions may have been very different but the use made of them for political purposes was virtually identical. While retaining its Hellenic features and appearance, what had been the bastion of Europe against Asia had itself become orientalized.

It was during the reign of Heraclius (610–41) that the name of the eastern Roman Empire was officially changed to the Byzantine Empire, representing the completion of the process of at least a linguistic Hellenization. By that time it had detached itself completely from the barbarian-dominated west in all except religion, where the authority of the pope, the bishop of Rome, was still recognized. In 1054 this situation came to an end and the Orthodox Christian Church declared itself autonomous. The patriarch was now head of a completely independent church with Constantinople, and the great church of Hagia Sofia in particular, as its undisputed centre.

Heraclius was soon victorious over the Persians but the Byzantine triumph was to be short lived. The biggest change since the establishment of the Persian Empire more than a millennium earlier was soon to take place in the Middle East. In the early seventh century a new religion came into being in the Arab world, arising from the revelatory ideas of the Prophet Mohammed. This was Islam and in 632, following the death of the Prophet, the Arabs began the process of creating their own theocratic empire. Both Byzantium and Persia were attacked by increasingly

Mosaic of Emperor Justinian presenting a model of Hagia Sofia to the Virgin.

powerful Arab armies imbued with the new faith. While the Byzantines successfully resisted the onslaught, the Persians did not. In 637 the Persian capital, Ctesiphon, fell and within twenty years their empire had ceased to exist, becoming absorbed into the growing Arab empire which soon covered most of the Middle East. Although the Byzantine Empire lost a good deal of its newly acquired eastern territory, it was able to hold the Arabs at bay and survive their onslaught. The forces of Islam, successful across the southern shores of the Mediterranean and Spain, were halted well before the gates of Constantinople. The following centuries, however, were to be turbulent ones and in 1204 Constantinople was occupied by the Crusaders who established a Latin kingdom there. Although this lasted less than 60 years, the empire had been greatly weakened by the episode and its boundaries continued to contract. The relative smallness of its territory now made it easier to defend and this, in part at least, accounts for its endurance.

By the eleventh century a new and dynamic people had arrived in the Islamic world. These were the Seljuk Turks from Central Asia. Moving westwards against the Byzantines, they wrested control of Anatolia from them, something the Arabs had never succeeded in doing. There they became sedentary and established their own version of Rome, the Sultanate of Rum, which for a time coexisted relatively peacefully alongside the Byzantine Empire. The desire to replicate Rome was present even in these Islamic people.

Finally, in the thirteenth century a new and still more warlike Turkish tribe moved southwards. These were the Osmanlis, the men of Osman, who were to become known to history as the Ottomans. They established themselves in Anatolia on the frontiers of the Byzantine Empire and in so doing defeated and replaced the Seljuks. Moving westwards, they made the old Byzantine city of Bursa their capital and this positioned them to endanger Constantinople itself. By the middle of the century they had reached the Sea of Marmara and were soon able to threaten the Byzantine heartland. In 1355 they crossed the Hellespont – Dardanelles – and were soon occupying much of the Balkan peninsula. Constantinople, stripped of most of its possessions, had contracted to a small strip of territory around the old Propontis, surrounded by the fast-growing might of the rapidly forming Ottoman Empire. It was perhaps a fitting conclusion to the second Rome, and to the whole Roman imperial enterprise, that the empire which had set out to protect the Hellenic world of city-states should, in its final stages, revert to being one itself.

Its powerful walls and the great chain across the entrance to the Golden Horn made Constantinople a formidable city which for most of its history had proved to be virtually impregnable. Only the shortage of foodstuffs and supplies could force its surrender and for a time it was able to retain sea communications with its few remaining possessions. Finally, in 1453 the Ottomans mounted a successful attack on the city which fell with little resistance. Not only was this the end of the Roman Empire but of Constantinople as the centre of the Orthodox Christian Church. Yet Orthodoxy was alive and well in other parts of Europe, and a third Rome was waiting in the wings to take over its role.

This third Rome was, of course, Moscow. The first Russian state, Kievan Rus, had become virtually a northern mirror image of Byzantium. While the main Russian city-states had been established along the great routeway 'from the Varangians to the Greeks', by the twelfth century Kiev, 'Byzantium on Dnieper', had established a quasi-imperial hegemony over the whole of the southern section of these Russian lands. Around its extensive boundaries, and in particular in the forests on its eastern flanks, was a smaller line of settlements, and Moscow began its life as one of these. The first mention of it was in 1147 as an *ostrog* – a wooden fort – built deep in the mixed deciduous forest by Prince Yuri Dolgoruky, son of Vladimir II Monomakh, Prince of Vladimir. Over the years a *gorod* – a small fortified town – grew up around this. Unlike the cities of the north–south routeway which looked southwards towards the Black Sea and Byzantium, Moscow was on the eastern side of Kievan Rus and was naturally oriented eastwards. This was because it was in the basin of the Volga, the largest river in European Russia, which flowed southeastwards into the Caspian Sea. It was actually located on the banks of the small Moskva river which is in the *mezhdurechie*, the Mesopotamian land between the rivers Volga and Oka. Although loosely within the boundaries of Kievan Rus, it was subject to far less influence from Byzantium than was Kiev itself.

Unlike Byzantium, the first major danger to confront Kievan Rus was neither from Persia nor Islam but from a people from much further to the east. These were the Mongols, known to the Russians as 'Tatars', who in the early thirteenth century under their great leader Genghis Khan began a process of expansion which was to lead to the creation of an enormous empire stretching across Asia and into Europe. Genghis Khan soon conquered much of Central Asia and by the time of his death in 1227 the Mongols were poised to invade the Russian lands. This they did after the death of the Khan under his son and successor Ogedai and in 1237

Kiev itself was attacked by a massive Mongol army. The city was quite unprepared to withstand the onslaught. It soon fell and Kievan Rus fell with it. This cataclysm produced a huge influx of refugees fleeing from the Mongols into the forest lands to the north and this increased the significance of Moscow and the other similar *gorod* in the forested upper Volga region. With Kievan Rus gone, this area, together with Novgorod on the Volkhov river to the west, was almost all that was not in the hands of the Mongols. Although Moscow and the other towns in the forest area were forced to pay tribute to the Mongols, and were punished if they failed to do so, they were never permanently occupied by them.

The Mongols were a people of the steppes, the great temperate grasslands, and their huge armies of cavalry were not able to cope well with the unfamiliar forest environment. As a result, Moscow was able to retain a degree of independence during these hard times which came to be known in Russian history as the 'Tatar Yoke'.

At first the *gorod* became a centre of resistance to the Mongols but, realizing that this was futile, the princes cleverly changed their policies and took on the role of collectors of *jassak*, the tribute exacted by their overlords. This arrangement was accepted by the Mongols and the princes of Moscow were expected to make the annual journey to Sarai, the Mongol capital on the lower Volga, to deliver it in person. This arrangement enabled them to build up their strength secretly, unbeknown to their Mongol overlords who just required the tribute and were not concerned with how it was gathered. This was all perfected during the reign of Ivan Danilovich 'Kalita' (the Moneygatherer), who secretly retained part of the tribute collected and used it to strengthen the fortifications of Moscow. After the fall of Kiev, the metropolitan had initially fled to Vladimir but in 1326 he saw that it was in his best interests to move to Moscow. He still styled himself 'Metropolitan of Kiev and All Russia' and from this time the princes began to style themselves 'Prince of Moscow and All Russia'. This was the beginning of Moscow's leading role which led to the term 'Muscovite Russia' being used for this period in Russian history. It was characterized by the steady expansion of Muscovite power across the great forests of northern Russia and eventually southwards to confront the Mongols themselves.

This rise of Moscow to a pre-eminent position had certainly much to do with the tactics of its princes, but there were also sound geographical reasons for the assumption of this role. Hunczak went so far as to be quite deterministic about the significance of the location of the city. He maintained that:

In retrospect there seems something inevitable about the expansion (of Muscovy). From its situation on the Moskva river in the Russian heartland – the *mezhdurechie* – bounded by the upper Volga and the Oka, Moscow had access to the Volga, the Msta, the Dnieper, the Western Dvina and the Lovat. To the west and north of the Valdai hills, three routes led to the Baltic . . . To the northeast of Moscow, tributaries of the Volga brought contact with the northern Dvina basin with its egress to the White Sea.[II]

Most importantly, this relationship to the river system also facilitated communication with Novgorod, the greatest and most prosperous of the free Russian cities, and later on the advance eastwards down the Volga. Moscow was located in the area of rich black forest soil in the middle of the *mezhdurechie* which enabled agriculture to flourish and so support a larger population than elsewhere in the forests. There were certainly many powerful geographical reasons for the rise of Moscow to a pre-eminent position among the Russian cities and, eventually, over the whole of Russia itself.

Although the people of this Muscovite Russian state were, like Kiev, culturally part of the Byzantine world, they had by the thirteenth century become geographically quite isolated from it. Direct contacts with Byzantium, so important in earlier centuries, had now been cut off by the Mongols who occupied the great steppe lands stretching across what is now Ukraine. This isolation was gradually made greater by the fact that the Byzantine Empire was continuing to contract under pressure from the Arabs and Turks. This made Muscovy look more to its own potential than had Kiev and the state that emerged can be seen as more truly the beginnings of the Russian nation.

In 1453 Constantinople finally fell to the Turks and the Russians, now led by the prince of Moscow 'and all Russia', rapidly moved to assume the legacy of Byzantium. The great change actually took place during the reign of Ivan III (1462–1505). He used the insignia of Byzantium, and was crowned ceremonially with the Cap of Monomakh. By tradition, this had been presented by the emperor Constantine IV Monomachus (1042–55) to Prince Vladimir of Kiev. From then on the double-headed eagle of Rome also became the new symbol of Muscovite Russia. In his dealings with the outside world Ivan also styled himself 'tsar' (Caesar), indicating the new status he had assigned himself. In his assertion of power over both Church and state he also used the title *samoderzhets*, the Russian form of the Greek *autokratos*. He ensured the continuation of the bloodline when he married the niece of the last Roman emperor, Constantine XI Palaeologus. Ivan, known as the 'Gatherer' then continued to extend the territory of Muscovite Russia, including Novgorod in 1478, and making Moscow the capital of a very large state.

As the most tangible confirmation of the pre-eminent role of his capital, Ivan began the building of a new Moscow, replacing wood with stone and brick. Although rising on the site of the old wooden *gorod*, this was very much a new city and its grandeur was in keeping with its greatly enhanced status. It was built on the northern bank of the Moskva river in the form of a *Kreml*, a stronghold surrounded by a wall. At its centre was the Granovitaya Palace (the Palace of the Facets), which was the residence of the prince himself. This was designed by Italian architects in the Italian style but the churches that sprang up around it were still very much in the Byzantine architectural style. The first of these was the Uspensky (Assumption) Cathedral which took on the primary role as the state church. Towering over the new complex was the magnificent Ivan III bell tower, begun in Ivan's reign and becoming the most striking feature of the skyline of the Kremlin. The word Kremlin, from *Kreml*, also came to be used at this time.

Ivan's son and heir, Vasili III, continued his father's building project. During his reign the magnificent cathedrals of the Archangel Michael and the Annunciation were added, together with a second royal palace intended for assemblies and the reception of foreign dignitaries. The close proximity of religious and secular buildings demonstrated the

The Moscow Kremlin, a magnificent display of the combined power of state and Church.

closeness of the link between tsar and metropolitan, state and Church. In the last years of the reign of Ivan III the foundations of bigger Kreml walls had been laid and this project was continued by Vasili. These formidable red brick walls with their huge towers put the finishing touches to the massive impressiveness of the Kremlin. In this way, within a matter of decades, a new and splendid capital had risen on the site of the old wooden gorod. The frontier fortress had been transformed into a powerful symbol of the new Russia. From the outset this Muscovite state was highly centralized and the Kremlin was its undoubted centre. Besides being a formidable stronghold, it was also the principal royal residence and the place from which ecclesiastical, administrative and military power was wielded.

Vasili was followed by his son Ivan IV who was given the name Ivan Grozny – 'the Dread'; in the English-speaking world this tsar has always been known as 'the Terrible'. He was the first prince actually to be crowned 'tsar' of all Russia. He continued his father's policy of the expansion of the Muscovite state, deciding that it was time to make a move against the Mongols. By this time this warrior people had become much weakened but they still occupied a great deal of territory west of the Urals. The empire of Genghis Khan had long broken up and the western branch, known to the Russians as the Golden Horde, had become an independent Khanate centring on the lower Volga. Muscovite Russia was well placed to advance eastwards against them and in 1552 Ivan's army captured the great Mongol stronghold of Kazan on the Volga. Advancing on down the Volga, Ivan's army reached the Caspian and occupied the important port of Astrakhan. They attacked the Mongol capital, Sarai, which soon surrendered to them. After 300 years the power of the Mongols in Russia had at last been broken.

When Ivan returned to Moscow, there were great services of thanksgiving for the defeat of the old enemy and the end of the Tatar Yoke. As a culmination to this thanksgiving, the tsar decreed that a new Cathedral should be built and work on it soon commenced. This was the Cathedral of St Basil the Blessed which was built between 1555 and 1560. Named after the Russian saint Basil Yurodivy, it is significant that this new cathedral owed a great deal more to traditional Russian architecture than to the Byzantine. With its central tent-shaped spire, it resembled the old Russian wooden churches found in villages throughout the land. St Basil's is situated just outside the walls of the Kremlin on the eastern side of the great open space known as the Red Square.[12] At the same time this cathedral and other buildings adjacent to it were incorporated

The Cathedral of St Basil the Blessed in Moscow, built to commemorate the defeat of the Tatars by the forces of Ivan the Terrible.

into the city by the extension of the walls to include the newer parts of the city. This was Ivan's major addition to Moscow and for the time being completed the building of the spectacular capital of Muscovite Russia. Few coming upon it could now doubt the power of the Muscovite tsar.

In 1589 the metropolitan enhanced his status and powers by becoming the patriarch and the Kremlin became the heart of the autonomous Russian Orthodox Church. At the same time the tsar of the 'third Rome' was pronounced the successor to the Roman emperors and protector of the Church. Ivan proceeded to take *autokratos* to an extreme degree by creating the *oprichnina*, a huge secret organization which he used to achieve his obsessive aim of bringing everything in the state under his direct control. This led to considerable conflict with the *boyars*, the Russian aristocracy, but Ivan maintained his position and set tsarist Russia on that autocratic path which it was to retain into modern times. This *oprichnina* was the ancestor of many later secret organizations of state, leading eventually to the KGB of Soviet times.

At this time the Uspensky Cathedral was greatly embellished with further decoration. It contained the throne on which Ivan had been crowned and this was used for the same purpose by all later tsars. It was in this cathedral that many of the great ceremonies of state were subsequently held. Although an emulation of the Byzantine practice, this took place in architectural and artistic surroundings which had become far more indigenously Russian. These included paintings, and especially icons, by great Russian painters, notably Rublyev and Feofan (Theophanes). From then on the cathedral of the Archangel Michael, built in 1509, became the burial place of the tsars.

The splendour with which Ivan surrounded himself was evidently observed by an English delegation arriving in Moscow in 1555. These were the remains of the expedition led by Willoughby and Chancellor to find the legendary 'northeast passage' to China and the East. When this failed, the survivors led by Richard Chancellor travelled south to Moscow instead. There they were clearly impressed by the splendour of the Kremlin and the magnificence of the Russian court. This initial contact led to the beginning of trading relations between England and Russia and the setting up of the Muscovy Company to handle them.

Moscow now had no rival in the Russian lands although its expansionist policies had earned it many enemies in Europe, notably its neighbours Sweden and Poland. Poland was a Catholic country, Sweden had become a Protestant one and neither was at all sympathetic to Moscow's assertion of its role as the 'third Rome'. From this time on, as protector of the Orthodox Church the country also came to be known as 'Holy Russia', thus adding strongly to the religious justification for its actions.

While Ivan had been mainly preoccupied with enemies in the east and west, it was from the south that the greatest long-term danger to Muscovite Russia was about to come. The Mongols had been so weakened that they represented no danger at all, but by the sixteenth century another powerful people had arrived on the scene. These were the Ottoman Turks who had defeated Byzantium and attained a dominant position within the Islamic world. In the later stages of its existence, the Golden Horde had become Muslim, as had another remnant of the Mongol Empire, the Khanate of the Crimea. This encouraged the Turks to look northwards and after the conquest of the Balkans they were poised to invade the northern shores of the Black Sea. They subsequently moved into the Ukraine and eventually converted the Black Sea into what was virtually a Turkish lake. In so doing they became close neighbours of the Russians.

Moscow considered itself the third Rome and so the protector of Orthodox Christians everywhere, but by the seventeenth century the new

Islamic power had moved uncomfortably close. Even more disturbing, Constantinople, for 500 years the Orthodox Christian capital towards which the Russians had looked for their religion and culture, had now been transformed into the capital of this Islamic power. The Cross and the Crescent were in close proximity and this fact was to have a profound influence on the histories of both powers during the next two centuries.

3
Constantinople and the New Lords of the Golden Horn

For the efficient control and administration of their new theocratic empire, the Arabs soon found Mecca and Medina, the original centres of their new religion, too peripheral and inconvenient and in 661 the seat of the Omayyad caliphate was moved north to Damascus. This city was in a far more central location, particularly in relation to the newly conquered lands. After the initial movement northwards out of Arabia, the most powerful thrust was directed westwards towards the Byzantine Empire. This was seen by the Arabs as being the heart of Christendom which it was their intention that Islam supersede. Everything changed in the later seventh century with the rapid defeat of the Persian Empire. Since the Byzantines proved to be a much tougher nut to crack, the victory over the Persians reoriented the Islamic empire eastwards. In 750 the successors of the Omayyads, the Abassids, transferred their capital eastwards to Al Kufah (Baghdad). This was situated in the heart of Mesopotamia between the Tigris and Euphrates rivers and close to the ancient capitals of Babylon and Ctesiphon. As a result the Arab empire became more the geopolitical heir to the Babylonians and Persians rather than the Byzantines as they had originally intended.

Baghdad was a new Arab foundation, one of many which the Arabs built at this time. Like Alexander the Great, the Arabs were great builders and 'new towns' sprang up widely across their empire. Important among these were Cordoba in Spain, Kairuan in Tunisia, Fustat in Egypt and Basra in the Tigris-Euphrates delta. Although it was chosen by the Abassids to be their principal seat of power, from the outset Baghdad became more a religious and cultural capital than an imperial one. As it evolved, its fine mosques and madrasas, together with its great library, were soon to make it the most important centre of learning in the whole of the Islamic world. Scientists and scholars from other parts of the empire, notably Central Asia, North Africa and Spain, converged on the city. Beside the study of religion, important contributions were soon made in such fields as astronomy, geography, history, medicine and philosophy. The city is associated with such distinguished names as Al Biruni and Avicenna, who came from Central Asia but found Baghdad a more stimulating intellectual environment. In this way, while Baghdad became the great centre of Islamic learning, specific displays of imperial power were less in evidence. This also reflects the fact that central control of the massive Arab empire was difficult to maintain and the devolution of power to regional centres took place at an early stage in its history.

Many of the other new cities built by the Arabs across their empire were soon transformed into important economic, cultural and political centres in their own right. By the eleventh century many of the provinces of which they became the chief cities had become independent emirates conducting their own affairs and even foreign policies. An early example of this was the Emirate of Cordoba, which initially covered virtually the whole of the Iberian peninsula. Meanwhile Cordoba itself became a great centre of Arab learning which had an important influence on Christendom. However, despite an attempt in the eighth century, the Arabs were no more successful in subduing Christendom by attacking it from Iberia than they had been in their earlier assault on Byzantium. While all the emirates existed within the overall embrace of Islam, political control was soon increasingly in their own hands. In this way the great Arabian Islamic empire did not so much fall as gradually fall apart.

This high level of devolution all changed with the arrival of the Turks whom the Arabs had converted to Islam in the eighth century after the conquest of Persia, and who soon became among the most active proselytizers for the faith. It was these Men of Osman, the Osmanlis, who were the most successful in bringing the Islamic empire together again.

The Osmanlis built their first capital at Yenisehir in the interior of Anatolia, but when they were victorious against the Byzantines they moved their capital to the old city of Bursa, closer to the Sea of Marmara and in the main thrust of their advance. This was their new forward capital and, after successfully crossing the Bosphorus at Gallipoli in 1354, followed by a rapid occupation of the southern Balkans, they again transferred their capital westwards to an even more strategic location. The Roman city of Adrianopolis, which they renamed Edirne, was to the north of Constantinople and as a result the great city had by now been virtually surrounded.

It was not until 1453 that they successfully attacked Constantinople itself and the city surrendered after only a short siege. The Sultan Mehmed II was astonished to see the extent to which the great city had been allowed to deteriorate. He made the momentous decision that the city should be his capital. Much as Constantine had done over 1,000 years earlier, Mehmed and his advisers saw the advantages of the site both militarily and economically and this put the Turks in the position of being heirs to the empire that now lay in ruins. This is something that from the outset the Arabs had always wished to do but had never succeeded.

Thus no sooner had the last Byzantine emperor, Constantine XI, died in the fighting than Mehmed, 'The Conqueror', proclaimed himself heir to the great city. A Greek scholar is said to have told the sultan, 'The seat of the Roman Empire is Constantinople . . . Therefore you are the legitimate emperor of the Romans.'[1]

Mehmed would certainly have accepted this role with alacrity. He considered himself to be both the supreme *ghazi* – warrior of Islam – and a new Alexander the Great, thus combining in his person the glorious achievements of past and present. Beside Constantinople's undoubted geographical advantages, the fact that it had been the capital of the Roman Empire may have been the most conclusive factor in the decision to move the capital once more. It was from here that the Turks now embarked on the creation of their own imperial state which was to become known to history as the Ottoman Empire.

By this time Islam had already been in existence for 800 years but had never had a really effective imperial capital. The Turks, the new masters of Islam, inherited what had 1,000 years earlier been a purpose-built imperial city and they immediately began to adapt it to their own imperial aspirations. Located on the periphery between Europe and Asia, the city which had always been orientated towards Europe was now reoriented eastwards. The golden city of medieval Europe became the golden city of the Islamic world and the leading city of the eastern half of the Christian world was adapted to become the new centre of Islam. In order to do this, new buildings had to be constructed and old ones removed or adapted to their new functions.

The first such building was the great church of Hagia Sofia, the heart of the fallen empire. Mehmed entered this immediately after the conquest and there gave thanks for his victory. He immediately claimed the magnificent building for Islam and proclaimed it to be from then on the mosque of the Aya Sofya. To the Byzantines it had been 'the earthly heaven, throne of God's glory' and it would still discharge this function but now for Islam.

Despite this peremptory beginning, the Ottomans were quite prepared to exercise tolerance, and this particularly applied to Christianity. A year after the conquest, the Patriarchate was reinstated. The new patriarch was consecrated and enthroned with considerable pomp in the great church of the Holy Apostles which became from then on the centre of Christianity in the city. From the outset the new empire displayed a large measure of religious toleration. However, while the religious symbols were usually preserved or turned to new use, the political ones were treated somewhat differently. For instance, the great statue of Justinian, the emperor in whose reign Hagia Sofia had been built, was destroyed, as were many other reminders of Roman imperial power.

Mehmed immediately embarked on a great building programme and for this he needed expertise of many kinds which the Turks did not themselves possess. To obtain it he encouraged a variety of different peoples to come, or to return, to the city. These included Greeks, Jews and Armenians together with people from the newly conquered Balkan lands, notably Serbs and Bosnians. These people brought their knowledge and skills in many areas such as trade and industry, but most of all the sultan was looking for those with expertise in building, architecture and painting. A huge variety of different skills were needed for the grandiose projects he envisaged for his new capital on the shores of the Bosphorus. These people also brought with them their own religions and cultures, and tolerance was extended to them. As Mansel puts it, the city soon became a 'multinational microcosm' with each nationality, including the Turks themselves, making their own particular contribution to the functioning of the whole.[2]

One of the most interesting and unusual of these were the Janissaries, who were given the massive task of running the empire and, if necessary, fighting for it. Originally these were European children, mainly from the Balkans, who had been captured and brought to the Ottoman court. There they were trained in the particular functions for which they were needed and for the offices they were destined to hold. As with the Byzantine eunuchs, they were officially designated as slaves, but many of them rose to positions of authority in the court and army. Eventually they became so indispensable that they were soon virtually in charge of the running the empire. This bizarre system arose from the belief that since these Janissaries did not have associations with particular Turkish families, tribes or regions, their advancement was entirely dependent on the sultan himself. It was believed that their absolute loyalty therefore would be to the Sultanate and there would be none of those other loyalties that Turks might have. Many of them rose to the highest offices of state and even to the highest of all, that of grand vizier, who fulfilled the role of prime minister and confidential adviser to the sultan. The vizier sometimes came to possess more power than the sultan himself and intrigue in the court sometimes resulted in the violent removal of the over-powerful official.

The first specifically Ottoman addition to the architecture of Constantinople was the Rumeli Hisar, the castle, built at great speed immediately after the fall of the city in 1453. It was on the western edge of the city adjacent to the great Wall of Constantine and fitted well into the ring of protective fortifications. It is said that Mehmed himself was involved closely in the architectural planning and even helped out as a labourer. The relationship of the castle to the city was similar to that of the Tower to London, representing both an assertion of the power of the new overlords and a place of security for the sultan and his court should that be necessary.

The real centre of Ottoman imperial power, however, was built in a more leisurely manner. This was the Serai (palace) which occupied the whole of the eastern end of the peninsula. The construction of this huge complex was begun in 1459 and took some twenty years to complete. It was surrounded by a formidable wall, the principal entrance through which was the Imperial Gate. Inside the wall was a series of courtyards surrounded by buildings, each designed for a specific set of purposes.

These courtyards were connected to one another by a series of 'gates' which were in fact highly decorated archways. The First Courtyard was designed to be an impressive entrance leading to the Second Courtyard, which housed the Imperial Divan where the grand vizier conducted the business of state, often watched from behind a curtain by the sultan. At the end of this courtyard the Bab-i-Aali (High Gate) connected to the Third Courtyard in which were the harem (women's quarters), the bathhouses and the private apartments of the sultan. In the centre of this courtyard was the Throne Room of the sultan which was said to be 'like a jewel box' in its magnificence. This was the epicentre of the palace and the heart of the power structure of the whole vast Ottoman Empire. Here the sultan, seated on his throne and robed in great splendour, would receive his ministers, foreign embassies and honoured guests. The Bab-i-Aali was also known as the Bab-i Sa'adet, the Gate of Felicity, and this became a synonym for the Ottoman government. This government came to be known simply as 'The Gate' and the officials of the palace the Kapi Kulu, meaning 'Slaves of the Gate'. This concept of 'The Gate' eventually came to be known to Europeans, who referred to the Ottoman government as the 'Porte'. 'The Sublime Porte' soon became a synonym for the Sultanate and its power and the term added to the increasing respect and even fear felt by Europeans towards the Islamic empire which by then occupied a large part of eastern Europe. The inscription in Arabic above the Imperial Gate read, 'The Sultan of the Two Continents, the Emperor of the Two Seas, the Shadow of God in this world and the next . . . the Monarch of the Terraqueous Orb'. The palace later became known as the Topkapserai – or just the Topkapi – from Top Kapi, meaning cannon gate.

Aya Sofya, the central church of eastern Christendom, now transformed into the central mosque of Islam, continued to retain its special role under its new masters. It was changed and adapted to its new function with the addition of four minarets and the interior was given the usual Islamic geometrical decoration with quotations from the Koran in Arabic. Mehmed II also embarked on the construction of his own mosque some distance away. This was the Fatih (Conqueror) Mosque, the principal architect of which, known as Atik ('Old') Sinan, was probably Greek and had made a very careful study of the architecture of Aya Sofya. The great dome was replicated in the new mosque and many other Byzantine influences can be detected. It was a building of considerable magnificence and was surrounded by a complex of other buildings which included a madrasa and a library. It was in this mosque that the conqueror was himself buried in 1481 and from that time on it always held a special place in Islamic worship. A number of other mosques, with their domes and minarets, were subsequently added to the skyline of the city and many later sultans built their own mosques which they dedicated to themselves. They all followed the same architectural patterns, with domes, semi-domes, minarets, columns and fine stone carving.

The most splendid of these was the Süleymaniye built during the reign of Süleyman the Magnificent (1520–66). This was intended by the sultan not only to be a place of religious worship but also an 'assertion in stone' of the power of the dynasty and in particular of the sultan himself, 'God's Shadow on Earth'.[3] At the beginning of his reign he had added another title to all the others he held: caliph, successor to the Prophet, an office surrendered to him by the Mameluks in 1520. The Caliphate had remained in Baghdad until 1258 but, following the turbulence of the Mongol conquests, it had been transferred to the relative safety of Egypt. Now it moved to Constantinople where it was to remain for the rest of its existence. The Süleymaniye mosque, designed by the sultan's chief architect Sinan (c. 1500–1588), was in many ways a celebration of the bringing together of the secular and religious in the Turkish Islamic empire. This mosque is at the heart of a large complex of buildings which included colleges, a bathhouse (hamam), kitchens and a hostel for pilgrims and visitors.

The reign of Süleyman proved to be the high-water mark of Ottoman power. By then the empire covered a vast area, including much of North Africa, Arabia, the Balkans and the lands around the Black Sea. Its wealth was enormous, and much of this was spent on the continued embellishment of the capital and other cities with more mosques and further additions to the palace. Little was spent on improving the conditions of the people. As with other empires before and since, this neglect was a major cause of the onset of decline.

Another important reason for the decline of the empire in the seventeenth century was the poor quality of the sultans themselves. This was caused by the bizarre selection process which resulted in the pretenders to the throne, and even the heir himself, being imprisoned in the palace for long periods of time before they succeeded. This incarceration was to ensure that there were no rivalries or alternative centres of power to the sultan and that no disputes over the succession could break out. The Empire had one indisputable head and no potential rivals were permitted. The incarceration was usually in the so-called 'Cage', a building in the third courtyard of the palace on the edge of the harem. In this, heirs were kept for most of their lives as virtual prisoners until they eventually succeeded to the throne. By the time they did so they were often mentally ill or so weak that they were incapable of exercising power. This produced a situation of almost perpetual intrigue in the palace in which the grand vizier and other officials exercised an absolute, if often precarious, hold on the reins of power of the empire.

At the end of the seventeenth century the Ottomans began to lose territory in eastern Europe to the newly expanding Austrian Empire, and by the nineteenth century the contraction had become a constant process. The Ottoman Empire was so weakened that it came to be

The Süleymaniye Mosque, Istanbul.

labelled 'the sick man of Europe', and a famous cartoon in *Punch* depict-ed the sultan being propped up by the other European powers. By this time the Ottoman Empire was in fact only still in existence because the great powers needed it. They were so suspicious of one another, and particularly of their conflicting ambitions in the Middle East, that they found that allowing the continued existence of the Ottomans was for the time being more convenient. The two most strident of these powers were Britain and Russia, both of whom had considerable interest in the region. Russia still retained the idea of Byzantium as the true heart of Orthodox Christianity, and a revived Christian empire with its capital in Constantinople which they called Tzarigrad – the City of the Emperor – remained an ever-present dream. The British had their own interests and were not prepared to accept any such outcome. In fact in the Crimean War (1854–6) the British, together with the French, took the side of the Turks in an attempt to thwart the ambitions of the Russians. By then Constantinople had virtually lost its historic role as a centre of power that it had possessed since the fourth century. However, located on the vital 'straits' routeway between the Mediterranean and the Black Sea, it had gained a new significance in the nineteenth century as a focus of the global imperial rivalries.

It was not until the First World War that the Ottoman Empire finally collapsed. The Ottomans took the German side and their defeat came together with that of their ally. In 1918 much of the Ottoman Empire was occupied by the victorious powers led by Britain. A Turkish republic was proclaimed and the new republican government led by Mustafa Kemal, 'Atatürk', moved the capital away to the old Turkish stronghold of Ankara in the middle of Anatolia. This was thought by the Turks to be their real homeland in contrast to the cosmopolitanism of Constantinople and the Marmara region. They had become increasingly suspicious of the non-Turkish inhabitants of the empire and this was a cause of the perpetration of many of the wartime atrocities of which the Turks were accused.

The sultan remained in Constantinople until 1922 when the republican government in Ankara finally abolished the sultanate. The Caliphate, however, remained and the former sultan retained the title of caliph only. One year later this was also abolished and the Islamic unity imposed four centuries earlier by the Ottoman Empire finally came to an end. The former sultan and caliph was taken away on a British ship and spent his final years in San Remo on the Italian Riviera, well away from both the new republic and Islam.

Constantinople, no longer capital but still the largest city in the new Turkey, was renamed 'Istanbul'. Interestingly, this was a Turkish corruption of the Greek 'eis ten polin', meaning quite simply 'into the city'. It had ceased to be an imperial city, and even lost its role as capital, but its new name retained in it a reminder of the Greek *polis* which it had been in ancient times. For many centuries it had been considered the most magnificent – and most desirable – place in Europe and in the Middle Ages had come to be known throughout Europe simply as 'the city'. Was this name change a final tacit recognition by the Turks of the role which they and those before them had always accorded to it as the greatest city in their world?

After 1,700 years, the purpose for which 'the city' had been originally intended had at last come to an end. It had first been built as the new Rome, capital of the Christian empire. In the seventh century it had been designated capital of the newly styled Byzantine Empire, centre of the eastern Christian world. Finally it had become capital of the Ottoman Empire and the seat of the Caliphate. Now, for the first time in its long history, it was no longer a capital city. The principal centres of world power had long moved away and the Mediterranean had declined into a backwater. The nineteenth-century empires were far more global than those of the Mediterranean and the Middle East had ever been. However, centuries before their rise, an earlier people had paved the way for them with the creation of the first empire to possess a truly global reach – that of the Mongols in the thirteenth century.

4

From Karakorum to Shakhrisabz: Centres of Power of the Imperial Nomads

The great empires and their imperial cities which have so far been examined were all basically regional and centred mainly on the Mediterranean and in the Middle East. Both Persia and Rome may have thought of themselves as being 'world' empires, but their worlds actually consisted of fairly limited areas of the globe. Most of the original creators of these empires were nomadic tribes who migrated from far poorer areas in search of a better life. The Arabs came from the desert regions to the south, while the Medes, Persians and Turks came from the steppes, the great temperate grasslands, of Central Asia. Their conquests of sedentary indigenous peoples then resulted in the establishment of powerful imperial states. The steppe peoples were also engaged in similar conquests in south and east Asia and, like those of the Mediterranean and Middle East, the empires resulting from this were powerful but also of an essentially regional character.

Many attempts had been made to bring peace to the Central Asian steppes by attempting to unite their warlike peoples, but until the thirteenth century none of these were successful. In the thirteenth century one of these peoples, the Mongols, was at last successful in defeating the others and the extent of their conquests resulted in the rapid creation of an enormous imperial state. Unlike earlier conquests, this was in Central Asia itself and eventually it became by far the largest empire to have existed anywhere up to that time. In view of this vastness, it could with some justification, more than any previous empire, be considered a 'world' empire.

The whole process was begun by Yesugai, the leader of the Borjigid tribe. Following his murder by the Tatars, a rival people, his efforts were taken up by his son Temuchin.[1] Such was Temuchin's success that in 1206 he was proclaimed 'Genghis Khan', the universal khan, at a kuriltai, a great assembly of the Mongol chieftains, which took place on the Onon river in eastern Mongolia. The new Genghis Khan then embarked on a series of conquests which were to take the Mongols across Asia from Europe to China and southwards into the Middle East.

The Mongols were a pastoral nomadic people whose origins lay deep in the heart of Central Asia. Their homelands were south of Lake Baikal around the headwaters of the Kerulen and Onon rivers, which flow eastwards into the basin of the Amur river. Life was hard in these poorer areas of the steppe grasslands. The reasons for their successful and dramatic expansion have been variously explained. Like others before them they were attempting to bring peace to a lawless region but they were also in search of better lands and in so doing became aware of the far richer life led by other tribes on the steppes and, more importantly, by the sedentary peoples around its fringes. This was made all the more obvious to them by the trade routes across Asia from China to the western lands, bearing riches they could barely have dreamed of. Most famous of these routes was the 'Silk Road' between the old Chinese capital of Sian and Constantinople. Linking the two greatest cities of West and East, this carried not just silk but an enormous variety of rare and costly products between Europe and Asia. In reality this 'road' consisted of a number of different routes across Asia, the northernmost of which passed close to the Mongol lands. At this time China, the power that had historically controlled much of Central Asia, was ruled by the Song dynasty which had concentrated its efforts on the improvement of the Han lands, so-called 'China proper', and had retreated from the peripheral regions that China had formerly occupied and in which it had usually enforced some kind of order. This Chinese retreat from their wider sphere of influence had added considerably to the lawlessness endured by these areas by the twelfth century. Genghis Khan himself had experienced this in his younger days and had spent much of his childhood in hiding. This was clearly a powerful motive for his desire to bring peace to the steppes. In the first instance, he proposed to do this by securing the dominance of his own people over the territory of what is now Mongolia. The Mongols were also influenced by the Uighurs, an advanced Turkic people who had formerly occupied these lands. What the Mongols learned from them would certainly have added considerably to their ability to secure a position of dominance over the surrounding peoples.

While Genghis Khan accomplished this with little difficulty, the whole project set the Mongols against other peoples living around the edges of the conquered areas. As a result, the khan came to believe that the best solution to this was to attack and defeat them, bringing them into the ever larger territories controlled – and so pacified – by his regime. According to the *Secret History of the Mongols*, a written record purporting to be from around this time, Genghis expressed the belief that, 'To bring peace you must have war! . . . When you have killed your enemy all is quiet all around. But I have not yet killed my enemy . . . And the other half of the world is still not under my heel.'[2] Given the nature of Central Asia, there was no natural or easily defined boundary to expansion and the Mongol conquests continued across the steppes, defeating one 'enemy' after another. As they moved, Genghis Khan and his horsemen were finding out about hitherto unknown places well away from the Mongol heartlands. They knew much about China, within whose sphere of influence they had been in the past, but the rest was largely unknown to them. The *Secret History* also talks of uniting 'the two halves of the world' and in doing this the great khan explored as far as the Russian lands in the west and the fringes of India and the Middle East to the south.

However, since China was the foreign land that they knew best, it was decided at another kuriltai that this should be the next country to be dealt with. The first to face the Mongol onslaught was the state of Northern Chin which, as the Sung dynasty declined, had gained power over the northern part of the country. By 1215 the Mongols had occupied much of its territory and established a military base in the Chin stronghold of Ta-tu. This was on, or very close to, the site of the city which was later to become Beijing. Genghis Khan was killed in 1227 while campaigning on this eastern front. His exact burial place still remains unknown.[3]

He was succeeded by his third son, Ogedei (1229–41), a thoughtful and careful man who was more administrator than warrior, which was why he was chosen by his father over the older brothers who took more after himself. Such a man was exactly what was needed at this time. However, although he concentrated on attempting to create an administrative framework for the enormous empire, Ogedei continued the expansion largely because by this time the conquest had gained its own momentum and because there were still many enemies who resented the great power which the Mongols had gained in so short a time. Further advances were made in northern China but the most important event in Ogedei's reign was the attack on Kievan Rus and the subjugation of Kiev in 1237. The fall of Rus' produced great geopolitical changes in the Russian lands, leading to the rise of Moscow and Muscovite Russia. The Mongols also moved southwards to Persia and there established a khanate under the rule of the Ilkhanids, another branch of the Chinghizid ruling family. This destabilized the whole Middle East and contributed to the weakening of the Baghdad Caliphate and eventually the rise of the Turks to a position of dominance in Islam. The great outpouring of the Mongols from Central Asia therefore had a profound effect on empires and empire building throughout the Middle East and Europe.

However, despite all this frenetic activity, Ogedei's priority was to give the empire, which was still in the course of formation, a coherent administrative structure. In order to do this he grasped the necessity for this nomadic people to have a fixed centre of power, a capital city, in the manner of the sedentary societies. This was, of course, something quite new to the Mongols who were constantly on the move and had never possessed fixed settlements of any sort. In the days of Genghis Khan the centre of power was where the khan happened to be at any time, and this was most often with his army. However, the Mongol homelands were the place to which the army always returned to recuperate after any campaign and this was where the kuriltais were held. These assemblies were called whenever major policy decisions had to be taken and, most importantly, on the death of the khan and the necessity to agree on his successor. Although the former great khan could express a wish as to who he wanted his successor to be, the Mongol ruling family, the Chinghizids, had an elective khanate. Usually the kuriltais were summoned to take place in the Mongol heartland of the Onon-Kerulen region on the slopes of the Burkhan Kaldun, the holy mountain. Initially the meeting places for these great gatherings gained the role of peripatetic capitals and they certainly had the decision-making function of a capital city. However, for the purposes of running the expanding empire, peripatetic capitals were not adequate and, in any case, this region was judged to be too remote. Genghis Khan on his return from his conquests normally pitched his tents, the Royal Ger, well to the west in the valley of the Orkhon river. This was part of the Selenge river system which flowed northwards into Lake Baikal. It provided far easier communications than the lands to the east, together with good grassland for the animals, always of the greatest importance for these pastoral nomads. In view of the increasing size of the Mongol army, the importance of adequate fodder became ever greater.

Thus even in the time of Genghis Khan a certain stabilization of the centre of power was beginning to take place and Ogedei continued with this. Soon after his accession to the throne, he began the construction of a capital city in the Orkhon valley very close to the place that Genghis had chosen for his Royal Ger. The new capital was named Karakorum, a Turkish word meaning the black stronghold. This provides another clue to the choice of location. The new capital was built close to an earlier capital which had belonged to the Turkish Uighurs who had established themselves in these lands in the middle of the eighth century. They were also a nomadic people but they had become sedentarized and went on to found a large and impressive state, the Orkhon Empire. Their capital was Ordu Balik, later known as Kara Balghashan, and the archaeological evidence shows it to have been a powerful stronghold. The Uighurs were among the first sedentarized nomads in Central Asia and they developed high levels of workmanship, including building and metal working. The achievements of the Mongols and their superiority over the other steppe peoples owed much to what they learnt from the Uighurs. These people also created their own script and this was something else which was adopted by the Mongols. This was the script used in most Mongol texts, including the *Secret History*. The advantages of having a fixed centre of power was perhaps the most important thing they learned from the Uighurs. They may even have thought of themselves as being heirs to the Orkhon Empire and they certainly moved rapidly to take over what had been its core region.

The walls of Karakorum were built in 1235 and by that time much other work had already been carried out. Much of what we know about what it might have been like comes from travellers who visited it during the time of the khans. Most of these came as ambassadors from European courts such as those of the pope and the Holy Roman Emperor. Famous among them were the Franciscan friars John of Plano Carpini, who visited the city in the 1240s, and William of Rubruck, who was there at around the same time. Both wrote about what they had seen, as did another traveller, Benedict the Pole, who travelled with his amanuensis, Simon of St Quentin. From these travellers we learn of the construction of walls and other building projects, most important among them the palace of the khan itself. We learn also that there were a number of religious buildings including Buddhist temples and Christian churches. The Mongols seem to have had great tolerance of most religions, and there was little desire to impose their own, something which was very rare among imperial peoples. Their own religion was a form of nature worship, widely practised throughout Central Asia at this time. At the centre of this was Tengri, the sky, a god-like presence which was the heart of their ideas of the universe. Their intermediaries with nature were the priests, the shamans, who were of great importance in Mongol life. They were called in to deal with evil spirits and to pray for rain or whatever weather the Mongols most needed at any given time.[4] Tengri also gave the orders for the great conquests and it was always necessary to secure the active support of the god in order to ensure success.

Plano Carpini was in Karakorum at the time of the coronation of Ogedei's successor, his son Guyuk (1246–8). This seems to have been a magnificent affair, the main ceremonies of which took place not in the capital itself in but in the Royal Ger just outside the walls. Although by then the Mongols had their one and only purpose-built city, they clearly preferred the old nomadic gers and used them whenever they could. The Royal Ger was closer to the hearts of the Mongols than the Royal Palace ever could be. Plano Carpini reports that during the ceremony homage was paid to the new great khan by members of the Chinghizid family and others of the Mongol aristocracy.

Today virtually nothing is left of Karakorum, even less than the remains of the much earlier Uighur stronghold of Karabalgas not far away. Russian archaeologists have dug the site of Karakorum and produced plans of what they think its layout may have been. These show the site of the palace of the khan, the treasury and the private quarters. They also reveal what is believed to be the site of the Great Ger retained by the khan within the precincts of the palace. If this is really the case,

Ruins of the old Uighur stronghold of Karabalgas.

then the Royal Ger, formerly at some distance, must have been brought in to become part of the whole complex. In this way the old nomadic culture represented by the Ger, together with the new sedentary life represented by the palace, became fused into one over the years.

The reports tell us that the palace was itself of considerable splendour and that travellers were highly impressed on first catching sight of it. This is, of course, exactly what the khans intended. William of Rubruck describes it as being 'like a church, with a middle nave and two side aisles'.[5] There was always much gold and silver on display. The throne of the great khan was of gold and had been made by the Russian goldsmith Cosmas. It was raised on a plinth and there the khan would sit in state on ceremonial occasions. Among the most important of these ceremonies was the bearing of tribute by the subject peoples. In the manner of other great rulers, the khan would have wished the subject peoples to be impressed by his power and one of the principal functions of Karakorum, like Persepolis built by an earlier nomadic people, was to ensure that this was achieved.

Another amazing feature in the centre of the great hall was a silver tree for the purpose of keeping the various beverages which were consumed most liberally by the Mongols. William of Rubruck describes this as follows:

> Master William of Paris has made for him [the khan] a large silver tree at the foot of which are four silver lions each having a pipe and belching forth white mares' milk. Inside the trunk four pipes lead up to the top of the tree. One of these pipes pours out wine, another caracosmos, that is the refined milk of mares, another bowl which is a honey drink and another rice mead, which is called terracina . . . At the very top he fashioned an angel holding a trumpet . . . The tree has branches, leaves and fruits of silver around which were four golden lions from whose jaws flowed wine, mead, fermented mare's, milk and arak.[6]

A nice touch was that when the angel blew its trumpet it was time for the supplies of drink to be replenished. The Mongol artist Purevsukh has produced an imaginative recreation of what the whole amazing scene may have looked like. Such was the splendour with which the khans intended to impress their visitors and demonstrate the wealth and power of their empire.

By the middle of the thirteenth century the empire had reached a gigantic size and the exercise of control from the centre was becoming

The Main Hall of the Palace of the Great Khan at Karakorum, with the 'Silver Tree' in the centre.

ever more difficult. Autonomous khanates were being established, most notably in Russia, the so-called 'Golden Horde', and in Persia. These khans were invariably members of the Chinghizid family and were subordinate to the great khan in Karakorum, but this subordination became ever more nominal after the reign of Guyuk. However, Mongolia itself remained the heart of the empire and it was there that the kuriltais continued to take place during which the overall strategy of the empire was discussed. However, the centre of the empire which Genghis had seen as unifying the two halves of the world was looking increasingly towards its eastern half. Even when the Chinese under the Song had retreated to their own Han heartland, the Mongols had always been subject to their influence. Although they had originally been highly influenced by the Uighurs, after attaining their great empire it was towards the Chinese civilization that they looked for further guidance. Genghis Khan had himself begun the move towards China and was influenced by the Chinese sage Chang Chun, who began to guide his ideas of empire. In the administration of the growing territories, Ogedei turned to Chinese mandarins. This privileged and highly educated class had been running the Chinese empire for centuries and Ogedei increasingly came to find them of great value. The Mongols needed their expertise and their new wealth meant that they were able to pay for it. It seems therefore that it was the combination of what they learned from the old Uighur steppe people together with the expertise they found in China that gave the nomadic Mongol tribes the ability to create an empire which was far larger and more impressive than any that had existed up to then.

Following the death of Guyuk there were disputes over the succession, and the imperial line moved to descendants of Tolui, the fourth son of Genghis Khan. The disputes came to centre on two sons, Qubilai (Kublai) and Ariq-böke, who represented very different views of how the empire should proceed. While Qubilai was in favour of continuing to concentrate on China, Ariq-böke believed, like his grandfather, that the centre of the empire should remain in Mongolia and that too much emphasis on China would result in the softening of the Mongols. It was Qubilai who eventually ascended the throne as great khan, although Mongolia remained for a long time in the hands of those who had been supporters of the views of Ariq-böke. In 1270 the Southern Song dynasty came to an end and the whole empire fell into the hands of the Mongols. This was the greatest prize of all and it largely determined the orientation of the empire from then on. During his years in China, Qubilai had been greatly influenced by the country and came increasingly under its spell. He was essentially an easterner seeing the Mongols as being part of the greater Chinese sphere which they had now come themselves to dominate.

Qubilai then took the most important geopolitical decision since Genghis Khan began his conquests – to move the capital of his empire eastwards to China. He decided that the location of this would be the old stronghold of Ta-tu, which had been the principal military base chosen by Genghis. This had the twin advantages of being in a strategic position for exercising control over China to the south and having good communications with Mongolia to the north. This facilitated ease of commerce between the two and enabled essentials from the steppes, above all cattle and horses, to be brought to China with relative ease. It was also congenial for the Mongols, since it had a climate as close as anywhere in China to that of Mongolia. The wet and humid conditions of the south did not suit them at all and they always felt alien to that part of the country.

In Ta-tu, Qubilai embarked on the construction of his new capital city which, although originally intended to be the capital of the whole Mongol Empire, became increasingly the capital of China alone. By doing this Qubilai made his empire ever more Chinese and as such heir to the Song and earlier dynasties. The Mongols replaced the Song with their own dynasty, the Yuan, and, following the Chinese custom, Qubilai gave himself the Chinese dynastic name of Yuan Zhi. By this time the Chinese influence was very strong, and the mandarins were made much use of in the administration of the Yuan empire. The building of the new capital also owed much to the skills of Chinese architects and craftsmen.

In 1272 the new capital was officially named Ta-tu, 'the great capital', but it seems doubtful whether most people would have used this name. Marco Polo, who visited it soon afterwards, called it Khanibalu which was his version of Khanbaliq, Turkish for City of the Khan. Once more, even in China itself, some of the old Turkish influence must have lingered. The city was built on a strict geometrical plan, quite different from the higgledy-piggledy of Karakorum. This was obviously also something learned from the Chinese and earlier Chinese capitals, such as Chengdu, which had been built in this way. Marco Polo emphasized that if one stood by the gate at one end of the city it was possible to look right through to the other end, a fact which clearly impressed the traveller. Running through the city was the river Kao-liang Ho which was dammed to form two large lakes. Besides beauty and tranquillity at the heart of the empire, these also supplied fish and helped the city's water supply. Marco Polo described the whole plan as being like a chessboard, having a number of walls, one inside the other, with the palace of the Yuan emperor in the middle.[7]

At that time this palace was the residence of Qubilai and as such was the heart of the power of the empire. Ceremonial took place in the Great Hall which Marco Polo describes as being painted in all sorts of vivid colours and ornamented with carved dragons, figures of warriors and representations of battles. The roof was also gilded and had colourful paintings. In the centre of this Great Hall was what he called a 'contrivance', which seems to have borne a striking resemblance to the silver tree in Karakorum:

> In the middle of the hall where the Great Khan holds the banquet, stands a beautiful contrivance, very large and richly decorated, made like a square coffer and cunningly wrought with beautiful gilt and sculptures of animals. In the middle it is hollow, and in it stands a great vessel of pure gold, holding as much as a large cask; it is full of wine. All around this vessel . . . there are smaller ones . . . in one there is mare's milk, in another camel's milk, and so on.[8]

These 'milks' were actually alcoholic and it seems that many of the old habits and customs of the steppe nomads had been transferred to the magnificence of the new Yuan capital. The ceremonial as witnessed by travellers to Khanbaliq appeared in many ways to replicate on an even grander scale what took place in Karakorum.

Nevertheless, despite all this wealth and splendour, it soon came to be widely felt among the Mongols that living in China was debilitating to those very qualities which had enabled them to get there in the first place. Ariq-böke may have been defeated by his brother but his ideas had survived. Genghis Khan himself would have agreed with these when he set out his ideas of how the empire should be governed. His plan was that the Mongols should use the knowledge and skills of the Chinese and other subject peoples to fulfil those functions which they were unable to fulfil and to produce those things they could not produce. In this way, they should use Chinese expertise whenever possible and necessary. But the Mongols themselves should always preserve their own culture. In order to do this they should continue to live in the steppe lands and maintain their pastoral nomadic lifestyle. They should also continue to rear an ample supply of horses and other livestock and bring up the next generation of young warriors to be well versed in steppe ways and warfare.[9]

By moving into China, his grandson had ignored this advice. Qubilai, himself a great warrior in the Mongol tradition, had become increasingly seduced by the ease and luxury that the conquered country had to offer. Nevertheless, the Mongols still took every opportunity to return to the steppes to ride their horses and enjoy the old lifestyle. Qubilai had a summer capital built at Chang-du to which he and the court retreated in the summer when it became unbearably hot in Ta-tu. This was the Xanadu of Coleridge's poem where Kubla Khan did 'a stately pleasure dome decree'.[10]

This city was situated close to the steppe lands lying to the northeast of the capital and to a degree replicated the physical conditions in Mongolia itself. There is little evidence of the pleasure dome or of Alph, the sacred river which, according to Coleridge, was supposed to run through it, but archaeologists have discovered evidence of a large complex of buildings and of the summer palace itself. Here it was possible for the Mongol rulers to engage in such traditional sports as archery and horsemanship and, for a time at least, to return to the traditional Mongol ways. Kuriltais remained a regular feature and some of these actually took place in Chang-du, but most of them were still in Mongolia itself, usually in the Onon-Kerulen heartland.

In Mongolia the Mongols had been nature worshippers and the old shamanistic religion, focusing on Tengri, was central to their beliefs. However, apart from this, the religion which appears to have had the greatest appeal was Buddhism and there were a number of Buddhist temples in Karakorum. Qubilai Khan, being inclined towards all things Chinese, appears to have taken readily to Buddhism which by this time had become an important religion in China. As part of the whole Ta-tu project, a great temple complex was constructed on the northern flank of the city. This was the Miao Ying Temple and it included, among other things, a large lamasery dedicated to 'Greatness, Longevity, Everlasting Peace and Tranquillity'. These were sentiments which Genghis Khan, at least after his conquests had been completed, would certainly have endorsed. In the centre of the temple was a magnificent pagoda which at the time must have been one of the most impressive structures in the city. Completed in 1279 and known as the White Pagoda, it stands to this day as evidence of the importance of Buddhism to the Yuan. The design of the pagoda is that of an alms bowl and its splendid interior contains many treasures including an effigy of the enthroned Buddha and other Buddhist deities. This pagoda was the largest to be constructed any-where in China during the Yuan period. The khan himself worshipped in this pagoda. The magnificence of the Miao Ying Temple complex must certainly have rivalled that of the palace itself and demonstrated the importance of Buddhism to the Mongols during the Yuan period. Although never a theocracy, Buddhism was a demonstration of the Chinese character of the Yuan, and their adoption of a religion which was so widespread in China served to give added legitimacy to the dynasty.

One of the motives of Genghis Khan as he built up his empire had been to secure control over the trade routes crossing Central Asia, and this the Mongols succeeded in doing. Since their conquests produced peace in the steppes, the trade routes became far safer than they had ever been. This *Pax Mongolica* greatly stimulated trade between West and East and the 'Silk Road' thrived during this period.

While the location of the Yuan capital made it quite accessible to this Central Asian communication system, the city also became the focus of a comprehensive network of roads across China. These could be used by travellers and merchants, but their main purpose was to enable the khan, his army and his emissaries to reach all parts of the country as speedily as possible. This enabled the Mongols to keep control of an increasingly restless Chinese population for the best part of a century.

One of the most spectacular projects in the improvement of the transport network was the rebuilding of the Grand Canal which by this time had fallen into disuse. It had originally been constructed during the Sui dynasty (581–618) with the aim of connecting the basins of the two great rivers Yangtse and Huang He. As a result of this, the two independent axes of China and its civilization were linked together for the first time. Under the Mongols this canal was extended northwards from Hangchow, the old capital of the Southern Song, as far as the Yuan capital. The prolific and diverse produce of the south, notably tea, silk, cotton and spices, and, most important of all, rice, was transported more cheaply and with greater ease to the capital. This added greatly to the wealth of the Yuan and to the commercial importance of Khanbaliq itself, since much of what was then taken westwards on the Silk Road was also brought in the same way.

Despite the influence which China had on them, the Mongols remained quite separate from the Chinese population they ruled. They never really became fully part of China in the way that other, even foreign, dynasties had eventually done. The Mongols always had one eye on the steppe lands, their true home, and this led to their being regarded as outsiders in the Middle Kingdom. They always 'ruled from the saddle' and to the end they ruled as conquerors. This contrasted starkly with the Song, their immediate predecessors, who had been the most peaceful dynasty in Chinese history. This marked contrast between the two dynasties made the Chinese even less willing to accept the Mongols as their overlords. Even during the reign of Qubilai, Marco Polo reported on the fear of rebellion which made the Mongols reluctant to allow large numbers of Chinese to live in their capital. As the Yuan weakened in the middle of the fourteenth century there was a succession of revolts against the current incumbent of the throne and Karakorum also played some part in this destabilization. The chronicles of Ibn Batuta report how the khan was away in the steppes for this reason when the Arab traveller paid a visit to the capital.

In the 1340s there was a successful Chinese revolt against the Yuan and this had its origins, like so many other Chinese revolts, in the Yangtse valley of central China. By this time the Mongols had certainly become debilitated and, disliking the south of China, they were eventually defeated by this peasant army and forced to retreat northwards. In 1368 Toghon Temur, the last Yuan emperor of China, was forced to flee and he returned to the old capital, Karakorum. Officially it was announced that this move was a strategic one and the khan was assembling new forces in order to deal more effectively with the rebels. But this was never to be and the khan died in Karakorum two years later. For a time his Yuan successors continued the fiction that they were still the emperors of China, and this went on until 1388 when the last of the Yuan dynasty, Togus Temur, was murdered in the old capital. After barely two centuries, the great Mongol imperial venture came to an end in the city which had been built to commemorate its triumphant beginnings. However, by this time much had changed in Central Asia and a new centre of power had arisen in the west.

The great khans had built capitals in Karakorum and Ta-tu/ Khanbaliq. In both, the splendid buildings were potent demonstrations of their power. Yet in Karakorum it was in the Royal Ger that the khans clearly felt more at home, and when in China the desire to return to the steppe life always produced a certain uneasiness. Perhaps the most potent symbol of Mongol power was really the Royal Gerlug, a ger on wheels which was carried across the steppes by horses or oxen. Purevsukh produced an artist's impression of how this might have looked as it was travelling across the Central Asian steppe. It was the nomadic lifestyle of these people that engendered their unsurpassed martial qualities in the first place. Despite the splendour of the capitals they built, this ger on wheels was most evocative of the way in which this steppe people had created an empire extending across Eurasia from

The Royal Ger on wheels; this ger was the real centre of power in the Mongol Empire during the great period of conquests.

Europe to China. It had linked the 'Two Worlds' in a way that had never been done before. Yet in the end, despite the immense wealth and economic power which it gave to the Mongols, it was China that eventually destroyed them.

In 1370, when news of the last Yuan emperor's death reached the western regions of Central Asia, a warlord of the region proclaimed himself to be the successor to Genghis Khan and so to the Chinghizid dynasty. He was Timur Lenk, the Emir of Transoxania.[11] Timur was a member of the Turkish Barlas clan who originally came from near Fez, now known as Shakhrisabz, then a small settlement to the south of Samarkand. Ambitious for himself and his clan, Timur had attained power as a young man by defeating the Chinghizid ruler of Transoxania. Claiming to be of mixed Turkish-Mongolian descent, he sought to find links to the Chinghizid family itself. After the proclamation of 1370 his stated aim became the revival of the great Mongolian empire which had completely disintegrated. By 1380 he had established control over the whole of the Chaghatai khanate and went on to use this as a base for the further expansion of his domains. In his conquests he displayed great cruelty to those he regarded as his enemies, and usually this included any who had the temerity to stand up against him. Although a cultured man with a love of Persian art and literature, and enjoying nothing more than having discussions with other educated men, he retained this cruel streak throughout his life.

In 1388 he attacked and defeated the Golden Horde, forcing them to flee northwards. There they became an easy target for the growing power of Muscovite Russia, which was soon able to begin the process of freeing itself from the hated 'Tatar Yoke'. By now Timur had gained control of a large territory covering much of the western part of Central Asia but he did not feel confident enough of his credentials to take the title of khan. Rather he preferred to install a puppet khan of the Chinghizid family to be the nominal ruler of his expanding domains. However, he married a princess of the Chinghizid line and from then on he always referred to himself as 'Gurgan', meaning the son-in-law.

Timur's capital and centre of power was Samarkand which he had taken in 1366. As the ancient city of Maracanda it dated back to the time of the Achaemenid dynasty and had been one of the most important trading centres on the Silk Road. Timur always returned to this city after his conquests to rest and prepare for his next campaign. During these interludes he began to embellish the city with many fine buildings, including mosques and madrasas. He lavished wealth and resources on the city, founding academies and libraries, with the intention of making it into a great centre of the arts and learning. The Spanish ambassador Ruy González de Clavijo tells us that 'Samarkand . . . was the first of all the cities that he had conquered and the one that he had since ennobled above all others, by his buildings making it the treasure house of his conquests'.[12]

At the centre of the city was his highly fortified stronghold, the Gok Sarai – the Blue Palace – around which were laid out beautiful parks and gardens. After his visit in 1404 Clavijo observed that Samarkand was a town set in the midst of a forest in which there were gardens and running water, fruit trees, olive groves and aqueducts.[13] One of Timur's favourite gardens was the Baghi Dilkusha, the Garden of Heart's Delight, which had been laid out to commemorate his marriage to Tukal-khanum, the daughter of the khan. Babur, writing over a century later, was of the opinion that the magnificent summer palace in the middle of it was 'a building of imperial dimensions'.[14] Everything about it was calculated to dazzle the visitor. The largest and most splendid of the mosques was the Cathedral Mosque built in Timur's later years. This has been described in glowing terms as being of surpassing grandeur with pillars, arches, much marble and gilt doors. The traveller Yazdi considered it to be a building of perfect beauty and in Marozzi's opinion it was 'the apotheosis of Timur's architectural creation'.[15] Like Baghdad before it, Samarkand was above all a city of culture. At the heart of the empire, which had been won with much blood and destruction, lay this oasis of tranquillity, this 'Rome of the east' built with the spoils taken from the rest of the vast empire. In creating this gem, Timur laid the foundations of what was to be the great age of the Timurid khanate during the following century, when Samarkand was its glittering capital.

However, Timur also needed a capital that would reflect his great power and military achievements. This reflected the hard side of his nature in which he saw himself as 'emperor of the world' rather than the softer side in which he was the patron of cultural and intellectual attainments. With this in mind, he embarked on the building of another capital which was very different in character from Samarkand. For this he chose Shakhrisabz, in the territory of the Barlas clan. The new city was adjacent to the old settlement and centred on the Ak Sarai, the White Palace, the building of which commenced around 1385. This was the largest building ever built by Timur and its sheer size amazed and overawed all those who saw it. Clavijo described in some detail how it looked in 1404. On approaching it, the first things to be seen were the huge twin entrance towers rising 200 ft from the ground and flanking a grand entrance arch 130 ft high. From there a courtyard led to a series of chambers which extended straight to the hall at the heart of the palace. This was the magnificent domed reception hall where Timur received ambassadors and other distinguished visitors. 'The walls are panelled with gold and blue tiles, and the ceiling is entirely of gold work', reported Clavijo. It was there that visitors first met 'the Terror of the World', who also styled himself 'the Shadow of Allah on Earth', a title which was written in Arabic above the entrance. At such receptions he would be seated on a splendid golden throne raised above the floor level of the hall. However, in contrast to all this splendour, it is reported that he himself was usually dressed quite simply in a plain gown and had little decoration on his person.

The scale of the palace was tremendous and was clearly intended for the specific purpose of impressing visitors and making them aware that they were at the court of a great and powerful king. Here more than anywhere was to be seen the truth of Timur's assertion: 'Let he who doubts our power look upon our buildings.' At the other end of the great avenue leading from Ak Sarai, Timur began the construction of a mosque which was on an equally gigantic scale. This was the Kok Gumbaz mosque, and its size and location fittingly demonstrated that this was the other, although less evident, pillar on which Timur's empire was founded.

While Samarkand, his great love, was first and foremost intended as a display of the civilization of his empire, Shakhrisabz, on the other hand, was intended as a demonstration of his overwhelming power. This and many other buildings were still under construction when Timur set off on his final military expedition. We hear of 'feverish construction' in Samarkand at this time and this contrasted markedly with the destruction which the conqueror left elsewhere. According to Marozzi, 'Timur threw himself into the glorification of his capital with all the furious energy of war.'[16] By the early fifteenth century, Timur's empire stretched from its Central Asian core into Persia, Mesopotamia, the Caucasus and Afghanistan. He had defeated the Golden Horde, the Chaghatai khanate and, most significantly, the Ottoman Empire. This emerging power, which was soon to dominate Islam, clearly struck terror into the hearts of the Europeans of the time. Timur joined the list of fearsome eastern conquerors who incarnated that 'danger from the east' which had become an entrenched belief in the European mind. The sixteenth-century English playwright Christopher Marlowe, who called Timur

'Tamburlaine', presents a picture both of his power and his destructiveness. In his play *Tamburlaine the Great* the Ottoman emperor, Bajazeth (Bayazit I), is captured and displayed in a cage so that all can see his humiliation. The formidable power which had already crossed into the Balkans and conquered its people had been itself defeated by a far more fearsome warrior. The fear this engendered is expressed vividly by Marlowe:

> The god of war resigns his room to me
> Meaning to make me general of the world;
> Jove viewing me in arms, looks pale and wan,
> Fearing my power should pull him from his throne.
> *Tamburlaine the Great, Part One, Act v, Scene 1*

Nevertheless, the more creative side of Timur is also acknowledged by Marlowe, who sees this as having been used to promote his glory. The conqueror boasts:

> Then shall my native city Samarcanda . . .
> Be famous through the furthest continents;
> For there my palace royal shall be plac'd,
> Whose shining turrets shall dismay the heavens
> And cast the fame of Ilion's tower to hell
> *Tamburlaine the Great, Part Two, Act iv, Scene 3*

Marlowe calls Timur a 'Scythian Shepherd', so going along with the myth of the close association between his empire and that of Genghis Khan's nomads. However, this was never really the case. The Barlas clan had become more urban than rural and Timur always sought solace in the beauties of Samarkand rather than in a ger on the steppes as preferred by Genghis Khan. Here we have a clear case of a sedentary people attempting to take over the empire of pastoral nomads and justifying it by creating their own myth. There would certainly have been many pastoral nomads from the steppes recruited into Timur's army but its leadership was firmly of urban and sedentary origins.

The one major part of the old Mongol Empire which had not been conquered by Timur was China. In 1405 the conqueror decided that this was to be his next and last conquest and he spent that summer assembling a formidable force which set forth eastwards from Samarkand in the autumn. Timur intended to conquer China as Qubilai Khan had done a century and a half earlier. However, the old warrior was now 69 years old and had been in poor health for some time. On the border of northern China the army ran into ferocious winter weather which held it up for weeks. Timur's health deteriorated in the appalling conditions and he died there in January 1406. This put an end to the attempted conquest of China. His body was brought back to Samarkand where he was buried in the Gur Emir mausoleum built by his successor. The inscription on his tomb reads, 'Here lies the illustrious and merciful Lord Timur . . . Conqueror of the World.' Illustrious he may have been but he was certainly not merciful and his empire, while enormous by European or Middle Eastern standards, was only a fraction of the size of that of his alleged ancestor, Genghis Khan.

Perhaps it is in the splendour of his capitals that one can see the most marked difference between Timur and the earlier conqueror. Genghis Khan was always happier in his ger and he thought of a fixed capital as being a Chinese idea which had to be reluctantly accepted. Timur, on the other hand, saw both his capitals as being the centres of his empire and statements of its ultimate purpose. Geoffrey Moorhouse pointed out that while Genghis Khan had laid waste to Samarkand and to many other cities, Samarkand in particular was Timur's greatest pleasure. 'Marlowe's "Scourge of God and terror of the world"', as

The tomb of Timur Lenk (Tamerlane) in Samarkand.

Moorhouse put it, 'never failed to send back treasure and skilled craftsmen from his conquests, with one end in view; to make Samarkand
worthier than ever of its long renown: not only Mirror of the World,
but garden of souls and Fourth Paradise as well. He had a creative streak
which was lacking in Genghis Khan or his heirs.'[17]

Nevertheless, the fear of the eastern conqueror, so vividly expressed
by Marlowe, continued to influence European perceptions of Asia. It
was seen as a place of barbarism and violence more than of any real
cultural or intellectual attainment. Yet this was very far from being true
of Timur. Samarkand had already become in his lifetime one of the
great centres of science, learning and the arts. However, Shakhrisabz was
designed to present quite a different image, which was the one with
which Europeans of the time had become far more familiar.

Following Timur's death in 1406 the period of Central Asian
imperial conquest came to an end. It was exactly 200 years since
Temuchin had been proclaimed Genghis Khan at the great kuriltai of
1206 and during this time Central Asia had been home to the largest
and most fearsome empires on the globe. The size of these great empires
was never to be repeated and from then on Central Asia changed its
role to a place of conquered people rather than of conquerors. This was
not just a matter of warlords and dynasties but was the result of important
underlying geopolitical changes. Following the death of Timur the great
land routes across Eurasia soon lost their importance. Even during his
lifetime they had been in decline and his fearsome reputation was already
beginning to deter traders from venturing across his domains. The *Pax
Mongolica*, which had for so long ensured the safety of merchants and
travellers, came to an end and the political divisions and strife which had
preceded it again came to characterize the area.

In addition to this, the peripheral peoples were themselves becoming
stronger and more powerful and were seeking other ways to ensure the
safety of their growing commerce. These were soon provided by the
new sea routes which were pioneered during the fifteenth century. Little
more than a decade after Timur's death the Portuguese Prince Henry
the Navigator began the great maritime explorations which were to
change the world communications system for good. The death of Timur
was thus momentous since it saw not only the collapse of a great Asiatic
empire but also the end of an age. The 'Chinghizid' age, which had
been most symbolized by the so-called Silk Road, came to an end and
the 'Columbian' age was about to begin. However, the immediate legacy
of Timur was not what might have been expected. It was the legacy of his

Registan Square in Samarkand, which Lord Curzon considered to be the most beautiful square in the world.

civilization rather than his power which was to be most in evidence during the following century.

Timur was succeeded by his son Shah Rukh who, together with his grandson Ulugh Beg, presided over a golden age of achievement in Central Asia. This Timurid age spanned architecture, science, painting, astronomy and many other fields. It was at this time that perhaps the most magnificent addition to Samarkand, the Registan Square, was completed. The British statesman Lord Curzon, while journeying across Asia in the late nineteenth century, expressed the opinion that this was the most beautiful square in the world. Ulugh Beg was more comfortable as an astronomer than as a ruler and he constructed a huge observatory on a hill overlooking Samarkand. The astronomers of Samarkand went on to make significant advances in astronomical knowledge. The Samarkand region also produced many scientists and scholars at this time who went on to make important contributions in the wider Islamic world. This changed the whole picture of a region which had been at the heart of one of the largest and most ruthless of empires. It was the legacy of the Timur of Samarkand which now went on to define the region for the following century, while the legacy of the Timur of Shakhrisabz, 'the once luminous jewel of an ever-expanding empire', as Marozzi put it, died with the great conqueror in the snows of China.[18]

Statue of Ulugh Beg, grandson of Timur Lenk, outside the observatory which he built in Samarkand. The 'Timurid' dynasty produced some of the greatest Islamic art and science.

While Samarkand went on to become one of the greatest and most renowned cities in Central Asia, Shakhrisabz soon declined into insignificance. By the twentieth century the Ak Sarai had deteriorated into a colossal ruin and little remained except its vast size to indicate what it had once been. While 'Look on our buildings' may have been Timur's comment on his power, few of those built to demonstrate his power have actually survived.

In Karakorum, the old heart of the Mongol Empire, great changes were also taking place. Following the murder of Togus Temur, the last of the Yuan, in the city in 1388, Mongolia soon broke up into two halves. The eastern Mongols, the Khalkha, continued to be ruled by a branch of the Chinghizids, while the western Mongols, the Oirats, broke away and established a separate state. In the early sixteenth century Altan Khan, a Khalkha leader, using Karakorum as his power base, endeavoured to reunite the Mongols and by the middle of the century he had become the acknowledged ruler of the whole country. There was again prosperity thanks to trade with Central Asia and China. In 1575 came a visit by Sonam Gyatso, an eminent Buddhist lama from Tibet. He soon had a profound effect on Altan Khan who, as a result, converted to Tibetan Gelugpa (Yellow Hat) Buddhism. Buddhism had, of course, been present in Mongolia since the time of Genghis Khan and was strong at the court of his grandson Qubilai. However, after the return of the last Yuan emperor there was little sign of Buddhist influence remaining. Altan Khan became so impressed with his guest that he proclaimed Sonam Gyatso to be the 'Dalai Lama', the Universal Lama, and after his death his successors were declared to be his reincarnations. Mass conversion to Buddhism soon took place and Mongolia became a deeply Buddhist country, this time looking to Tibet for its spiritual inspiration. However, Sonam Gyatso's successors eventually decided to return to Tibet, taking the title of Dalai Lama with them. This left the Mongols bereft of the very reincarnation which Altan Khan had proclaimed and it was decided that Mongolia must have its own separate reincarnation. This reincarnation was given the title of khutuktu. He was believed to be the 'Living Buddha' and immediately became and remained the central figure of Mongolian Buddhism.

After his conversion, Altan Khan began the construction of a massive lamasery, Erdene Zuu, in Karakorum. Stones and other materials from the old city were used in its construction. It was surrounded by massive walls which contained over 100 stupas, dome-shaped Buddhist memorial shrines. The lamasery included living quarters for the lamas together with temples and secular buildings for administration. The temples were filled with statues of the Buddha and major figures in Tibetan Buddhism. They were eclectic in their architectural style, displaying Chinese, Tibetan and Mongolian influences. It is said that at its maximum size over 10,000 lamas lived in it. Karakorum now became the residence of both the khan and the khutuktu. A theocratic state was established in which Buddhism played a major role and the close religious links with Tibet were retained. In the great courtyard at the centre of the monastery was the Royal Ger of the khan and this was also the place where kuriltais took place. The tombs of Altan Khan and other Khalkha nobles were within the walls of this lamasery. In this way, Karakorum resumed for a time its old position as capital, but now it was the capital of a far smaller theocratic state in which the Buddha had replaced Tengri.

In 1691 at a kuriltai that took place in Inner Mongolia, the Mongolian nobles made a formal submission to accept the hegemony of the Ming dynasty. After nearly 700 years of Mongolian independence, during which the largest empires the world had ever seen had risen and fallen, the Chinese were once more back in control.

Karakorum remained the religious centre and the residence of the khutuktu until the nineteenth century when he transferred his capital to Urga, now renamed Ulaan Baatar. This was on the newly opened routeway from Russia to China via Mongolia and so in a far more convenient location than Karakorum. After 500 years the centre of power in the country had moved back eastwards, closer to the old Mongol heartlands.

While the imperial cities of Karakorum and Shakhrisabz both fell into ruins, the fate of Ta-tu, the second Mongol capital, was to be rather different. While much of the old Mongol city disappeared, it soon became the site of the building of yet another imperial capital which was to prove far more enduring than either of the others had been.

5
Power over East Asia: The Forbidden City and the Middle Kingdom

The fall of the Yuan dynasty had been brought about by a successful rebellion against Mongol rule that had its origins in the middle Yangtze region of central China. It was a peasant revolt against the appalling conditions of life under the Yuan who, still possessing the psychology of pastoral nomads, always despised the peasantry. The revolt was led by Zhu Yuanzhang, a man of humble origins who soon proved himself a capable leader. Zhu proceeded to establish a new dynasty which, unlike its predecessor, was Han Chinese. To this he gave the name Ming, meaning bright, and Zhu himself took the imperial title of Hong Wu.

During the rebellion Nanjing had been Zhu's headquarters and as the new emperor he decided that this city in the heart of China should become his dynastic capital. It had always been an important centre of power in the Yangtze region and had been favoured by indigenous as opposed to foreign dynasties. In any case, the Ming emperor considered Ta-tu/Khanbaliq to have been far too much identified with the hated rule of the Mongols.

During his 30-year reign (1368–98) Zhu returned to the traditional systems which had been either ignored or abandoned by the Yuan. As part of this the old Chinese class system was revived and the mandarins were reinstated to their prime position in government. The lot of the peasantry, which had been dire under the Mongols, soon greatly improved. There was also a revived interest in the south of China and in opening up trade with the east Asian maritime world. Despite their defeat, the Mongols were still considered a danger and the stated aim of the Yuan, now back in Karakorum, was to collect together sufficient force to reconquer China. In view of this the Ming continued to keep large forces in the north and among the generals in command was the emperor's own son, Zhu Di.

Since the heir to the throne had predeceased his father, on the death of Hong Wu in 1398 the successor and second Ming emperor was his grandson, Zhu Yunwen. This young man proved to be an ineffective ruler and he was deposed in 1402 by his uncle Zhu Di who then ascended the imperial throne as the third Ming emperor, taking the title of Yong Le. A man of great strength and ability, but quite ruthless and brutal, he came to be known as 'Black Dragon'. Until then he had spent much of his life on the northern frontier fighting the Mongols and other tribes in this dangerous and turbulent region.

On becoming emperor, Yong Le made the surprising decision to return the capital back north to the old Yuan capital. He did this despite the fact that the ruling house was firmly based in the Yangtze area, from whence it had always drawn its support. There had also been considerable emphasis under Hong Wu on China's southern and maritime connections which had, for understandable reasons, been largely ignored by the Yuan.

However, the move to the north took place in 1417 and the building of a new imperial palace began. Three years later the capital was formally returned to Khanbaliq which was renamed Beijing, the northern capital. By this time the old Mongol city was mostly in ruins and a completely new city was rising in its place. For the Chinese, moving the nation's capital to a different location involved more than just an adjustment to changed geopolitical circumstances. The site and situation of the capital had since the earliest times been governed by the geomantic principles contained in feng shui, a form of geomancy. The capital had ideally to be located at the 'pivot of the four quarters', the point at which the emperor was in closest contact with the realms above and below the earth. These always had to be borne in mind when planning a new city and the necessity to face in the right direction and to take into account the nature of the local topography were paramount. The legend of a holy man well versed in the principles of feng shui who strongly influenced the decisions of Yong Le helped give the necessary celestial approval for what was being done.

This decision by a southern dynasty to return the capital to the north has been considered by some to be inexplicable. The most plausible explanation appears to be that the new Ming emperor had been a military man and had spent most of his adult life around the northern frontiers. As a result he had grown to feel more at home in this area. However, in addition to this personal motive, a powerful geopolitical reason for the move, and for the particular choice of site, may also have been the perceived need to reinforce the power of the north as protection in the direction from which the greatest dangers in Chinese history had usually come. The new Ming northern capital was just to the south of the Great Wall which had been originally built in the time of the Qin dynasty but which had fallen into disuse, for obvious reasons, during the Mongol period. A priority was now the rebuilding and reinforcement of the Wall, together with the strengthening of the whole system of northern defences. The new Beijing was thus a 'forward' capital in the sense used by Cornish, and its location was linked to the overall defence of the country.[1]

Nevertheless, Yong Le was as aware as the first Ming emperor had been of the importance of the country's south and its maritime connections. This was clearly demonstrated by the new emperor's other major decision to equip a grand fleet of impressive ships under Grand Admiral Zheng He to explore the lands to the south and west of China and to forge links with them. Although these expeditions were largely discontinued after the death of Yong Le, there was a final one as late as 1433. After that there was a surprising reversal in policy and the whole great enterprise was wound up.

It would seem that as a result of the move to the north, continental thinking had taken over and even under this indigenous southern dynasty the country had resumed its northern orientation. There were still those who yearned for a return of the capital to Nanjing, and on the death of Yong Le one last attempt was made to do this. However, by the 1440s the Ming northern capital was so well established that there could be no question of any further change taking place. In any case, by then a new city of surpassing magnificence was growing up among the ruins of the old Yuan capital and this was clearly intended to be a powerful demonstration of both Ming power and of the dynasty's intentions.

The new city which sprang up on and near the ruins of the old capital was in fact made up of four quite distinct quarters, all closely linked within a series of powerful walls. In the north was the 'Inner City', later known as the 'Tartar City', and in the south was the 'Chinese' or 'Outer City'. Inside the area covered by the Inner City was the imperial city incorporating some of the beautiful lakes which had been originally made for Khanbaliq. In the heart of this Imperial City was the Forbidden City. This was 'forbidden' in that only the imperial family and the court and retainers were allowed to live there. Apart from those of the imperial family, the only males allowed were the palace eunuchs. These were the 'servants' of the emperor in the widest sense, some of them, like those of the Byzantines and Ottomans in Constantinople, eventually rising to the highest positions in the state.

Since the Forbidden City was intended to be the centre of Ming power it contained the major buildings directly associated with this power. Nevertheless, there were some important buildings outside it, notably the examination halls and a number of temples, the most important of these being the Temple of Heaven.

It has been said that the Ming capital represented the final stage in the development of traditional Chinese architecture and certainly the ideas which went into it were very similar to those of the earlier capitals. Not one of those, however, had been so clearly built to be a magnificent display of power. The nearest was perhaps Chang'an, the centre of power of the Sui and Tang dynasties, which was close to the first Chinese capital, Xianyang. This city was built on a geometrical pattern surrounded by gigantic protective walls. However, within the walls were palaces and gardens clearly intended more for the pleasure of the emperor, the empress, the harem and the court than for the display of power. The opulent lifestyle of the imperial family was kept well out of sight of their subjects.

In contrast to this, the Forbidden City was intended as a display of imperial power both for the Chinese people and for the foreigners who visited the capital. Most of the latter would be expected to be bringing tribute to the emperor. China was, after all, the Zhong guo, the Middle Kingdom, and it was necessary for both the Chinese people and the barbarians beyond to be kept fully aware of this fact and of its implications. As has been observed, the basic factors underlying its construction were the traditional Chinese ones enshrined in feng shui. The nature of the activities which took place within the Forbidden City, and for which it was built, also owed much to Confucian precepts which since early times had underlain the Chinese concept of government.

In the original plan, geomancy and cosmology played the major role, determining the disposition of all the major buildings. From the outset it was understood that the city would face southwards. This was the direction of the sun and in any case it always made sense for buildings to be orientated towards the maximum light. But besides these practical considerations, the sun was also seen as being the centre of the universe and the capital city had to reflect the fact that it was the seat of the emperor who ruled his domains as the sun ruled the sky. It was also essential that the precise orientation accorded with the celestial systems centred on the Pole Star. As it was the centre of the Chinese universe, the capital was therefore like the Pole Star in the sky. The emperor was considered to be the 'Son of Heaven' and it was his task to rule on earth as the Heavenly Being, Tien, rules in the Heavens. Tien is the Lord of Heaven and, as his son, the emperor has celestial authority bestowed on him. This son–father relationship tied the Ming into the celestial world and it was this above all that was deemed to give the dynasty its legitimacy.

The highly geometrical character of the Forbidden City was also intended to represent order as opposed to chaos. One of the principal functions of the emperor was to bring order to the country and therefore his own capital had to reflect this. In this way the capital demonstrated the contrast both with the disorder of nature and with the disorder that accompanies the lack of a firm and powerful authority.

The emperor having had the Tien Min bestowed on him is responsible for ensuring that there is peace and order throughout his lands and the achievement of this requires an overall situation of harmony. This is the harmonious linking together of all things in the empire so that they will live and work together peacefully and constructively for the good of the whole.

On earth the enforcement of this requires the use of power and its display is intended as being something to deter, and if necessary strike terror into, those who would upset the imperial state of peace and harmony. As Osvald Sirén put it, the Forbidden City was built 'in accordance with the architectural principles and the ancient traditions of might and splendour, which have prevailed in the construction of all the great imperial palaces in China'.[2] Sirén also noted that nothing could be seen as an individual creation but that everything was part of a greater whole and that symbols of imperial power were to be found everywhere. The most important of these was the dragon which was symbolic of many types and grades of power. The dragon of the emperor was always yellow and had five claws, while those of the nobility had only four. The lion was also a symbol of imperial power and was often placed in a position to guard the emperor and his palaces. In fact, everything in the Forbidden City was representative of something, none more so than numbers which were linked to mathematical principles and so to order. The number five always had a very special significance and this was because of the belief in the five elements which constituted the basis of the preservation of order. These were earth, wood, metal, fire and water and each had its particular place

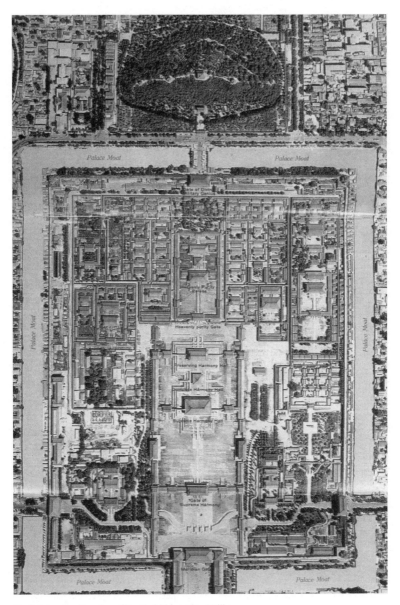

Model showing the plan of the Forbidden City, Beijing.

in the overall scheme of things. Every age was believed to be governed by one of these elements and the age possessed the virtues and also the weaknesses of that particular element.

Colours were also important and each had its own particular significance. An example of this is that while the name Forbidden City

The imperial throne in the Hall of Supreme Harmony at the heart of the Forbidden City, Beijing.

indicates the closed and mystical character of the place in which only the selected few were allowed to reside, the additional name of 'Purple' Forbidden City was a reference to the colour associated with the heavenly bodies. In this way the palace-city would proclaim the close relationship between the Lord of Heaven, who ruled above and dwelt in the 'purple' cluster of stars around the Pole Star, and the Son of Heaven who ruled in the Purple City below. This accorded well with the Confucian precept that 'A virtuous ruler is like the Pole Star that keeps its place while all other stars do homage to it.'[3] While its great walls protected the city from any dangers around it, the city was open to the heavens above. It was 'the great within', the heart of the Middle Kingdom, and from inside its walls all the important decisions concerning its government emanated.

The plan of the Forbidden City was absolutely in accordance with the prime objective of displaying power. In the first instance, this was achieved by the routeway which was necessarily taken by those who visited the city on official business. They would have included imperial servants, provincial governors from distant provinces of the empire and embassies from the surrounding countries bearing tribute. On occasion there were foreigners from the barbarian lands beyond. These would all have been expected to enter through the Tiananmen Gate, the Gate of Heavenly Peace, which linked the sanctum with the Inner City around it. From there a walled avenue led to the Meridian Gate from where the emperor was displayed to his people on the great occasions of state. The emperor alone was allowed to pass through this gate which was otherwise normally kept firmly bolted. Only on the rarest occasions and for the most important of guests would it be opened; such guests included the candidate who came top in the imperial examinations. After this illustrious student had been accorded the honour of a congratulatory audience with the emperor he was allowed to leave in grand style through the Meridian Gate. Such students were then destined for the highest offices of state.

The main avenue through the Forbidden City went on past this outer Gateway to the Gate of Supreme Harmony which led to the centrepiece of the whole city, the Hall of Supreme Harmony. As has been observed, harmony was at the heart of the imperial purpose and a central function of the emperor was to preserve this at all costs. It was in this Hall that some of the most important ceremonies of state took place, including the observation of the Chinese New Year and the solstices. The Hall itself was built on the top of three terraces known as the Dragon Pavement and so raised on a great platform above the level of the other buildings of the city. At the top of the steps stood a pair of bronze tortoises which symbolized the strength of the empire and the firm foundations on which it was built. In the Hall was the Dragon Throne which was elevated on a great dais, lifting it well above the already high level of the Hall. Here

the emperor would be seated in order to be the main focus of all ceremonial. The Hall was filled with symbolism including the dragon and the
repetition of the number five which appears in the five colours and the
five directions leading out of the Hall.

On the occasion of the great ceremonies of state the emperor was
conveyed on the Chair of State covered by a yellow canopy and on his
arrival heralds would cry, 'The Lord of Ten Thousand Years approaches'.
He then ascended the throne but was covered so that he could be seen
only by those closest to him. The 'Great Presence' was too sacred to be
seen by others on these ceremonial occasions. All present were then
instructed to give thanks for the imperial bounty and to kowtow to
the emperor.

Behind the Hall of Supreme Harmony was a succession of lesser
halls which were also associated with imperial ceremonial and government. The Gate of Heavenly Purity led on to the Palace of Heavenly Purity
which was another place where the emperor presided over ceremonies
and also met with his ministers and the high officials of state. Most of
the activities of the emperor took place within the Forbidden City but
some ceremonies were also held outside it. For this purpose the great

Interior of the Temple of Heaven, Beijing.

Meridian Gate was thrown open and the emperor emerged. The populace were then ordered to prostrate themselves as the emperor passed by. They were certainly never allowed to look on the sacred one. The most important of all such ceremonies took place in the splendour of the Temple of Heaven located in the Chinese or Outer City to the south. This was the most important temple in the city and it had functions analogous to those of the church of Hagia Sofia in Constantinople. At the centre of the Temple of Heaven was the great Altar of Heaven which was a magnificent circular building constructed in the fifteenth century. It was here that the emperor came to pray for good fortune for the Chinese people and, most importantly, for the harvest. However, the longest of all the ceremonies was the annual celebration of the Chinese New Year. This was also considered to commemorate the birth of the Chinese empire and was an event of the greatest significance, taking many days and involving much complicated ritual. Nearby in the complex were many other temples including the Altar of Soil and Grain and the Temple of the Imperial Ancestors. They all had their place in the endless rituals and ceremonials which took place throughout the year and at the most important of which the emperor would normally be expected to officiate.

Besides these great state occasions, the Forbidden City was intended to impress both those who saw it from outside and the privileged few who were allowed to pass through its sacred portals. The intention to link Heaven and Earth, the human and the celestial, is clearly seen from the description of one traveller many centuries later. In the early twentieth century Osbert Sitwell described how 'The huge buildings floated upon clouds, were borne up by them . . . The glory that shone from the ground imparted a brilliance beyond belief to the interiors, to the great red pillars, up the length of which golden dragons clawed their way to doors and frescoed walls.'4 By that time most of the glory of the empire had passed away but the great buildings continued to impress as they had in earlier centuries.

Immediately to the north of Beijing the Ming dynasty constructed two further important symbols of their power. The first of these were the Ming tombs which covered a large area some 20 km from the capital. This vast complex contains the mausoleums of thirteen of the Ming emperors but by far the largest and most splendid of these was that of Yong Le himself. Entry to the tombs is via the Sacred Way, guarded by massive statues of animals including camels, lions, elephants and horses. A huge underground chamber containing vases, incense burners and candlesticks puts one in mind of the great subterranean tomb complex of the first emperor Qin Shi Huangdi, which contained all the preparations for the afterlife together with the terracotta army to guard him.

The second symbol was both a very real statement of Ming power and also something of practical use. This was the Great Wall which, originally dating back to the first Chinese empire, had long fallen into decay. During the Yuan period its existence had been of no relevance but now it became important again. The rebuilding instigated by Yong Le was done over a long period during the fifteenth and sixteenth centuries. However, by the time it was finished, the lingering threat posed by the Mongols, and later on the far more real one from Timur, had long passed and the Khalkha Mongols had once more submitted to the Chinese as their overlords. As a result it turned out after all that the newly restored Great Wall had become to all intents and purposes little more than a symbol. Its enormous size and length was both a demonstration of Ming power and a clear demarcation between the civilized Middle Kingdom and the barbarian lands beyond.

Despite its early power, by the middle of the seventeenth century the dynasty was in a much weakened state. A series of natural catastrophes such as earthquakes, floods and bad harvests had brought great suffering and had shaken the faith of the people in their rulers. In 1628 there was a severe famine in which millions died. It was coming increasingly to be believed that the dynasty had lost that Tien Min – Mandate of Heaven – which was essential for the successful governing of the Zhong guo. The last Ming emperor, Chongzhen, who came to the throne in 1627, inherited a discredited administration. In desperation he turned to the Jesuits who had been present at the imperial court for some time. This powerful religious order, which had first come to China in the wake of the Portuguese in the sixteenth century, was able to acquaint the Chinese with many of the technical advances taking place in Europe, but even they could not help a dynasty in the terminal stages of decline. All their intervention did was to cause more trouble by making even the mandarins, always suspicious of the Jesuits, begin to doubt the legitimacy of the emperor and of the Ming dynasty itself.

Beyond the Great Wall, historically always the place of greatest danger to the Chinese, there had been further menacing developments. The peoples living immediately to the north were becoming increasingly restive. These were the Manchus, the people of Manchuria, who had been historically within the Chinese sphere of influence but had usually been strong enough to maintain independence. Whenever

China was weak this was seen as an opportunity by the peoples of the north. China was now showing all the signs of degenerating into chaos and the Manchu, who had been expanding their territories for some time, saw their opportunity. By the 1630s their army reached Shantung where they displayed their martial prowess and were successful in defeating a far larger Ming army. In 1644 they breached the Great Wall and soon reached the gates of Beijing. In response, the last Ming emperor called a council and proclaimed that, 'I, feeble and of small virtue, have offended against Heaven.'[5] He proceeded to remove his imperial robes and retired to the hill north of the Forbidden City where he committed suicide. The Ming dynasty, which had been so triumphant in removing the Mongols, had been forced to submit to another non-Chinese people.

Very soon afterwards the Manchu army entered Beijing and a Manchu dynasty was proclaimed. This took the name of the Qing, and the Manchu king, Aisin-Gioro Fu Lin, became its first emperor. He took the imperial title of Shun Zhi. The reign of this young man was dominated by his uncle Dorgon and it was mainly spent in consolidating Manchu power over the whole of China. It was the second Qing emperor, Kangxi (1661–1722), who set the seal on what was to be a very successful dynasty by showing himself to be deeply respectful of all aspects of Chinese culture and prepared to continue the system of imperial governance which had been developed and perfected by the Ming. First and foremost the imperial capital was to remain in Beijing and very few changes were made to it for fear that the whole system of imperial governance would come tumbling down. Qing Beijing remained essentially Ming Beijing. As Cotterell put it, the new dynasty saw that nothing was to be gained in disturbing the cosmic layout of the imperial capital 'which had been built in the centre of the earth in order to govern the whole world'.[6]

The only major innovation was the building by Kangxi of the summer palace to the north of Beijing. The site chosen included hills and lakes and this magnificent natural location was used to great advantage. Kangxi wrote:

In harmony with the natural contours of the country I have built pavilions in the pine groves thereby enhancing the natural beauties of the hills . . . I have made water flow past the summer houses as if leading the mountain mists out of the valleys . . . I think of virtue.[7]

In this place an imperial palace, temples and other buildings constituted a magnificent retreat well away from the heat and dust of summers in the capital.

However, the Qing dynasty, like their predecessors, ruled most of the time from the Forbidden City and dutifully carried out the Ming rituals. Although Manchus, they adapted well to China and came rapidly to be looked on as virtually an indigenous dynasty. Already subjected to Chinese influences in their homeland, they were accepted easily by their new subjects. This was something the Mongols had never been able to achieve.

By the eighteenth century, large parts of the world were either under direct European political control or at least were in the sphere of the maritime powers. However, like the Ming before them, the Qing were not interested in having much to do with the 'foreign devils', as the Europeans were by this time known, and did all they could to keep them at arm's length. Like the Ming, they found the Jesuits both interesting and, to a certain extent, useful, but they were certainly not prepared to accept the notion of European superiority in any way or to make any real concessions to them.

As Britain moved into its position as the leading world maritime power in the eighteenth century, the urge to forge closer relations with China became irresistible. China had been able to retain its position as a closed kingdom outside the Eurocentric global system that had been in the course of creation for two centuries. Despite the huge changes taking place around it, the *Zhong guo* still considered itself the centre of the world and far superior in the arts of civilization to the barbarians outside its borders. However, the Europeans were becoming ever less prepared to accept this Chinese isolation and were bent on the creation of their own maritime version of the Silk Road. Largely as a result of pressure from the East India Company, which dominated the eastern trade, in 1792 a British diplomatic mission led by Lord Macartney was dispatched to Beijing for the purpose of paving the way for the opening of diplomatic relations which would lead to trade. It was the biggest mission ever sent to China by a western power and was at first received with great courtesy and formality. An audience with the Qianlong emperor was arranged and this took place in the summer palace. However, despite many meetings with officials and the exchange of presents and platitudes, in the end the mission proved unsuccessful. Among other failings in the eyes of the Chinese, the British did not show the required degree of deference. The idea that the British would treat the Zhong guo as some kind of equal power was quite shocking to them. As the mission drew to a close, the reply of the emperor was finally delivered at a grand ceremony in the Hall of the Gate of Supreme Harmony in the Forbidden City. The emperor was not present and the imperial letter of reply to King George III was placed on the imperial throne and had to be itself kowtowed to as though the emperor were actually sitting there. In the reply, the request for an exchange of embassies was flatly refused in the most peremptory terms. The emperor referred to 'wanton' proposals for an ambassador to stay at 'the Celestial Court', something which was quite out of the question. It was firmly ruled out as being 'not in harmony with the state system of our dynasty and so will definitely not be permitted'.[8] It is significant that this final meeting took place at the Gate of Supreme Harmony and that the word 'harmony' was also used in the imperial letter. This was, after all, the ultimate and supreme function of the emperor and he certainly was not going to allow it to be interfered with by these dubious foreigners. For the emperor to have had anything to do with foreign devils would certainly not have accorded with the required harmony prescribed by the names of the halls of the Forbidden City itself.

However, despite this display of contempt, the reality was that China was already much weakened in both actual and relative terms. The idea of the all-powerful Zhong guo, which might still have been a reality during the rule of the Ming, became more and more unreal during that of their successors. This was soon realized by many within China itself and a few years after the Macartney Mission the conflict between the traditionalists who wished to keep the foreigners at bay and the modernizers who were prepared to allow them in had come to a head.

By the nineteenth century the material progress of the Europeans had become spectacular. Those inventions which the Jesuits had in earlier centuries displayed to the Chinese were nothing compared to what the Europeans, led by the British, now possessed. The introduction of such wonders as the railway, the telegraph and coalmining was something the modernizers saw as necessary if China was to keep up, but the traditionalists resisted them tenaciously. They believed that such things did not accord with feng shui and so would destroy the harmony so essential to the smooth and proper functioning of the celestial empire. This opposition was led by the mandarins who had always been suspicious of the Europeans and their inventions.

As custodians of Chinese culture and civilization they saw their pre-eminence at the heart of government being threatened by the

Europeans. The attempt to force trade on the Chinese, later done in the most brutal and disastrous manner by the British in the Opium Wars, caused many Chinese to distrust and hate foreigners, especially the British, even more. Nevertheless, it also made them realize that these foreigners could no longer be resisted. The defensive walls of China were quite inadequate to keep out this new and all-pervasive invasion.

No Great Wall could keep out the modern world for ever and by the end of the nineteenth century the great powers had secured a number of bases in the country by various means, including the use of military force. By then they had been accorded territorial 'concessions' in many ports and were permitted to set up embassies in Beijing. The British had established themselves in Hong Kong as an entry point into China from the south and were using it to extend their trade. The diplomatic quarter housing the embassies in Beijing was close to the Forbidden City and so was a constant reminder to the imperial government of the much changed world situation in which the country now found itself. A century after Qianlong's dismissive letter the outside world was closing in on the *Zhong guo*. At the same time the 'harmony' which isolation had promoted and encouraged was fast breaking down and with it the hold of the dynasty itself. After 250 years in power the Qing dynasty were losing the Mandate of Heaven but, like all dynasties before them, they were extremely reluctant to accept that the end was in sight.

The last effective Qing ruler of China was the Empress Dowager Ci-xi, daughter of a Manchu nobleman and one of the wives of Emperor Xian Feng. She was the real ruler of the country for half a century, following the death of her husband in 1861. She was able to maintain her power through intrigue and manipulation during the reigns of a succession of weak or child emperors. For most of this time rebellion was in the air, and in 1900 came the rebellion of the Society of Harmonious Fists, more popularly known as the Boxer Rebellion. The Boxers sought a return to traditional values and blamed the dynasty for allowing outsiders to gain such a hold and bring with them such things as the railway. This aroused great suspicion and was widely felt to represent the unwelcome changes being imposed on the country. In order to protect their embassies and their concessions, which were under threat of violence, the powers assembled a joint military force and intervened. Their success in breaking through Boxer resistance to reach Beijing and relieve their embassies was a clear demonstration of their power and of the weakness of China. The Empress Dowager and her court were forced to flee from Beijing and the great powers were left virtually in charge of the city. The heart of the Zhong guo was now at the feet of the foreigners and the humiliation of China was complete.

It is significant that the Empress Dowager fled to the old Qin capital, Xianyang, and for a time set up her court there. When she was at last allowed to return in 1902 her magnificent imperial procession made a detour to visit the former capitals, beginning with Chang'an, before arriving back in Beijing. The final part of her journey to the capital actually took place by rail, a clear demonstration that the modernizers had in effect won. During her final years in power, the Europeans continued to tighten their grip on the country.

The Empress Dowager and the puppet emperor Guang Xu, in whose name she ruled, both died within months of each other in 1908. The funeral of Ci-xi was the last great imperial event not only of the Qing dynasty but in the whole of Chinese history. Ci-xi's great nephew Pu Yi ascended the dragon throne as the last emperor, taking the title of Xuan Tong. Two years later an uprising took place, centring on the middle Yangtze region, and the country was again thrown into turmoil. On 1 January 1912 a republic was proclaimed in the southern capital, Nanjing, and a month later Pu Yi abdicated the throne. The official announcement of the abdication, which came from the Forbidden City, was accompanied by the pronouncement that 'Tien min is clear and the wishes of the people are plain.'[9]

With this announcement the power of Beijing, which had dominated China for most of the previous 650 years, came to an abrupt end. The new nationalist regime was firmly southern in its origins, its attitudes and its choice of capital. While the former emperor Pu Yi was allowed to go on living in Beijing for a few more years, the Forbidden City was otherwise empty and abandoned. The mystique that had surrounded it over the centuries had vanished.

Within two decades China was to face a whole generation of massive turmoil caused by the invasion by the Japanese and the subsequent Civil War. During this turbulent and divisive period in the country's history, what was left of it was ruled from a number of capitals, mainly in the south and centre. Yet, as had been the case with the Ming centuries earlier, with the return of stability a new government would again be seduced by the lure of the north. Although it might have seemed highly unlikely in 1912, the role of Beijing as the centre of power was far from being over.

6

Power over South Asia: The 'Seven Cities' of Delhi and the *Saptusindhu* Capital Region

Like China, south Asia has had many capitals in its long history, but few of these have actually controlled the whole of its vast territory. The most enduring of Indian capitals, and the one which, with a single notable exception, has been the centre of power over the largest part of the subcontinent, is Delhi. This has been the dominant capital of the subcontinent throughout much – but by no means all – of its modern history.

As a capital Delhi goes back further than Beijing, but in reality it has over this long period been not so much a single city as a cluster of cities occupying contiguous sites. Delhi, asserted Percival Spear, 'has undergone transformations as numerous as the incarnations of the God Vishnu'. Yet, 'it has preserved through all a continuous thread of existence'.[1] According to legend there have been seven cities of Delhi, but Spear was of the opinion that there have in reality been as many as double that number. Stretching around this cluster of cities is the territory known as the *Saptusindhu*, the principal core region of India.[2] The *Saptusindhu*, Hindi for 'seven rivers', stretches from the Punjab, the land drained by the five main eastern tributaries of the Indus, to the *Doab*, the area stretching between the middle courses of the Ganga and its major tributary, the Yamuna. This has been overwhelmingly the most powerful geopolitical focus of power in the whole of south Asia.

As with the other great imperial cities, there are many legends concerning the origins of Delhi. An interesting one comes from the *Mahabharata*, the epic poem which has its origins in the time of, or before, the Aryan invasions of India. It has been suggested by scholars that *Indraprastha*, the capital city of the Pandavas, was in fact the first Delhi. The likelihood that this is true is, according to Spear, 'a circumstantial probability'. The oldest evidence of a city on the site are the ruins at Purana Kila in the heart of modern Delhi, dated by pottery to the tenth century BC. Just to the north was another legendary site, that of Kurukshetra, the great battlefield between the Pandavas and the Kauravas in the *Mahabharata*. Thus the Delhi region has from the outset been linked to legendary political and military power. This is something which has over the years considerably strengthened its hold on the Indian imagination and added legitimacy to its position as capital.

As with all capitals, there are also powerful geopolitical factors accounting for the importance of Delhi through the centuries. One of these suggests that there is some basis for the *Mahabharata* legend since very close to the city is the historical battlefield of Panipat, the site of a number of important battles in Indian history. Most of these have been between the forces of the indigenous Hindu population and invaders from the north. It is on the great plain north of Delhi that the confrontation between the two has most frequently taken place. Since the earliest times, Delhi has been the location where successful invaders have set up their centre of power. It lies strategically at the centre of the *Saptusindhu*, and is well connected to most other routes. As a result, it is the place from where invaders have been best able to assert their control over the rest of the subcontinent. Besides these powerful geographical advantages, the Delhi region is also central to the whole of the *madhyadesa*, the huge plain stretching from the Indus valley to the Ganga-Brahmaputra valley, the territory with the largest population and the greatest agricultural and industrial potential. This is the area which, above all others, invaders have sought to conquer. The city is also situated close to the watershed between the two major rivers in northern India, the Ganga and the Indus. This has given it control over routeways to the west and east and also to the south between the Aravalli hills of Rajasthan and the escarpments of the northern Deccan. This strategic location is reinforced by the fact that Delhi is where the Aravallis finally dip beneath the alluvium of the Indo-Gangetic plain. At this point it forms the Ridge, a long series of hills on the northeastern side of the city. Yet despite these formidable geographical advantages, Delhi was not actually the first city chosen to be the capital of an Indian imperial state.

The first unification of India, the Mauryan Empire in the third century BC, chose Pataliputra, now Patna, in the middle Ganga basin, to be its capital. This is located well to the east of the *Doab*. The successor Gupta Empire in the third century AD inherited the same capital. Outside the legends, Delhi does not actually appear as a leading centre of power until the twelfth century and this related to the arrival of powerful invaders from the north. These were the Turks from Central Asia who, following their conversion to Islam, used their new religion as a justification for expansion and conquest. They arrived through the mountains of Afghanistan using the natural routes, notably the Khyber Pass, which led down into the Indus valley. The first such invasion was that of Mahmud of Ghazni in 997, who for a time was able to occupy much of the upper Indus region. This was followed in 1191 by another invasion from Afghanistan by Muhammad of Ghur. His army was met by the army of a Hindu confederacy led by the Rajput prince Prithviraj at Tarain, close to the legendary battlefield of Kurukshetra. At the second of the two battles on this site the invaders were successful in defeating Prithviraj in 1192, moving on from there to capture Delhi. This had been one of the strongholds of Prithviraj, one of whose titles had been 'Lord of Delhi'. The city is thought by some to have been his capital but there is no positive proof of this.

Whatever the truth of this, the invaders chose Delhi as their capital and there established the Delhi Sultanate, which was to be the major power in the subcontinent for the next 300 years. During this period there were a number of dynasties and until the last of them the Delhi area remained the site of the capital and principal seat of power.

The Sultanate actually came into being in 1206, the first sultan being Qutb-ud-Din Aibak. Qutb had been a slave of Muhammad of Ghur but when Muhammad returned to Afghanistan he seized power himself. It was his immediate successor Iltutmish who really established the dynasty and was responsible for the first buildings of the Sultanate in Delhi. The place chosen for these was Lal Cot, which had been the site of Prithviraj's city about 5 km from the first Delhi at Purana Kila. There Iltutmish first built a great victory tower, the Qutb Minar, named after the founder of the dynasty, which proclaimed the triumph and supremacy both of the dynasty and of Islam. It was modelled on the great tower of Ghazni in Afghanistan where the first projected conquest of India had originated in the tenth century. This immense structure towered over the surrounding countryside and was clearly intended as an unmistakable assertion of the new dominant power in India. It was certainly an uncompromising demonstration of power in stone, which was exactly what the Sultanate wished to achieve. In the fourteenth century Ibn Batuta, who for a time lived in Delhi, described it thus:

> (The Minar) has no parallel in the lands of Islam. It is built of red
> stone . . . ornamented with sculptures and is of great height. The

The Qutb Minar, Delhi. Constructed around 1200, this minar was a powerful symbol of the arrival of Islam in India.

ball at the top is of glistening white marble and its 'apples' [small balls surmounting a minaret] are of pure gold. The passage is so wide that elephants could go up it.[3]

At the same time the building of the Quwwat-al-Islam mosque was begun nearby. In this immense structure the humiliation of the Hindus was made even more evident by the use of stones from existing Hindu temples which had been destroyed. The remains of these Hindu sculptures are still to be seen in the mosque's stonework. The great citadel built at Lal Cot was the centre of the dynasty's power and became the principal residence of the sultan. By the end of the Slave dynasty the size of this capital city had grown considerably but its principal purpose was clearly to be an overwhelming demonstration of the new power dominating the land. The centre of power of the Sultanate always remained, said Spear, not so much a capital as 'the headquarters of an army of occupation'.[4]

The Slave dynasty was followed by the Khilji, the most important sultan of which was Ala-ud-Din Kilji. This sultan, who styled himself the 'second Alexander', is historically significant for a number of reasons, in particular the fact that he resisted and defeated the attempt by the Mongols to extend their domains into India. He continued to embellish the impressive Qutb site with varying results. The great mosque of the Quwwat was further enlarged but the most ambitious of all his projects was the attempt to construct another victory column close to the Minar which was intended to be even larger. In fact it was on a truly immense scale and its projected height would have dwarfed the Qutb Minar itself. However, he did not complete this huge structure in his lifetime and all attempts to continue with it after his death met with complete failure. Ibn Batuta was, however, clearly impressed even by the ruin:

This minar is one of the wonders of the world for size, and the width of its passage is such that three elephants could mount it abreast. The third of it built equals in height the whole of the other minaret . . . though to one looking at it from below it does not seem so high because of its bulk.[5]

Only the base of this gigantic tower actually remains today. It proved beyond the capacity of the architects of the time and it stands today as a kind of Ozymandian reminder of the fragility of power.

Close to the Qutb Minar is yet another great column made of pure iron. For a long time this was thought to have been intended as another

The remains of the gigantic minar built by Ala-ud-Din Kilji. Intended originally to surpass the height of the nearby Qutb, it was never fully completed and soon collapsed.

demonstration of the power of the Sultanate, this time using metal. However, analysis has now shown it to date from the Gupta period and to have come from the Pataliputra area in the heart of the Gupta Empire. It must have been brought to its present site and erected there as a suitable addition to the Qutb site. It would certainly have been used as another symbol to complement the Minar and, in particular, yet another demonstration of the Sultanate's domination over the native Hindus.

Ala-ud-Din also built an imperial palace at Siri some 3 km to the northeast of the Qutb site. This lavish building came to be known as the 'Hall of a Thousand Pillars' and was the place where the sultan preferred to live and to conduct much of the business of state.

In 1320, after only thirty years, the Khiljis were replaced by a third dynasty. These were the Tughluqs, the most important sultan of which was Muhammad bin Tughluq. His reign has been referred to as the golden age of the Sultanate during which the lands controlled by Delhi were at their most extensive. During this period northern India had a stable government and for a long time enjoyed relative prosperity. However, it was during the reign of his predecessor and founder of the dynasty, Ghiyas ud Din Tughluq, that the third Delhi of the Sultanate was built. This was Tughluqabad, built on a defensive site using a rock outcrop. The Tughluqs were a severe military dynasty and this is reflected in the nature of their seat of power. Built like a fortress and surrounded by formidable stone walls, at its centre was a massive citadel. It was redolent of military strength and what has been called 'the stark cyclopean grandeur of Tughluqabad' reflected all aspects of their austere regime.[6] Muhammad bin Tughluq did not much favour this enormous and grim fortress city and for a time even transferred the capital south to Daulatabad in the Deccan, where he was engaged in military operations. However, he soon returned to Delhi which the sultans had always seen as being the best and most effective centre for the government of their domains.

Following their defeat of the Arabs and the Ottoman Turks, the Mongols by the fourteenth century had achieved a position of dominance over Eurasia. As a result of this, Muhammad now considered the Sultanate to have become the real centre of Islam and the Islam in which he believed was in tune with the dynasty's overall characteristics. Everything they built was in an uncompromising, grim style and this included their religious buildings. Muhammad's main contribution to the Tughluq building operations was at Jahanpannah between Qutb and Siri where he built a new palace and mosque, both in the unmistakable Tughluq style. The Tughluqs were aiming above all to present a statement of power and this they achieved most effectively. Muhammad was now a leader of considerable importance in the Muslim world and he was visited in Tughluqabad by emissaries from as far afield as Baghdad. The records show that these emissaries were impressed by the stark grandeur of the Tughluq capital and by the distinctive and puritanical picture of Islam it conveyed.

Muhammad was succeeded by his nephew Firoz who, as well as continuing with the embellishment of the existing buildings of Delhi, built his own fortress-palace at Firozabad close to the Yamuna river about 10 km to the north. In so doing, he transferred his capital to a completely fresh site which has been described as a kind of 'New Delhi' of the fourteenth century.[7] Here the sultan built a magnificent royal palace, the Ferozshah Kotla, which he seems to have used particularly for grand receptions and ceremonies of state in preference to either Tughluqabad or Qutb. It was also the place where this particular sultan preferred to make his residence. This seems to have impressed one British traveller who went so far as to refer to it as being the 'Windsor' of Delhi.[8]

Nevertheless, despite all these changes, both Tughlaqabad, as a grim and uncompromising statement of power, and Qutb, as a triumphal symbol of victory, remained the two most potent symbols of the power

of the Sultanate. Qutb itself seems to have been regarded as the official
capital and it certainly remained the most impressive and enduring
symbol of their power throughout the period of the Sultanate.

In 1398, ten years after the death of Firoz, Timur Lenk – Tamerlane
– invaded India and, as in so many other places, the results were rapid
and catastrophic for much of the north of the country. Delhi was plun-
dered and sacked and the sultan was humiliated and reduced to being
a vassal of the great Central Asian conqueror. The Tughluq Sultanate
never fully recovered from this and the last of the dynasty died in 1414.
The Sultanate continued in name only under the Sayyid dynasty which
at times ruled little more than Delhi itself and remained, nominally at
least, vassals of Timur's successors.

In 1451 power was seized by the Lodis, warlords from the Punjab,
who left little more than their tombs in Delhi as memorials to their rule.
The first of the Lodis, Buhlul Khan, re-established the power of the Sultanate
and this was continued by his son, interestingly – and inappropriately –
named Sikander (Alexander). Initially, Sikander made Qutb his capital
and built there another new mosque, the Moti Masjid, the only major
addition to the architecture of Delhi during the whole period of this
dynasty. So Qutb, the first great symbol of the new power in India two
and a half centuries earlier, continued to retain its hold and became the
principal symbol of the power of the revived Sultanate in the middle of
the fifteenth century. However, Delhi's role as capital was to be brief and
the stern heavy tombs of the Lodis remain the most telling memorials to
their rule. Sikander came increasingly to see Delhi as being far too
vulnerable to new attacks from the north. As a result he forsook what had
been the centre of the power of the Sultanate since its inception, with
its dramatic symbols of former glory, and embarked on the building of a
new capital further east in the *Doab*. This was Sikanderbad, close to
Agra, and the sultan moved there around 1500. From there he judged
the Sultanate could exert control over the rich Ganga-Brahmaputra
plain and would be safer from attacks by the northern tribes. In the
final stages of its existence, the Sultanate was edging its centre of power
closer to the old Hindu capital of Pataliputra. Nevertheless, some of
the mystique of Delhi must have remained because Sikander's tomb is
in the old capital.

However, the Sultanate was not made any safer by this move.
Afghanistan remained a turbulent centre of expansionist activity and
this related to the events taking place in the lands of the Timurid dynasty.
In 1526 the Sultanate was forced to do battle with the next invaders on

the fateful field of Panipat, north of Delhi. These were the Mughals, also Turks from Central Asia, and they defeated the army of the sultan and rapidly occupied northern India. The new rulers decided to keep the capital near to Sikanderbad, establishing themselves in Agra, about 10 km further east. Their leader was Babur, a product of the great Timurid civilization of Central Asia. He was said to be the most brilliant Asiatic prince of his age and claimed descent from both the Mongol Genghis Khan and the Turkish-Mongol Timur. Like the Sultanate, the Mughals were also Muslim and so were able to fit easily as successors to the Lodis. Their religion still separated them from the great majority of their new subjects, in particular the large population of the Ganga-Brahmaputra plain together with the whole of the Deccan. As had happened before, a large Hindu force was assembled, led again by the Rajputs, which sought to defeat these new invaders. However, like the forces of Prithviraj, they were defeated and the Mughals were able to consolidate their regime.

Successful as they were in battle, the military prowess of the Mughals was by no means truly representative of the nature of this new dynasty. They were certainly far from being another version of the warlike Tughluqs. The early Mughals at least proved civilized rulers who introduced a great tradition of art and architecture which they brought with them from their Timurid homeland. They spoke Persian and had been considerably influenced by Persian art, architecture and literature. As a result, during the centuries of their rule, they left an indelible mark on the culture of India. Babur, himself a highly cultivated man, had a poor opinion of the people of his new domains. India's great attraction was 'an abundance of gold and silver' and the fact that 'workmen of every profession and trade are innumerable and without end'.[9] In other words, India's main virtue was that it could be exploited easily and was a good base for the creation of an empire. This is what the Mughals then proceeded to do, in the course of which they bequeathed to India some of its most stunning and memorable architecture.

Babur's son Humayun, bookish and intellectual, was attracted back to Delhi where he engaged in considerable building near the old Purana Kila site. However, he proved a weak and ineffectual ruler and his reign was a turbulent one which endangered the continuation of the new dynasty. For a time he was removed from the throne but he was eventually reinstated. Babur had loved his Afghan homeland and on his death in 1530 his body was taken back to Kabul for burial. Humayun was the first Mughal emperor to be buried in India and his splendid tomb in

Delhi is an early and magnificent example of Mughal architecture. His son Akbar was a complete contrast to his father and his reign was the most important in the whole of Mughal history. It was he who secured the dynasty's full control over its Indian possessions.

THE FIRST SIX GREAT MUGHALS
Babur 1526–30
Humayun 1530–56*
Akbar 1556–1605
Jahangir 1605–27
Shah Jahan 1627–58
Aurangzeb 1658–1707

*Humayun was faced with many rebellions during his reign and for a time he was forced into exile. The most important of the rebels was Sher Shah who himself ruled from 1540 to 1545.

Akbar proved a resolute and effective ruler, introducing many measures to improve governance. His domains were divided for administrative purposes into provinces, each of which had a governor. The coinage was reformed and new silver coins were minted. The taxation system was also reformed and made fairer to the peasantry. Most importantly, an attempt was made to break down the great gulf between Muslims and Hindus and to integrate the whole of the population more effectively. Hindus were introduced into the higher levels of the administration and often even reached the level of provincial governors. An important symbolic gesture was that a Hindu was appointed to be the governor of Afghanistan, the home province of the empire and always dear to the hearts of the Mughals. This all helped produce greater stability and so promoted trade and general prosperity.

Akbar decided that he needed a strong fortress in Agra, making use of the easily worked local red sandstone as a building material. When completed in 1570 this massive building was a powerful statement of Mughal power and, apart from the fact that it was in red stone, it was hardly less uncompromising and forbidding than Tughluqabad. However, the Mughals were in most ways very different from the Tughluqs and, while the fort may have displayed their power, it gave little indication of the great civilization they brought to India. They were after all Timurids, and this division between power and civilization was in many ways a duality similar to that found in the buildings of Timur himself.

In 1570 Akbar embarked on the building of a new capital which he clearly intended to be the principal symbol of his own reign and policies. This capital was Fatehpur Sikri, the 'City of Victory', located some 40 km to the south of Agra. It may have been a city which celebrated Mughal victories, but its origins lay in much more personal matters. The story is that Akbar had no son to continue the dynasty and this greatly concerned him. One day he stopped to rest at the village of Sikri where he was told of a holy man, a hermit, who lived in a cave nearby. This was Salim Chisti who was believed to possess miraculous powers. Akbar visited the holy man and revealed his plight to him. Salim suggested that Akbar's wife, Maryam-uz-Zamani, daughter of a Hindu prince, should come to reside at Sikri for a time and this she did. Within a year she had given birth to a son, the future emperor Jahanghir. Akbar was overwhelmed with joy and, as an act of thanksgiving, announced that the capital was being transferred to Sikri where a great city would be built. Work began immediately and by 1574 the citadel was complete and Akbar and his court moved into it. No sooner had the Agra fort been completed than it was abandoned for this new city.

While the legend is very telling, there were, of course, other factors involved in this choice of site. It was located on the route from the *Doab* to the south, following the river Chambal deep into the Deccan, and

The Panch Mahal, Fatehpur Sikri.

The Jama Masjid Mosque, Fatehpur Sikri.

the Gulf of Cambay. This gave the capital ready access to the west of the country with its important sea communications. The region was also blessed with a ready supply of fine red sandstone which became the basic building material for the city as it had for Agra. It had the added advantage of being very close to Agra. Of course, the policies adopted by Akbar were designed to have the effect of pacifying his domains but the presence of the great fortress nearby must have been reassuring.

The city which rose in the desert to the south of Agra was indeed magnificent. It was surrounded by walls and had seven gates leading in all directions. One of the highest and most striking buildings was the Panch Mahal, the five-storeyed palace, used by Akbar and his court for rest and pleasure. Its architectural style showed considerable Hindu influence, something which is to be found in many of the other buildings throughout the city. Architecture was another aspect of the attempt by Akbar to create a fusion of Muslims and Hindus and put his empire on firmer foundations.

By far the largest and grandest building in Fatehpur Sikri was the Jama Masjid mosque. At the time it was also the largest mosque in India and was built on the plan of the great mosque at Mecca. Again its architecture represents a blend of the Mughal and Hindu styles. Akbar was himself a deeply religious man and initially his whole regime was closely associated with Islam. After all, religion, and particularly his veneration of the holy man, was at the heart of the whole project. In 1579 Akbar proclaimed himself imam, making himself head of the whole Muslim religious community of his empire. The inscription in Persian above the entrance to the mosque makes it clear that it was Akbar who was responsible for its building and adornment, which 'is second only to the chaste mosque' (in Mecca). The mosque complex is built in a large courtyard surrounded by cloistered walls. There are two great gateways, one leading into the city itself and the other facing outwards to the south.

Near to the mosque was the tomb of Salim Chisti, who had died around 1576. This is generally acknowledged to be one of the finest examples of a Mughal building. It is in white marble, and has been called a pearl set in a ring of sandstone. The mausoleum at its centre is faced in pure white marble and the tomb itself has a canopy of wood inlaid with mother-of-pearl. The existence of this magnificent tomb in the centre of the city shows clearly the importance given to religion at the heart of the activities of the empire.

Akbar's cultivation of the Hindu princes related to his eclectic religious policy which was formulated over a period of years in Fatehpur Sikri. In 1578 the emperor organized a series of debates in which he participated. At first they were confined to Muslims but were later extended to include Hindus, Parsees (Indian Zoroastrians), Buddhists, Jains and, eventually, Christians. These latter were in the first instance Portuguese missionaries. The debates took place in the Diwan-i-Khas, the hall of private audience which came now to be used as the Abadat Khana, 'the Hall of Worship'. The participants sat in small kiosks around the walls facing one another. In the debates, free speech was encouraged and the emperor listened carefully to the often highly divergent opinions being expressed. As a result of these debates Akbar began to cast a critical eye on Islam and in 1579 the 'Infallibility Decree' was promulgated. This was what officially made the emperor imam and the head of Islam in India. As imam, he took on the twin role of pope and emperor and decided what was and what was not acceptable Islamic practice.

Out of this ferment of activity the emperor then evolved the idea of a new eclectic religion which would contain the best elements from all the religions. This was the 'Din Allahi', the Divine Faith, established in 1582. Its exact contents remain a mystery but it appears to have centred on Akbar himself as its prophet. It postulated 'suh-i kul', tolerance of all religions, but paradoxically Islam itself came to be treated with increasing harshness.

Despite all the work and expenditure on his new capital city, the emperor did not actually remain there for very long. After fifteen years he abandoned the city and moved back to Agra. The reasons for this decision are still shrouded in mystery: one theory has been that the water supply in this dry area proved insufficient for the growing population. However, recent scholars have suggested that there were probably other reasons. Agra was on the great line of communication stretching from the northwestern frontier to the delta of the Ganga. This was the main axis of northern India, and so a capital located on it was better placed for the exercise of control over northern India. Later this came to be known as the 'Grand Trunk Road', made famous by Rudyard Kipling in *Kim*. In addition, as he became older Akbar became more conscious of security, particularly in view of the highly controversial policies he was pursuing. The fort at Agra was a formidable stronghold and far more secure than the relatively open city of Fatehpur, which did not have very high protective walls. While Fatehpur was built for a land at peace, Agra was built for a land in which peace was not so certain. For a time Akbar also moved to Lahore in the Punjab, which was a good base for dealing with northern frontier problems and for maintaining the links with Afghanistan which remained strong. It was not, however, the best location for his later campaigns in southern India and for these Fatehpur was occasionally used again.

This may explain why towards the end of his reign Akbar built his last great addition to Fatehpur Sikri, the Buland Darwaza, the 'Gate of Victory'. This triumphal gateway to the Jama Masjid mosque was added in 1601 to commemorate victories in southern India. The style once more blends the Mughal and Hindu and the inscription above the entrance reads 'Jesus, son of Mary, said, on whom be peace: the world is a bridge, pass over it but build no house upon it.' The image of the bridge, which can be found elsewhere in Fatehpur, encapsulated the idea of a link between the divergent peoples and religions of the empire which Akbar was striving for. It is a remarkable inscription to be found on a mosque.

The Buland Darwaza was built on a low hill with 40 steps leading up to it. In this way it towered impressively over the city and the surrounding countryside. It was described by the architectural historian James Fergusson as being 'noble beyond any portal attached to any mosque in India, perhaps in the whole world'.[10] Although leading to a mosque, this final addition to the architecture of Fatehpur Sikri is far more an expression of power than anything else in the city. While by this time engaged in many other projects, including the religious ones, the emperor still commanded his armies in the field and was conscious of being master of a great empire.

Akbar's final years were spent mostly in the fort at Agra, his first building project. It was a far more secure stronghold than any building in Fatehpur. There he died in 1605 and his son and successor Jahangir, the child born in Sikri, built his magnificent tomb nearby at Sikanderabad.

Jahangir did not return to Fatehpur but remained in the safety of the fort at Agra. An indolent emperor given more to the pursuit of pleasure than to governing the empire, he largely continued the policies of his illustrious father and, while he went back to Islam, the policy of religious toleration was maintained. Jesuits and members of other faiths were welcomed at his court, as were ambassadors from neighbouring countries and Europe. It is interesting to note that during the reign of Jahangir the first English trading settlements were established in India and later in the century the merchant Job Charnock founded Calcutta (Kolkata). This was eventually to become the main base for the power which two centuries later would replace the Mughals. Sir Thomas Roe was designated to be England's first ambassador to the court of the Great Mughal. His reception was a far friendlier one than that given a century and a half later by the Chinese emperor to Lord Macartney. The two great oriental empires behaved very differently towards the arrival of the Europeans and the events that unfolded during the following centuries reflected this difference.

Jahangir's son and successor, Shah Jahan, proved far more energetic and generally aggressive in his policies. The policy of religious toleration was revoked and Christian churches, including the one in Agra, were razed to the ground, as were a number of Hindu temples. For the first decade of his reign he remained in Agra and it was there that his beloved young wife Mumtaz Mahal died in 1631. Distraught at this calamity, he immediately threw himself into the great project of building a magnificent tomb for her. This was the Taj Mahal which for a number of years became his main preoccupation. It took an enormous amount of effort and was a considerable strain on the coffers of the state.

In 1638 Shah Jahan made the momentous decision to move the capital back to Delhi. It may have been that Agra, filled with memories, had become a sad place for him but he would also have seen the strategic superiority of Delhi as a location for the control of India. Agra had, after all, been chosen as a place of refuge by the beleaguered Sultanate, but expansion rather than defence was on the mind of the new emperor. Agra and Fatehpur were also indelibly associated with Akbar, and Shah Jahan certainly did not wish to remain in the shadow of his illustrious grandfather. Although the earlier Great Mughals had rarely used Delhi, it did have a special place for them since it had been the historic symbol of the triumph of Islam on the subcontinent. The place which Shah Jahan chose for his new city was close to the Yamuna river and about 15 km north of the Qutb site. Here between 1639 and 1648 the new city of Shahjahanabad rose on the low-lying land adjacent to the Yamuna. When completed the city was large and impressive. It had massive walls with 27 towers and eleven gates. Its population by the end of Shah Jahan's reign has been estimated as being around 400,000.

The city was planned on a grid pattern with a grand processional way, the Chandni Chowk, at its centre. Its most impressive and important feature was the Red Fort, the imperial residence and centre of government. This was modelled on the fort at Agra and, like the latter, overlooked the Yamuna river. From then on the emperor, himself a natural builder, spent the greater part of his time and effort on it. He had a special love for marble which he had used lavishly in the building of the Taj Mahal. Together with the red sandstone which gave the fort its name, this was the main building material, but many other precious and semi-precious stones and jewels were also used, usually inlaid into the stonework.

The basic purpose of the Red Fort was to be an impressive centre of government and to symbolize power in stone. That this purpose was achieved there can be little doubt. The comments of the English traveller Lovat Fraser make this quite clear:

> There is one place in Delhi, the first sight of which is unforgettable. It is enshrined behind the titanic rose-pink walls of the vast Fort, those huge masses that look as though they were built for all time. The great battlements tower above you as you enter a formidable gateway . . . and stand in the centre of a gigantic hall with vaulted roof. It is like the nave of a cathedral. Beyond it you enter an open space that is called a courtyard . . . You cross it, advance through another mighty archway and confront the Diwan-i-Am.[11]

The Diwan-i-Am, the hall of public audience, was one of its two most important buildings. It was the pivot of the whole Red Fort. The impressive approach is, as Fraser said, through two great archways and a courtyard. The Diwan was an open pavilion supported by arches. It was built on a low platform at the centre of which was the imperial throne. It was here that the emperor dealt with matters of state in a public way in front of his subjects. According to Nicholson, it was 'the Mughal Empire's centre stage for displaying its greatest pomp and ceremony'.[12] The whole pavilion was painted in bright colours and behind the throne was a panel with brightly coloured pictures of flowers and birds. Above this was a painting of the Greek god Orpheus playing his lyre. Since this was taken from a painting by Raphael on the same subject it strongly suggests that Italian artists and craftsmen had been hired for the building and decoration of the most important building in the fort.

The Diwan-i-Am was the splendid sight seen by those who entered the fort through the ceremonial arches and were witness to the display of the magnificence and power of the emperor. Coming from outside, one reached the Diwan by means of the great processional route of the Chandni Chowk and the Lahore Gate and the whole was clearly intended to constitute a complete experience. However, the real centre of the power of the Empire, where policies were discussed and decisions made, was not there but well behind it and hidden from public view. This was the Diwan-i-Khas, the private audience hall, where the really important business of the Mughal Empire was conducted. It was here that the emperor met with his ministers and others summoned to the palace to discuss the most important and secret matters. This Diwan was even more magnificent than the other. It was built of marble and inlaid with precious stones. As with the Diwan-i-Am, much use was made of colour and the walls were bedecked with paintings boasting an abundance of leaves and flowers. On a marble dais at the centre was the *pièce de résistance* of the whole Diwan, the Peacock Throne which Shah Jahan had had made for himself. It was inlaid with a variety of precious stones and seemingly no cost had been spared in its making. The Frenchman François Bernier was certainly impressed and has left a detailed description of one particular ceremonial which he witnessed there:

> The King appeared seated upon his throne, at the end of the great hall, in the most magnificent attire. His vest was of white and delicately flowered satin, with a silk and gold embroidery of the finest texture. The turban of gold cloth had an aigrette whose base was composed of diamonds of an extraordinary size and value, besides an Oriental topaz, which may be pronounced unparalleled, exhibiting a lustre like the sun. A necklace of immense pearls suspended from his neck . . . The throne was supported by six

The Diwan-i-Am, Red Fort, Delhi. The centre of power of the Mughal Empire and place where the Great Mughals gave audiences to their subjects and to representatives of foreign powers.

massy feet, said to be of solid gold, sprinkled over with rubies, emeralds and diamonds. I cannot tell you with accuracy the number or value of this vast collection of precious stones, because no person may approach sufficiently near to reckon them . . . But I can assure you that there is a confusion of diamonds, as well as other jewels . . . It was constructed by Chah-Jehan, the father of Aureng-Zebe, for the purpose of displaying the immense quantity of precious stones accumulated successively in the treasury from the spoils of ancient Rajas and Patans, and the annual presents to the monarch, which every omrah is bound to make on certain festivals.[13]

When Bernier returned to France this information was passed to Louis XIV who was himself involved in a similar project to demonstrate his power. The French monarch was no doubt curious to know how an oriental despot managed such things.

Visitors would certainly have been dazzled by the magnificence of the whole vast new centre of Mughal power. The intention to overawe was heightened by the elaborate ceremonial associated with the approach to the emperor. At every stage it was made abundantly clear that this was the ultimate source of unbridled power. However, for those in the sovereign's entourage who lived within the great walls this was a place of exquisite beauty which possessed everything to make life pleasant. On the central wall of the Diwan was inscribed the couplet by Khusrau in Persian,

> If on earth there be a paradise of bliss,
> It is this, Oh! It is this! It is this!

The many other buildings of the fort included the harem and the private quarters of the emperor. All were set off by the splendour of the large open spaces and the Mughal gardens which certainly would have given the idea that this was paradise.

The Mughals derived a great deal of their culture from the Persians and this was displayed in this ultimate centre of their power. But it was only incidentally a paradise and its real purpose was to make clear to all where the absolute power in the empire lay.

As always with the Mughals, and before them the Sultanate, there was the explicit acknowledgement that their power was not entirely of their own making but derived from and sanctioned by Islam. The other most impressive building of Shahjahanabad was the Jama Masjid mosque. When completed, it was designated as the royal mosque of the Empire, used by the emperor and his court for worship. It was built, like the fort, in red sandstone and inlaid with marble and brass. Three great marbled domes and two tall minarets dominate its skyline. On the east side the open arcading of the mosque faces towards the Red Fort and this emphasizes the strong relationship between these two dominating buildings. The mosque was built on a low hill, the highest part of the city, and so in order to enter it one had to ascend by a series of flights of steps. These led to a grand entrance arch much like the Buland Darwaza in Fatehpur. This was the entrance used by the emperor when he and his entourage arrived for Friday Prayers. The imperial procession would leave the fort by the Delhi Gate and proceed from there the short distance to the mosque. The imperial party then climbed the steps and went in through the grand entrance. Besides prayer, this was also intended as another demonstration of the close links between Islam and the state in the Mughal Empire.

In this 'New Delhi' of Shah Jahan the rituals of empire were conducted with great regularity and punctiliousness. Unlike Akbar's capital, here there was no debate or discussion, no openness to new ideas or willingness to make changes. There was just an immense certainty about the greatness and the rightness of the Mughal Empire and its domination over India. As one historian put it, 'The outspoken animation of Akbar's symposia had given way to a more awesome ceremonial and a more exalted symbolism. Now the "King of the World" ethereally presided from sun-drenched verandas of the whitest marble.'[14] It has been observed that, when sitting on his Peacock throne, the backdrop was designed to look as though there was a glowing halo around Shah Jahan's head in the saintly Christian manner.

Barely twenty years after the foundation of Shajahanabad it became clear that the grip of Shah Jahan was weakening. This produced a war of succession among his sons. One of them, Aurangzeb, was in command of the army of the Deccan which was aiming to bring the restive south of India more firmly into the Mughal grasp. In 1657 he moved back northwards to secure his succession to the throne. He defeated his brothers and imprisoned his father in the fort at Agra. From there the old emperor was able to look out towards the Taj Mahal, his most loved and beautiful creation, and to wait for his own death and entombment alongside his beloved Mumtaz Mahal.

Aurangzeb was a strict puritan and as emperor he enforced Islam in his domains with an iron will. In terms of building projects he was the complete opposite of his father. While Shah Jahan had been a great and enthusiastic builder, Aurangzeb was given more to destruction. He ravaged the north of India, destroying Hindu temples and monuments and leaving a trail of bitterness and hatred behind him. He was the complete opposite of Akbar who had attempted to bring together his diverse peoples and in whose architectural legacy this can be seen. Aurangzeb, on the other hand, left virtually no architectural legacy. When he was in Delhi he resided at the Red Fort and was careful to observe the rituals devised by his father. His one addition to the fort was the Delhi Gate which was rebuilt in an austere style. It was intended to match the great entrance gate of the mosque and to form an impressive backdrop for the imperial processions.

With the aggressive policy of Aurangzeb continuing undiminished, the banner of Hindu resistance to Islam, and to northern power, was taken up by the Marathas. They and their allies put up such a determined resistance to Mughal rule that in 1681 Aurangzeb moved south with his army and remained there for most his life. He established there a new capital, Aurangabad, which became his base. More a military camp than a city, it was abandoned soon after his death. By 1691 Mughal power, secured exclusively by military means, was at its height and almost the whole of the Indian subcontinent was in their hands. This had been achieved with great brutality and Aurangzeb was himself responsible for the most appalling atrocities. All this increased the implacable hostility of the Hindu population of both south and north. The huge campaigns drained the resources of the treasury in much the same way that the building projects of his father had, but with far less of a legacy.

Aurangzeb died in 1707 while on campaign in the south. He had attempted to put the whole of India into a straitjacket of his own making but in the end it all proved a complete failure. By the time of his death the empire had never been bigger but it was so weakened that it never fully recovered. His successors attempted to make peace with the Hindus of the south and to undo some of his excesses but with little success. Very soon after his death the empire began to show signs of disintegration.

In 1739 the king of Persia, Nadir Shah, invaded the now weak empire. He saw the increasing turmoil in India as his chance to add to his power and wealth. He came via the well-trodden route from Afghanistan and his forces confronted and defeated the army of the Mughals on the historic battlefield of Panipat. On reaching Delhi his troops engaged in the usual bout of destruction and looting. The loot taken by the king himself included the fabulous Peacock Throne, the most important symbol of Mughal power. This was taken back to Persia where it became the symbol of the Persian dynasty and its removal marked the end of the effective power of the Mughals. The emperors were from then on little more than shadows, pawns in the hands of adventurers. As Spear put it, 'The Great Moghuls of the seventeenth century degenerated into embarrassed phantoms in the eighteenth century.'[15] Finally, in 1804 the emperor Shah Alam put himself under the protection of the British. The fledgling maritime power which had established a tentative base in Calcutta during the reign of Jehangir had by the nineteenth century become the dominant power in India. The emperor received the British commander, Lord Lake, in the Diwan-i-Khas simply dressed and under a tattered canopy. The Peacock Throne was long gone and the old blind emperor was seated humbly on the ground. To the British he presented a pathetic sight. It was all so very different from the great audiences of Shah Jahan in the same Diwan 150 years earlier. Shah Alam's lack of any real power was expressed in the Persian couplet:

From Delhi to Palam,
Is the realm of Shah Alam.[16]

The great Mughal Empire did not so much fall as fade away, and a new power was poised to take over. This power was eventually to leave its own legacy among the 'seven cities' of Delhi.

7

Global Power: Philip II and the Escorial

At around the time when Babur conquered India and the Mughal Empire came into being, the dominating figure in Europe was the Habsburg Prince Charles who had succeeded to the Spanish throne as Charles I in 1516. Three years later he was elected Holy Roman Emperor and became Charles V. As emperor and king of Spain and its European and overseas possessions, Charles was now the most powerful ruler in Christendom, taking precedence, in theory at least, over all the other monarchs of Europe. However, the hold of Christendom was weakening and soon after his accession came that great split in the Catholic Church known as the Reformation.

The most powerful of Charles's many possessions was Spain and increasingly this became his main source of military strength in his attempt to curb the Reformation and to keep together the unwieldy edifice of Christendom over which he presided. In this he was ultimately unsuccessful and in 1565 the Council of Trent was forced to accept the existence of Protestantism. The centre of Protestantism was in the north of Europe and included some Habsburg possessions, most significantly the northern provinces of the Netherlands.

In 1556 Charles was succeeded on the throne of Spain by his son Philip II. Philip did not become Holy Roman Emperor, but his inheritance included the Netherlands and certain possessions in Italy. A deeply devout man, Philip took it upon himself to be both the leader of the Catholic cause against the Protestants and of Christendom against the Ottoman Empire which had been making considerable advances into the Mediterranean and Eastern Europe. By this time Spain was also in possession of a huge empire in the Americas which was becoming ever more important to the Spanish economy. A great variety of products were transported across the Atlantic to Spain, the most important of which were gold and silver. These became the fundamentals of the great wealth of the country in the sixteenth century.

The other major power involved in overseas exploration was Spain's close Iberian neighbour, Portugal. Portugal had in fact preceded Spain, leading the way in the previous century. While by the early sixteenth century Spain was looking westwards across the Atlantic, the Portuguese voyagers had much earlier sailed south and eastwards around the coasts of Africa. In 1498 they reached the coast of India by the maritime route. This was a transformational event for the whole relationship between Europe and the rest of the world. Very soon the Portuguese began to trade with India using this new route and so undermined the importance of the historic land route, the Silk Road. By the time of Charles v, Portugal possessed well-established bases around the coasts of Africa and India and was poised to move on to China and Japan. To avoid possible war between the two emerging maritime powers of the Iberian peninsula, in 1494 the Treaty of Tordesillas, brokered by the pope, set a dividing line through the middle of the Atlantic between the spheres of influence of Spain to the west and Portugal to the east.

Growing overseas connections had the effect of making Spanish foreign policy very divided. The country took on two important roles: champion of Christendom in Europe and overlord of vast non-European possessions. These two were brought uneasily together into the official objective of Christianizing the new lands but the tactics and strategy necessary for the two were very different. While in Europe Spain was a land power and used its huge armies to secure a dominating position over the Continent, for the overseas territories it needed a large fleet, of both merchant vessels for trade and naval vessels to protect the trade and territorial acquisitions. This was to become the great problem for Spain throughout the sixteenth century and was basic to the way in which the Spanish empire was governed and, in particular, the places it was governed from.

The capital of Spain on the accession of Charles was the historic city of Toledo. This was situated in a central location on the Meseta, the great plateau at the heart of the country which is surrounded by high mountain ranges. Its location on the river Tagus gave it good communications both to west and east. It had originated as the Roman fortress of Tolentum and subsequently became the Visigothic capital. For many centuries following the defeat of the Visigoths the Iberian peninsula was in the hands of the Moors, an Islamic people who had invaded from North Africa in the eighth century. Their main centre of power was

Cordoba in the south and the powerful Emirate of Cordoba gained considerable autonomy in the greater Islamic world.

All that remained of Christian Iberia was a small coastal stretch in the far north which was divided into a number of petty kingdoms. The eventual *Reconquista*, the Christian re-conquest, was led by Castile which was successful in conquering the central areas of the Meseta. Toledo was recovered in 1085 and in time became the kingdom's capital. In 1479, following the unification of the Crown of Castile with that of its smaller neighbour, Aragon, Toledo was accepted as the first capital of the newly united Spain. The Moors still occupied Granada in the southern mountains and were not finally dislodged from there until the fateful year 1492. In that same year Columbus crossed the Atlantic and so began that process of discovery which within fifty years resulted in the greater part of this 'New World' coming into the possession of Spain. As capital of Castile, Toledo had been the centre of power of a landlocked state which had thought entirely in terms of land power. It had a huge army that had been almost permanently on a war footing during the long centuries of the *Reconquista*.

As a result of this history, Castile considered itself the leading state of the Iberian peninsula and its capital the natural centre of power of the new Spain which came into being around it. Toledo was soon transformed into a splendid city with high defensive walls, an impressive stronghold, the Alhambra (the residence of the monarch) and a magnificent cathedral.

A problem soon arose out of this. Since the time of the *Reconquista* the Castilian cities had gained considerable rights of their own. These *fueros* gave them the right to build their own walls, to bear arms, to hold markets and to establish city institutions. This resulted in increasing conflict with the monarchs who now wished to assert their total power and this conflict came to a head during the reign of Charles. To guard their *fueros* the cities established their own organization, the *Junta de Tordesillas*, and united together as the *comunidad*.[1] The capital, Toledo, was one of the most vocal in asserting its rights and this did not endear it to the monarch. In the conflict that followed, the Spanish army was employed to smash the *comunidades* and this it proceeded to do with vigour. Among the last to resist was the capital itself but by 1522 all resistance had come to an end. Charles was able to assert his total control over Castile, putting his own governors in charge of the cities and adopting increasingly centralist policies. These included challenging the regional assemblies, the *Cortes*, which, like the cities, had accrued considerable powers over the centuries.[2]

While Charles was mainly concerned with wider European affairs and spent little time in Spain during his long reign, his son Philip was king of Spain exclusively and throughout his reign the country was his main place of residence. However, he increasingly found Toledo, despite its long history as the principal centre of power in the Iberian peninsula, unsatisfactory as his capital. It retained the memory of the lost *fueros* and the revolt of the *comunidades* and failed to show the solid support that he needed and expected. Philip, like his father, was in no sense a democrat and was as lacking in sympathy for the aspirations of the cities or the regions as his father had been. In 1560, after only two years, he moved the capital 70 km north to the site of the hitherto small and insignificant town of Madrid. This was also in the Meseta but was less well located as a centre for the effective exercise of power, being on the small Manzanares river which, despite being a tributary of the Tajo, was not navigable. Philip, however, hoped that it did not possess the traditions of *fueros* so strongly associated with the old capital. There he began building his own new capital city centred on a splendid square, the Plaza Major, which was intended among other things for the holding of great state and religious ceremonies. He also built a royal palace to be his principal residence and centre of government. However, it was not long before Madrid soon also proved unsatisfactory in the eyes of Philip. There were rumblings of discontent among the populace reminiscent of Toledo. The fact was that Charles and his son Philip did not find cities congenial. They displayed too much desire for freedom and self-government that had been encapsulated in the *fueros*. This was something to which the authoritarian Habsburgs were never going to consent.

Despite its free cities, Castile had been basically a rural state ruled by the *grandees*, the great rural aristocracy. From them came the military traditions that had kept the country almost permanently on a war footing. It was in the rural areas also that the belief in autocracy, strict Catholicism and loyalty to the monarch were at their strongest. Cities on the other hand had a tendency to be subversive and always seemed to be making demands for greater rights. As a result Philip came to the conclusion that his centre of power had to be separate and more associated with the country than the city. Only in such an environment would he be able to exercise the total power that he craved and to fulfil what he believed to be his divine mission unimpeded by irritants like *fueros*. He saw this mission as being the re-establishment of the unity of Christendom and the defence of the Christian lands against the danger posed by the Ottoman Empire.

Philip took great trouble in the selection of the site for his centre of power. It had to be isolated and to be in impressive and evocative surroundings. It also had to have ample stone for building, be in a central location and have good communications. Madrid, although it was no longer destined to be the centre of ultimate power in the state, was nevertheless to retain its role as the official capital and the main place of government. Too much had been done there for it to be completely abandoned. It was essential therefore that the new centre of power be close to Madrid and have good and rapid communications with the city. After much searching, a suitable site was found. This was El Escorial, a name derived from *scoriae*, meaning refuse from old mines on hillsides. It was in the foothills of the Sierra de Guadarrama, an impressive range of mountains reaching heights of 2,500 metres in the vicinity. This range divided the Meseta into two, the north centring on the old kingdom of Leon and the south centring on the great dry plains of La Mancha. There was ample water and stone and good and easy communications to Madrid just 40 km away. There were also adequate communications to the north using the passes through the Sierra. The architect chosen was Juan Bautista de Toledo and, following his death, Juan de Herrera. Work began in 1563 and took twenty years to complete.

However, by then events were moving fast and, besides its growing European possessions, which stretched along a great north–south axis from the Netherlands to Italy, Spain had accrued ever larger overseas possessions. In 1581 Philip inherited the throne of Portugal, unifying virtually the whole of the Iberian peninsula and adding the considerable Portuguese overseas possessions to his own. The result was the creation of a massive empire stretching from the Americas eastwards via Africa to India. This was the first global power and its management began to take up more and more of the monarch's time. Of course, there still remained the other great mission of reuniting a divided Christendom.

In order to accomplish these twin objectives, Philip moved his headquarters away from the Meseta to Lisbon, the Portuguese capital, where he stayed for some years. The move from a continental capital to a maritime one reflected a huge change in the priorities of the Spanish state. From Lisbon he supervised the building of an enormous fleet which was essential for the protection of Spanish convoys as they crossed the Atlantic. They were bringing silver and gold from the New World which were fundamental requirements for the continuation of Philip's great mission. Also from Lisbon he engaged in the biggest naval project of

The Monasterio del Escorial, built by Philip II north of Madrid to be both the centre of power of the Spanish Empire and a place of religious observance.

his reign, the building of the great Armada which was intended for the subjugation of the Protestant north, in particular the Netherlands and England. Lisbon proved to be the ideal place for the supervision of this work and it might have been thought that it would remain the permanent capital of the vast Spanish empire. However, this was not to be, and in 1584 Philip returned to the now largely completed Escorial which was to be his home and seat of power for most of the remaining years of his reign.

The full name of the enormous edifice was the Real Monasterio de San Lorenzo del Escorial. The fact that it was called a monastery, indeed the 'royal' monastery, tells us much about the mindset of Philip and the deeply religious nature of the whole Spanish imperial enterprise. However, the building was actually a combination of many things, including royal palace, seat of government, basilica, monastery, library and royal mausoleum.

The grand entrance to the Escorial was a huge and magnificent door around which were eight Doric columns. This led to a central courtyard, the Patio de los Reyes, and immediately in front of this was the impressive basilica which was at the centre of the whole project. This had a very large nave and was capped by a gigantic cupola which was one of the dominating features of the whole structure. The interior of the basilica had 40 altars and at its centre was a magnificent decorated altarpiece. To the right of the Patio was the Monasterio de San Lorenzo, dedicated to the saint who was one of the most venerated martyrs of the Christian Church. The monks who occupied this from 1571 belonged to the Hieronymite order. It was in a monastery at Yuste belonging to this order that Charles v had spent his final years and Philip therefore considered it appropriate that this should be the order chosen for his new monastery-palace. On the main staircase are a number of frescos, the most striking of which is Luca Giordano's St Lawrence in Glory, Adored by Charles v and Philip II (1692–4) in the vault. Depicted in scenes below are the Battle of Saint-Quentin and the building of the Escorial. In the front of the building near to the great door is Philip's library which contains a fine collection of books, mostly religious, and which links the secular part of the building with the monastery. The secular parts to the left include the royal palace, the personal quarters of Philip and the government offices. The huge Royal Pantheon housed the marble coffins of the monarchs of Spain. The first to be interred was Charles v, whose remains were moved there in a great ceremony in which both Church and state were represented.

The Escorial was intended as a multipurpose building, but as such it also demonstrated the unity of purpose of the monarch. The secular purposes of empire were fused together with the religious mission to form a degree of unity greater than that of most imperial buildings where, despite religion being used to underpin imperial ambitions, Church and state are usually set apart in separate buildings. This unity of purpose is also embedded in the nature of the building, which had a profound effect on all who saw it. For any foreign missions or ambassadors who might have been in doubt, the Escorial was an uncompromising statement of the self-proclaimed mission of the Spanish monarchy. 'Its rigid geometrical design', wrote Calvert, 'looks at us with petrifying effect.'[3] The austere and even menacing exterior sent a clear message about what could now be expected from Spain and from the religion it sought to uphold. Castile has been called 'the redoubt of the true faith' and certainly the Escorial had all the appearance of being a great redoubt, thus in many ways reflecting the Castilian mentality as well as that of Philip himself.

The building also fitted perfectly into its surroundings. The bleak and bare centre of the Meseta was a world away from the softer and richer lands of the Iberian periphery. This had nurtured a religious vision which was more austere than that found in most other parts of Christendom. Calvert, in his classic work on the Escorial, put this succinctly:

> This tabernacle in the wilderness is a symbol of the mind of Spain in the days of her power, the manifestation of her profound faith, and a tribute to the seriousness and quietism which were the ideals of one of the most remarkable and complex of her rulers. We feel the very stones of the building reveal the nature of Philip, the king who would be saint, the ambitious patriot who longed for power.

Calvert went on to assert that, 'The building instructs us in the temper of a memorable age, profound in faith, zealous in patriotism and conspicuous in martial valour.'[4]

The overall building style of the Escorial has been called 'desornamentado', which can be translated as 'unadorned'. It also represented a decisive move away from the Renaissance style and a return to the classical. This was described by Elliott as 'the cold symmetry of a constricting classicism, imperial, dignified and aloof', and 'a fitting symbol of . . . the triumph of authoritarian kingship over the disruptive forces'.[5] The 'disruptive forces' which Elliott had in mind were the Reformation together with the demands for more rights made by the *Cortes* and the persisting legacy of the *comunidades*. The massive symbol in the foothills of the Guadarrama was firm and square, the geometrical design asserting the unity of form and purpose that Philip sought to impose on his country. It was from there that Philip conducted the massive operations on land and sea which were aimed at realizing his dreams. In this bleak and formidable refuge he was, as Braudel put it, 'a spider sitting motionless at the centre of his web'.[6]

One could hardly imagine a greater contrast than that between the Escorial and the vibrant commercial city of Lisbon which would certainly have been the natural centre for those maritime operations so essential for the realization of Philip's mission. However, the Portuguese capital was also a world away from the monarch's bleak religious vision. He no doubt sensed this and hastened to return to the far more congenial surroundings of his monastery-palace deep in the heart of the Meseta.

Unfortunately for Philip, this sanctuary was not the best place from which to run a global empire. Those beliefs and values which the Escorial symbolized were never to be achieved and the dreams of Philip, no doubt fostered by the nature of the Escorial and its surroundings, did not come to fruition. The Armada proved a disaster and the aim of bringing England back to the faith proved not only a failure but also a complete humiliation for Spain. In addition to this, the European possessions remained restive and ever less willing to accept Spanish rule. Nowhere was this more so than the Netherlands, the seven northern provinces of which declared their independence as the United Provinces in 1579. With the English privateers increasingly harassing his treasure fleets and successive attempts to bring the Netherlands to heel proving unsuccessful, Philip's final years, spent mostly in the Escorial, were indeed gloomy ones. Confined to his small and simple bed chamber, the monarch died in his great monastery-palace in 1598 at a time when both the European and global pre-eminence of Spain were beginning to slip away. He was interred alongside his father in the great vault beneath the building he had constructed to symbolize his self-proclaimed mission.

At the beginning of the seventeenth century his son and successor, Philip III, faced a much changed European and world scene. He was forced to accept the independence of the United Provinces, and the Thirty Years War, which began in 1618, signalled the end of attempts to re-establish the unity of Christendom. One of the main characteristics of the 'Westphalian' Europe that came into being after the treaty in 1648 was its division into nation-states. Portugal regained its independence in 1640 and by this time Spain had many rivals in its quest for overseas empire. The other provinces of Spain, led by Aragon, never really accepted the dominance of Castile and the flame of freedom was kept alive there over the centuries.

These great changes also marked the end of the relatively brief period during which the Escorial was Spain's main centre of power. Philip's successors returned to Madrid and, after less than half a century, the huge monolith in the foothills of the Guadarrama was forsaken. It was left as a stark monument to the power of Spain and its self-proclaimed mission during the 'Golden Age' in the sixteenth century. While the other features, notably the monastery and the magnificent library, remained, all that was left of the monarchy that built it was the Royal Pantheon where all future Spanish monarchs were interred. In this way the Escorial became more a symbol of the past than it was of the present and a grim and austere reminder of ambitions and failures. Many centuries later, Hilaire Belloc described it interestingly:

I salute it: the supreme monument of human permanence in stone; the supreme symbol of majesty . . . In time it must be gone as must, for that matter, the pyramids; but it seems to me that works of this mighty sort are like dents inflicted on the armour of time.[7]

As the first global power in the sixteenth century, Spain naturally needed to look out to the surrounding oceans and for this Lisbon was the most obvious choice for a capital. However, the monarchy of Philip II had felt far more at ease in landlocked Castile, home of the *Reconquista* and of an uncompromising view both of Christianity and of royal power. This had meant more attention being paid to building a powerful army, the much feared *tercios*, than on developing a really effective naval power as Portugal had done. Considering this landlocked mentality, the defeat of the Armada by England can be seen as an almost inevitable consequence. In effect, when it came to it, Spain rejected the surrounding seas and persisted in looking inwards to a kind of mythical greater Castile. It took as its central mission a strange continuation of the *Reconquista* on a grand scale with the objective of bringing the whole of Europe forcibly within its orbit. The Escorial fitted well with this objective, having more in common with the castles and strongholds of Castile than with the new commercial world arising around it.

In the end the attempt by the first power of the modern age to put Europe into a straitjacket proved a complete failure. In this respect, Philip was much more like Aurangzeb than Akbar. He had Aurangzeb's stern frugality and uncompromising attitude to his mission and the imperial and religious dreams of both met the same fate at the hands of those who refused to accept them. Yet while Aurangzeb left scarcely any legacy in stone, this was certainly not the case with Philip. The Escorial is a stark reminder both of power and of its fragility and of the ultimate futility of attempts to impede mankind's natural desire for freedom.

Most importantly, significant changes were taking place in Europe which rendered Spain's attempt to dominate the Continent quite unrealistic. In a sonnet addressed to Philip II the poet Hernando de Acuña looked forward to the imminent arrival of the promised day on which there would be but one shepherd and one flock in the world, and 'one monarch, one empire, and one sword'. By the time of Philip's death such an outcome was looking ever more improbable.[8] As a consequence of the commercial and economic developments of the previous century, a major shift in geopolitical power had taken place on the Continent. After 2,000 years, during which the Mediterranean had been the main centre of power, this centre was now moving to northern Europe. The power which next emerged to a position of dominance in Europe very much reflected this fundamental change.

8

Grandeur: Louis XIV and Versailles

In the seventeenth century the principal centre of power in Europe shifted from the Mediterranean to northern Europe. This fundamental geopolitical change was marked by the Treaty of Westphalia of 1648 which ended the Thirty Years War. In 1618, at the beginning of that war, Spain was still the dominant power in Europe, but by the time it ended everything had changed. Spain had been greatly weakened and was not even a signatory to the treaty which dealt mainly with the new arrangements in post-Westphalian northern Europe. The power of the Holy Roman Empire was much curtailed and the Protestant kings and princes were accorded full recognition. In one of the treaty's constituent parts, known as the Treaty of Münster, the United Provinces were recognized as an independent state and became the Dutch Republic. This small but dynamic country was to dominate world trade for the rest of the century.

The country which now replaced Spain as the dominant power in Europe was France. For the rest of the century this power was engaged in the entrenchment of its position and in the further enlargement of its territory by steadily moving its frontier eastwards. In 1643 Louis XIII, who had been king throughout the Thirty Years War, died and his four-year-old son, Louis XIV, ascended the French throne. The country was run by a Regency with a dominant first minister, Cardinal Mazarin. The death of Mazarin in 1661 gave Louis the opportunity to assert his authority and he was able to take full charge of the government of his country. There were many who aspired to power of the sort which Mazarin, and before him Richelieu, had enjoyed but Louis was strong willed and did not allow this to happen. A later painting of the king emphasized this by depicting him as Jupiter with the inscription 'Le Roi gouverne par lui-même' (The King rules alone).

Louis XIV carried on a great deal of the foreign policy of his predecessors but with far greater vigour and aggression. Most of his
long reign was taken up with wars in which the French frontier moved
inexorably eastwards, adding large parts of the Spanish Netherlands,
Franche Comté and Alsace to the king's domains. By the closing years
of the seventeenth century the area of France had increased by about a
third over what it had been a century earlier. By then the country also had
the largest population in Europe and had become by far the continent's
strongest military and economic power.

Louis was determined to assert both the dominant position of his
country and his own position of dominance in France. In seeking to
achieve his goal, he embarked early in his reign on the building of a
new centre of royal power. This was symbolic of his intentions and was
intended to impress all who visited it with the power of his country and
the magnificence of his monarchy. Paris had been the French capital
since the country had first come into being in the ninth century and the
Louvre, the splendid royal palace, was at its heart. The city had
developed a hold on France far greater than either Toledo or Madrid
ever had on Spain. 'The reason why Olivares failed and Richelieu
succeeded', wrote Fisher, 'is that in France conditions were favourable
to centralization whereas in Spain they were adverse. All ways in France
lead to Paris. No ways in Spain lead to Madrid.'[1] Besides being the
capital, Paris was also a great economic and cultural centre. It was the
location of the Sorbonne, one of Europe's earliest and most prestigious
universities, and became a magnet for large numbers of people seeking
to avail themselves of the opportunities which a great capital afforded.
These ranged from merchants and craftsmen to students from both
France and the neighbouring countries.

However, like Philip II of Spain in the previous century, Louis
wished to detach himself from his capital. The reasons for this were
not dissimilar from those of the Spanish monarch as the city had
been far too closely associated with the turbulence of the recent past.
Most alarming had been the outbreak of disorder known as the Fronde
which had taken place during Louis' childhood and had resulted in
the monarchy for a time being in a precarious state and even being
forced to flee the capital. With such associations in mind, when he
assumed power in 1661 Louis did not feel that Paris was a safe place
to be. An underlying motive for the move away was therefore the
necessity to find somewhere where the monarch and the royal family
could be more easily protected.

Louis also had another motive which was to design a centre of power which would reflect his ambitions for France and enable him to carry them out more easily. He was an absolutist and his idea of the monarchy was that it should wield total power. This was encapsulated in the famous phrase attributed to him, 'L'Etat, c'est moi'. He wished to be unhindered by all the other elements that make up the kaleidoscope of a nation and are inevitably present in its capital city . However, since Paris was so much the undisputed centre of the country, he did not intend to disengage himself and his government totally from this prime location.

In considering the nature of his project Louis looked to other similar examples, but in Europe at that time there were few. Philip's monastic Escorial palace was not what he had in mind at all and he was more interested in the great city which Shah Jahan was building in Delhi at this time. News of this was brought back by travellers, notably François Bernier who submitted to Louis a detailed description of what was taking place. To what extent this actually influenced the construction of the new palace is uncertain but in some respects there are distinct similarities. The objectives of the two monarchs were, after all, very similar. However, there was another great chateau nearer home towards which Louis looked with some admiration and much envy. This was Vaux-le-Vicomte, the palace built for himself by Nicolas Fouquet, his first minister of finance. This impressive and costly project typified what Louis had in mind for himself. He felt strongly that such a grand palace should be for a king and not a minister. His resentment towards Fouquet grew both on account of the power he wielded and his display of wealth. The minister's fall as a result of charges of financial corruption freed Louis of this overpowerful and over-grand rival. Never after that was any minister of his allowed to attain such wealth and power.

Louis chose as the site for his palace the village of Versailles, some 20 km to the southwest of Paris. Here his father Louis XIII had a hunting lodge and it was around this that the building of the new royal palace began in 1664. The architect Le Vau was in charge of designing the first stage which consisted of enveloping the hunting lodge in a completely new structure. Later Le Brun and Hardouin-Mansart contributed to the building and its adornments and Le Nôtre designed the spacious gardens and their surroundings.

Despite the huge numbers of workers employed, the construction of the new palace was a slow and painstaking business and it was not until 1682 that the court was able finally to move to Versailles. In so doing the king made it his new centre of power and of the government of France. By that time the palace had grown to enormous proportions with hundreds of rooms intended to accommodate the large numbers who made up the court and government. All officials, members of the government, the royal family and, of course, aristocrats were expected to reside there either permanently or at least for part of the year.

The approach to the palace was itself a highly impressive experience, as one travelled through the grid pattern of avenues on which the new town of Versailles was planned. A long avenue led to the vast expanse of the Place d'Armes around which were the Royal Mews, barracks and other official buildings. At the end of this were the great gates beyond which were the courtyard and the main entrance to the palace. The whole was built in the classical style and its awesome vastness was clearly designed to impress all who made the short journey from Paris with the power and splendour of the monarch.

In the middle of the palace was the Grand Appartement du Roi, which initially was where the king resided and was also the most important centre of government activity. It consisted of seven principal rooms, each named after one of the known planets. The plan was heliocentric and centred on the Salon d'Apolon, the Greek god most associated with the sun. It was from this that Louis came to be known as 'le Roi-Soleil', signifying that the king was to France what the sun was to the solar system. This was a very similar notion to that of the Chinese emperors who were proclaimed to be the 'Sons of Heaven' and derived their authority from this. The salon was also originally the Throne Room in the centre of which the solid silver throne of the monarch was situated. On the walls of this salon and of the other rooms in the Appartement were paintings by Le Brun of scenes of the exploits of heroic figures such as Cyrus, Alexander the Great and Augustus. Louis XIV wished to associate himself with these great historical figures, giving a clear indication to all that he saw himself in this heroic tradition. It followed from this that he saw France as an imperial state with a historic role akin to the great empires of ancient times

Parallel to the king's apartment was the Grand Appartement de la Reine which consisted of another set of rooms decorated with similar splendour. Just as the king's apartment was decorated with paintings of legendary heroic figures, those of the queen were decorated with the heroines of antiquity.

Some changes to the whole structure were soon needed for the addition of what was to be one of the centrepieces of the palace, the Galerie des Glaces – the Hall of Mirrors – which was designed by Hardouin-Mansart and completed in 1690. This hall was the most magnificent and highly decorated in the whole palace and was intended for the purpose of holding grand receptions and conducting state ceremonial.

While initially the Grand Appartement du Roi was used as the centre of government, as the size of the palace increased and the Salon d'Apolon ceased to be used as the Throne Room, changes were made and the centre was moved to La Chambre du Roi, the king's bedchamber. In the centre of this was the enormous royal bed with its impressive fittings and decorations. This soon came to be regarded as the real heart of the palace and so the centre of the government of France. This might seem an extremely bizarre arrangement but it accords with the idea that the monarch was a public figure to be viewed at – almost – all times. The principal axes of the palace and the gardens radiated from this Chambre, thus symbolizing the fact that all power in France also radiated from there. It was there that the most important formal and ceremonial events associated with the monarch took place. These began in the morning with the *levée*, the rising of the monarch, followed by the ceremony of dressing and the partaking of breakfast, all of which were watched by

The Palace of Versailles in the early 18th century.

a large collection of people. Beside nobles and government ministers, this also included members of the public who wished to behold their monarch and to have some contact, however brief, with him. In order to enter the presence of the monarch it was necessary to observe a certain code of dress and swords had to be worn. Otherwise members of all classes could attend this ceremonial and were invariably greeted politely by the king. In the afternoon the king would often stroll in the gardens, and these walks too soon took on the role of ceremonial. In fact, the whole palace was designed as a backdrop for the grandeur of the king and through him the grandeur of the country over which he ruled. Louis' life became in many ways a day-long spectacle and, as Seward put it, the king 'resembled an actor perpetually on stage'.[2] According to Saint-Simon, with a calendar and a watch one could tell what the king was doing at any hour of the day.[3]

At the rear of the palace were the great gardens designed by André Le Nôtre. Highly geometrical in form, they were planned so that the whole vista could be seen at a glance. These gardens were intended to complement the chateau and to provide a suitably impressive setting for the whole project. The symmetrical layout had a central axis which followed that of the palace itself. Trees and plants were brought from far afield, including 3,000 orange trees from Italy. Water was diverted to provide sufficient for the great elongated lake at the centre and for the fountains on statues of Neptune. Supplying sufficient water for the whole vast complex proved problematic and the military engineer Vauban was called in to help rectify this. He attempted to build an aqueduct over the river Maintenan but this failed to resolve the issue and the inadequacy of the water supply remained a persistent problem for the palace and its gardens. While the taming of nature was successfully accomplished, the cooperation of nature proved more difficult to achieve. Vauban's precept that in order to tame nature it is necessary to obey her did not fit well with the prevailing ideas at Versailles. There the concept of man dominating nature fitted much better with the idea of the monarch dominating France and France dominating Europe. The best view of the whole garden was said to be from the Chambre du Roi itself and this meant that the centre of power was complemented by a vista to match. Or in Nikolaus Pevsner's words, 'Nature subdued by the hand of man to serve the greatness of the King, whose bedroom was placed right in the centre of the whole composition'.[4]

The palace of Versailles, together with its associated lodges, gardens and grand avenues, was the greatest and most impressive building project of the era anywhere in Europe. More than one commentator has dismissed it as being little more than a monumental piece of folly by a monarch who was intoxicated by his own splendour. According to Ashley, Versailles was 'the place he designed for his magnificence, in order to show by its adornment what a great king can do when he spares nothing to satisfy his wishes'.[5]

Be this as it may, it can hardly be denied that the existence of Versailles played a major role in the eventual collapse of the Bourbon dynasty. It is certainly true that it reflected Louis' love of the luxurious and the ostentatious and the monarch enthusiastically took on the role of principal actor on this massive stage. Nevertheless, as with the other great imperial cities which have been examined, there was more to it than this. Important *raisons d'état* underlay Louis' magnificent and costly project.

As the palace grew in size, it became ever more the heart of the government of France and Louis also came to see it as a way of controlling the great nobles who in the past had possessed so much power that they rivalled that of the king himself. Members of the nobility were called on to serve in the government and some were chosen to be ministers. These were referred to as the *noblesse de la robe* and they often became so involved with Versailles and its affairs that they left their estates to decline. Many nobles were soon bankrupt and had to be bailed out by the king, thus increasing their dependence on him. This was exactly the situation that he wanted to achieve. Versailles became the only route to preferment for the nobility and regular attendance at court was therefore essential. Even if they did not have such positions they were nevertheless required to attend the court and to live for at least part of the year in Versailles. The splendour of the court turned their heads and the rural life became ever more boring for them. La Bruyère's assertion that 'provincials are fools' became generally accepted. They were drawn to Versailles like moths to a candle. When their estates suffered, living in Versailles became their only option. In many ways it became a home for great nobles who were fast losing their *raison d'être*. Versailles had turned into the principal instrument for the taming of the nobility. The words 'He is never seen' became the greatest condemnation and the nobility fell in with this with surprising readiness. They came to believe that attendance on the king in Versailles was the only thing really worth doing and that remaining on their estates was very much a second best. The nobility, said Morris, had been placed in a gilded cage from which there was no real desire to escape.

Indeed, such sentiments applied not only to the nobility but to all who had the honour to serve the king. Cardinal Richelieu, Mazarin's predecessor, is on record as having said, 'I should rather die than not see the King.' Although this had been said before Louis XIV came to the throne it was very much a sentiment that came to be widely felt among the king's subjects. The visibility of the monarch was at the heart of the whole great project.

As the nobles luxuriated in their gilded cages, the king moved to secure tighter control over his domains. He placed royal officials, the *intendants*, as his representatives in different regions, thereby increasing his own direct grip on the country. They were the forerunners of the prefects, and this was the beginning of the process which was to make France the most centralized country in Europe.

The sheer magnificence of the monarchy was on display at Versailles and the splendour of the palace and its grounds spoke louder than words. All who visited, and there were many, were awestruck by what they saw. Colbert, Louis' finance minister after the fall of Fouquet, viewed the palace as being a 'showcase' for France. His aim was that everything, from the decor to the paintings and furniture should be French. The widespread belief of the time was that a country was stronger when it was self-sufficient and this was something that Colbert wished to bring about for France. Thus while Versailles was symbolic of the grandeur of the monarchy, it was also intended to be symbolic of the strength of France as the leading power in Europe.

The geometrical plan of the palace and the gardens also symbolized order, an order which tamed nature and imposed an organized pattern on it. Le Nôtre's idea of the '*jardin d'intelligence*' accorded well with the planned order which it was Louis' aim to bring to France. This was all very much in line with the developments in science taking place in the later seventeenth century, which were transforming the way Europeans thought about the world and the role of mankind within it. What was in nature diverse and chaotic was being unified into an organized and intelligent system. Far from 'obeying' nature as Vauban proposed, Versailles represented the imposition of order upon what was regarded as chaos. In the same way, in the human world, what had been diverse and chaotic was now also being given order and purpose. A unified taxation system was introduced, unified laws promulgated and even a unified culture promoted. This was accomplished by means of the establishment of academies. The Académie Française, Académie des Beaux-Arts and Académie de Musique were intended to exercise control over the French cultural scene and make it part of the system designed to unify the state. This search for order was epitomized in France by the ideas of Descartes. Cartesian logic underpinned most thinking, imparting the same mathematical order to the human world as was being discovered to exist in the physical. The overall objective was to create a France which through its unity of purpose would be the centre and focus of the new emerging Europe. As it turned out, it also entailed the creation of the first of those nation-states that were to become the principal heirs to medieval Christendom. Over this ordered world presided Louis, 'le Roi-Soleil', shining like the sun at the heart of his own solar system.

This represented a final break with the Middle Ages and the central role for Christianity and Christendom. Spain was the last power to devote itself to the preservation of this system and in this it had failed. The European world had undergone a massive change both geopolitically and in the realm of ideas, and the France of Louis was the principal exponent of this new post-Westphalian model. While the Catholic Church was still part of the new France, like most other things within the state it was also given more national characteristics. The idea of the 'Gallican' church fitted more readily into a state in which all the elements were linked together in a kind of living whole. The principal representative of this view was Jacques-Bénigne Bossuet, the bishop of Meaux, who believed in a balanced and tolerant Catholicism which would play its role as a component part of the French state. Bossuet drew up the 'Four Articles' which affirmed the independence of the French Church from that of Rome. He was an exponent of absolutism and talked of a 'loi fondamentale' which regarded the king as being God's image on earth. Louis himself paid sufficient heed to the important role of the Church within the state. He had his own chapel in Versailles and attended Mass every morning. Still, in what has been called 'the pagan paradise', religion had lost the central position it had held in Christendom. The main purpose of Philip II's state had been to promote Catholic values and support the Church. In Louis' France the opposite was true. The role of the church was to play its part in supporting and strengthening the monarchy. The whole idea of a sun king, after all, was hardly a Christian one. It and the god Apollo were drawn from the beliefs of the pagan world. Louis came to be regarded, and to regard himself, as a kind of god figure. In an early address to the sovereign, the Paris parlement effused, 'the realm's estates pay you honour and duty as they would to a god who can be seen'.[6] They referred to him as 'Louis le

Grand' and considered that his was 'the throne of the living God'. This all represented a massive break with the past and the beginning of that marginalization of religion that was to reach its apogee in the French Revolution. The unified and centralized state which Louis produced was also the most powerful in Europe and by the second half of the seventeenth century it had taken over from a much weakened Spain as the new centre of power on the Continent. The objective of creating a Europe united around France and subservient to it was seen as another way in which the mathematical order of the universe was being transposed to the human world.

The magnificence of Versailles, itself far more splendid than any other royal palace in Europe, symbolized this ambition. The geometrical plan of the great palace and its gardens focusing on the Chambre du Roi was akin to the geometric plan of a Europe in which France was the sun, the focus of power, around which the smaller and less powerful states revolved. This was the new – and even natural – political order replacing the old order of Christendom. However, this grand ambition was never to be fully achieved as a result of the coalition of states led by the Netherlands and England which were determined to restrain the territorial ambitions of the French monarch.

Louis XIV died in 1715 after one of the longest reigns in European history. The Treaty of Utrecht, ending the long War of Spanish Succession, had been signed two years earlier and had produced a very different order from that envisaged by Louis and his ministers. Rather than one power dominating, the new eighteenth-century Europe was to be one in which a number of rival powers sought advantage for themselves but in the end tended to balance one another out. Alliances formed among them kept aspirants for the prime position from achieving their goal. France certainly for the time being remained the most powerful of the European states but the others stubbornly refused to revolve around her alone. The sun with its satellite planets was certainly not the appropriate celestial analogy for the new Europe in the making. If there was such an analogy it was of many stars in the firmament, some bright and some less so but each maintaining its place within the whole.

Versailles remained the residence of Louis' successors and it continued to be the heart and symbol of that unified and centralized state which was his main legacy. However, to an increasing number of French men and women it also symbolized wealth and privilege and was the focus of the discontent that grew in the country as the gap between the privileged and the underprivileged, wealth and poverty, continued to widen. The things Versailles had been intended to symbolize came under increasing scrutiny as the military and economic power of France began to wane. The need for change came to be widely felt throughout the country, except in that 'gilded cage' which was Versailles itself. There the parade of power and privilege went on much as before. In 1789, three-quarters of a century after the death of Louis xiv, the country erupted into revolution. The famous – or infamous – remark put into the mouth of Queen Marie Antoinette in response to the growing conditions of famine, was 'Let them eat cake'. Whether this is true or not it is illustrative of the great chasm which had opened between a court isolated in luxury and the mass of the people in poverty.

Following the Revolution, the king and the royal family were forced to return to Paris where they were certainly confronted by the poverty and anger of the people. In 1793 both king and queen were guillotined alongside thousands of those aristocrats whom Louis xiv had made obsolete. They had nevertheless been able to retain their privileged positions and this is what sent them to the guillotine. From then on Versailles became an empty shell, its halls filled only with the memories of past greatness. For those regimes which ruled France during the nineteenth century, Paris was once more the undisputed capital.

However, the vast palace was still used occasionally for great ceremonial events. Ironically, one of the most splendid of these was the proclamation of the creation of the new German Empire after the Franco-Prussian War of 1870–71. While the building of Versailles had signalled the beginning of French hegemony in Europe, it was the unlikely setting for the rise of another hegemonial power. Half a century later the signing of the Treaty of Versailles in the Galerie des Glaces aimed to set the seal on yet another new European order after the First World War. With the beginning of the age of mass tourism, the palace became a magnificent museum visited by millions who marvelled at the wealth and power that had created something so incredible.

The most lasting legacy of Versailles was the creation of the highly centralized French nation-state. While the sun and its satellites had long ceased to be appropriate, the geometrical representation of France as a hexagon, its towns and cities arranged in a quasi-geometrical fashion around Paris, continued to give the idea of an order which could not and should not be interfered with. The order which had been enshrined in Versailles and its gardens became the model which modern France has continued to follow.

9
St Petersburg and the Imperial Vision of Peter the Great

A quarter of a century after the transfer of the French seat of government to its new home in Versailles, on the other side of Europe another grand project with a very similar objective was getting under way. This was the foundation of the city of St Petersburg which took place in 1703. Located at the eastern end of the Gulf of Finland on the deltaic estuary of the river Neva, from the outset it was intended by its founder, Tsar Peter I, 'the Great', to be the new capital city of the Russian Empire.

Peter reigned from 1689 to 1725. He was therefore a slightly younger contemporary of Louis XIV of France and, like the French monarch, he had visions of greatness for his country. These, however, entailed a far more radical transformation than had ever been the intention of Louis. Although Louis built a completely new seat of government, it was very close to Paris, which had been the capital of France since the country came into existence. The basic geopolitical structure of the French state remained largely unchanged and France continued to be ruled from a seat of power at the centre of the Paris basin. Peter, however, was responsible for the complete transformation of the geopolitical structure of Russia.

Peter was the greatest modernizer in Russian history, and he saw his role as lifting his backward-looking country out of the Middle Ages into the eighteenth century. Europe was undergoing a massive transformation in virtually all fields and by the later seventeenth century this transformation was most in evidence in the countries of northwestern Europe, in particular the Netherlands and England. Peter desperately wanted Russia to be a part of this but he realized that nothing could be accomplished without massive changes. The establishment of the new capital was without doubt his most important step in bringing this about.

Although Moscow had long been a fortress in the forests of central Russia, after the fall of Kievan Rus it had been completely transformed into a magnificent capital city in the late fifteenth and early sixteenth centuries during the reigns of Ivan III 'the Great', Vasili III and Ivan IV 'the Terrible'. It was planned specifically to be the capital of Muscovite Russia – 'Holy Russia' – and this entailed the unity of state and Church at the heart of power. The Muscovite state saw itself as being essentially the heir to the Byzantine Empire and thus indirectly the heir to Rome itself. However, while the Roman world and its heirs had dominated Europe for the best part of 2,000 years, by the seventeenth century the principal centre of power in Europe had moved northwards and Russia had fallen well behind the new developments taking place there. Peter put this backwardness down to the fact that his country was virtually landlocked and had looked towards the east and south rather than westwards towards Europe. A further factor was the dominant role of the Orthodox Church in the affairs of the state and the continuing prevalence of ideas inherited from the now defunct Byzantine Empire. Geography and history had thus combined to make Russia a backward-looking country cut off from the mainstream of new political and scientific ideas which were increasingly dominating European thinking. Peter wanted to change all that and to open the doors of Russia to Europe. He envisaged the future of Russia as a modern European power. Peter was a 'westerner' but on becoming tsar he found that the 'easterners' were very much in control in his capital. His radical solution to this situation was to get away from them and all they represented by moving to a new capital.

Much of Peter's thinking had its origins in his childhood experiences. Following the death of his father, Tsar Alexis, in 1676 problems arose due to the physical and mental weakness of the immediate successors Fedor and Ivan. Peter, the son by Alexis's second wife, was marginalized by his half-sister, the Regent Sophia, and forced to live away from court in the village of Preobrazhenskoe. He was a strong and intelligent young prince and quickly learned much, especially from the foreigners in the nearby German colony. It was there that he became acquainted with what was happening in western Europe and he was especially fascinated by boats which he sailed on the nearby river. His increasing knowledge led him to the lifelong conviction that maritime power was essential if Russia was to develop. The acquisition of such power presented a huge problem for a virtually landlocked country and one which could only be solved by acquiring a more suitable coastline.

In 1689 Peter became joint tsar with his feeble-minded half-brother, Ivan. This arrangement lasted until 1696 when Ivan died and from then on Peter reigned alone. Only then was he able to begin his grand project of modernization which had been in his young mind for so long. In order to achieve this, in 1697 he embarked on a great journey to western Europe in order to see for himself the wonders which he had been told about by the foreigners he had met in his childhood. This was the 'Grand Embassy' and in the first instance it went to the Netherlands, regarded as the most technologically and scientifically advanced country in the world at the time. There he was able to see for himself – and actually take part in – the advances in shipbuilding, navigation, artillery and a variety of other industries and to marvel at the construction of the huge dams and water-control projects. The Anglo-Dutch king William III invited him to visit England, an offer he accepted with alacrity. There he was able to witness similar activities and to see the commercial and industrial activity taking place in the English capital. He also experienced the rich cultural, scientific and political life of the great city. Unsurprisingly, the English Parliament does not seem to have impressed the Russian autocrat and political freedom was one thing he did not desire to import into Russia. As a result of these travels, he now knew how an advanced modern country worked and it prepared him to undertake the transformation of his own country along the same lines.

There was, of course, huge opposition to the envisaged changes and this was especially the case in Moscow, the centre of the old order. In 1698 the revolt of the powerful palace guard, the *streltsy*, gave Peter a warning of the problems which the project of modernization would face. Seemingly this was one of the factors which finally made him determined to move the centre of government to a new capital, well away from Moscow, where he would be able to put his ideas into practice without interference. He combined this with his other great desire to open up Russia by giving the country a more satisfactory maritime frontage and ready access to the sea. This presented Peter with his first major geopolitical problem and in order to resolve it he realized that he would have to go to war. This war, when it came, was to last for most of the rest of his reign.

In the west, Russia was hemmed in by three powerful states which completely prevented access to all but the icy northern seas. In the south was the Ottoman Empire which had controlled the eastern Mediterranean and the Black Sea since the fall of the Byzantine Empire in 1453. As the self-proclaimed successor to this empire, the Russians had always felt a powerful pull of destiny in this direction. They retained an underlying desire to liberate Constantinople and to free all Orthodox Christians from what they regarded as Islamic interlopers. However, the immense power of the Ottomans had always made this project unrealistic. In the centre was Poland, at the time a large and formidable country which itself had ambitions to unite all the Slavs around it. It was Catholic in faith and so was hostile to Orthodox Russia. Poland blocked the most direct contacts with Continental Europe by land or sea. In the north lay Sweden which in the late seventeenth century was at its most powerful and which, after the Thirty Years War, had converted the Baltic Sea into a Swedish lake.

It was to the north that Peter decided to make his principal move, since the Baltic provided the best maritime route westwards to the North Sea and to those advanced countries which he had visited. In 1700 war broke out between Russia and Sweden over a territorial dispute. This was the Great Northern War and it was to last more than two decades.

In 1702 Peter's forces captured the Swedish stronghold of Noteborg and so secured access to the Gulf of Finland. The following year construction commenced of a Russian fortress on one of the islands in the Neva delta. This was the beginning of St Petersburg. Traditionally, the date of its foundation was 16 May 1703 and the site chosen was on the island of Ianni Saari, close to the Swedish fortress of Nyenchants. Peter talked triumphantly of planting the Russian flag on this fortress in place of that of the Swedes.[1] The island was close to the northern bank of the Neva and many reasons have been given for its choice, including the more suitable terrain and the greater security afforded by this particular island. Many myths later arose, notably the one that Peter saw an eagle hovering in the sky above the island and immediately set about digging the first turf. This has resemblances to the myths associated with the choice of other sites, including Constantinople, showing that the links with old Russian beliefs and traditions were far from being entirely severed. Peter had a log cabin built nearby so that he could supervise closely, and even take part in, the work. It was a massive project and large numbers of Swedish prisoners were forced to labour on it. Since this was still very much in a war zone, the first building was a fortress which Peter named the Sancta Petropavlovsk (St Peter and Paul). It was the very first part of the construction of what was to become the new capital of Russia. From the outset, Peter seems to have made it clear that he intended his new capital to be there. In letters he used the Russian word *stolitsa*, meaning capital, rather than *gorod*, meaning town or city. It is significant that the *stolitsa* was first given the Dutch name of Pieterbruk and the first foreign merchant vessel which arrived in that year was Dutch. Likewise Noteborg was renamed not with a Russian but with a German name, Schlüsselberg, meaning the 'key' fortress. This indicated its importance for the defence of the new city. The new Russian fleet was soon to be based on another neighbouring island, renamed Kronstadt. These Dutch and German names clearly demonstrated the direction in which Peter was heading with his new Russian Empire. It seemed that becoming more European meant that it was also going to be less Russian.

It is interesting that at the time of its foundation Pieterbruk was legally still on Swedish territory and it required a considerable act of faith, and also of audacity, for Peter to begin the building of his new capital on the territory of another state which was still very powerful. However, Russia was becoming each year more confident both on land and sea. In 1709 the Swedes were defeated at the battle of Poltava and in 1714 came the decisive battle of Hangö which was Russia's first ever naval victory. This heralded the country's arrival on the scene as a naval power and also brought to an end the half century during which the Baltic had been a Swedish lake. In an address after the battle of Poltava, Peter asserted that 'now with God's help, the final stone has been laid in the foundation of St Petersburg'.[2] The following year, 1710, the court finally moved away from Moscow and settled in the new capital. However, it was not until 1721, with the Northern War ending in victory for Russia, that the country's capital was legally on Russian soil. By this time a considerable city had already arisen in the marshes and islands of the Neva delta. The Treaty of Nystadt ending the war also transferred to Russia the provinces of Karelia, Ingria, Estonia and Latvia, giving her control over the Gulf of Finland and ready access to the Baltic. The new capital was still highly peripheral to the enormous Russian Empire which stretched eastwards as far as the Pacific Ocean, leaving it dangerously vulnerable to attack. However, it was soon well protected by the forts in the Gulf of Finland, and the new acquisitions on the Baltic. Above all Russia now had a formidable navy which was based on the island of Kronstadt downstream of the capital. This build-up of power in the Baltic region represented a major geopolitical shift in the Russian Empire both from south to north and from continental to maritime.

The original St Petersburg was thus built on an island in the Neva river and was initially little more than a defensive fort, one of the many guarding the new Russian presence in the Baltic. It was designed in the Vauban style, another west European feature which displayed knowledge of the latest military engineering. Inside its massive walls there was ample room to accommodate other buildings. It was, in fact, a kind of maritime Kremlin which sheltered the combined elements of military, state and Church. In this way, despite the vigorous westernization in which Peter was engaged, the traditional Russian concentration of power within a fortress was still in evidence. Construction continued throughout the reign of Peter and into that of his successors, and western European architects were always prominent. At its centre is the Cathedral of ss Peter and Paul designed by the Swiss architect Domenico Trezzini. This was built in the European classical style hitherto unknown in Russia. The grand entrance gateway to the fort was also designed by Tressini. It is in the form of a triumphal arch with the two-headed imperial eagle prominently displayed and is topped by a bas-relief which gives thanks for Russia's victory in the Northern War. The tomb of Peter himself, together with those of all the subsequent tsars until the revolution, was in this magnificent building. Close to the cathedral is a small building housing the skiff in which Peter sailed during his childhood. This was intended as a reminder of how the great transformation of Russia had started.

Immediately to the north of the fortress was the first part of the emerging city. Known as the St Petersburg side, it is actually on another island between two arms of the Neva. It was there that Peter's log cabin was built. The Troitskaya Ploshad (Trinity Square), slightly to the east of it, was the first real centre of the city. On the northern side of this square stood the wooden Church of the Trinity and on the other side was a German hostelry, named rather grandly the Triumphal Hostelry of the Four Frigates. This was where Peter availed himself of ample alcoholic refreshment during respite from his labours.

However, Peter never intended the centre of the new capital to be there at all but on an adjacent island. This was Vasilievsky Island, located downstream between the Bolshaya and Malaya – Great and Little – Neva. He envisaged this as a kind of 'Baltic Amsterdam', possessing all the facilities for a great port and with waterways winding through it. To achieve this ambition he embarked on the construction of a canal system crossing the island. He also ordered the construction of official government buildings and houses for the army of civil servants and administrators whom he intended to bring from Moscow. One of the first buildings there was the Menshikov Palace, the residence of the governor of the city. The island, with its docks and ready access to the sea, soon became the city's first centre of commerce. However, there were as yet no bridges and the only links to the island were by sailing boat, on which

Plan of the Peter and Paul Fortress, St Petersburg.

Peter insisted in preference to the more practical rowing boats. Highly dependent on the weather, these proved to be to be unreliable and often hazardous and the Vasilievsky project had to be abandoned before the end of Peter's reign. As a result it came to be realized that the most practical place for future development would be on the mainland immediately to the south of the river. However, the eastern spit of Vasilievsky island, known as the Strelka, was soon to gain its own special character with the opening of the university in 1725, followed by a number of libraries, museums and institutes. In this way it evolved into the intellectual and cultural centre of the new capital. The island also remained the city's commercial and financial hub, retaining its port facilities and stock exchange. In the following century, with the erection of the Rostral Columns, it became more than anywhere else representative of the capital. These two impressive columns at the eastern end of the Strelka were intended to commemorate Russian naval victories and were imitative of the Roman practice of erecting symbols of victory. The figures at the base of the columns represented the four great rivers of Russia – the Dniepr, the Don, the Volkhov and the Volga. In this way the symbols of the overwhelmingly maritime character of the city, and of Peter's new Russia, were linked with symbols of the Russian past, so acknowledging the importance of the rivers in earlier Russian history.

From the outset Peter wished his new stolitsa to be beautiful as well as functional. To achieve this he not only took great interest in the architecture but sent for large numbers of plants and trees to fill the new parks and gardens which he was planning. As well as being the spearhead for the new orientation of his empire, Peter saw his new city as being a 'paradise on earth'. It was, he said, like living in Heaven. After his trials and tribulations in Moscow one can understand the emperor's sense of liberation when he established his own capital well away from the old one. The city was thus to combine the roles of paradise and centre of a revived Russian Empire.

In the opinion of Hughes, it was far from being another 'Third Rome' but rather more a recreation of the 'First Rome' – pre-Christian, imperial and pagan.[3] It certainly came to possess many features which could be termed pagan, but there were also many churches and the Christianity of Muscovite Russia was by no means abandoned. It was certainly intended to be the new Rome for Peter's Europeanized, and powerful, Russian Empire.

Those who were forcibly transferred to work in the new capital did not by any means share Peter's rosy image of it. Rather than being any kind of paradise, they were more likely to view it as a cold, damp, sunless and unhealthy place in which they had been forced to live under duress. For them, what were commonly referred to as 'the unhealthy Finnish marshes' were far from having that image of desirability which Peter sought to impart.

Whichever was the truer picture of the new capital, and its physical setting, for Peter it had one immense physical advantage over the old capital. It had maritime access and, as well as being the capital, it was also a vibrant port and the country's main naval base. In fact, in Peter's mind these factors were fused together in the forward thrust of his dream of a modern and European Russian Empire.

The Europeanization which Peter instigated in decrees issued from his new capital covered most aspects of Russian life. He decreed that the wearing of beards was henceforth forbidden and all the men were ordered to shave them off. Later, in the face of massive opposition to this decree, Peter compromised and introduced a beards licence. This was symbolic of the massive break with Moscow and the religious traditions of that city, since from the beginnings of Russian Orthodoxy the wearing of a beard had been a sign of saintliness. Furthermore, the introduction of European dress at court also represented a powerful symbolic break with the old culture.

Besides these externals, huge changes were made in political arrangements. A Senate was established which was given limited powers for the discussion of important issues and for lawmaking. This was, however, no parliament in the English sense and it was never allowed to interfere with the ultimate authority of Peter himself. The body remained advisory rather than legislative. The administration of the empire was divided into a new system of colleges, each of which was responsible for the handling of a particular aspect of state business. To bring Russia more closely into line with Europe, the old Russian calendar, which started from the beginning of the world, was abolished and a new European one was introduced that began on 1 January 1700. Finally, Peter himself took the Roman title of imperator in place of tsar. He ignored the Byzantine version, basileus, further emphasizing the strong message that he was modelling his new empire on Rome rather than Byzantium. Even in his view of the ancient world, Peter was looking to the west rather than the east. This alienated him all the more from the traditional Muscovite hierarchy which had looked to Constantinople rather than Rome and based itself on Byzantine rather than Roman religious and political traditions.

While the whole Russian Christian tradition had always been an Orthodox one, Peter set about its modernization by looking to western practices. He abolished the patriarchate and replaced it with a synod. The architectural style of the cathedral of ss Peter and Paul, at the centre of the great fortress bearing their name, was essentially European and this was also the style of most other churches later built in the capital. Most fundamentally, the role of the church in state affairs became more limited. The close link between Church and state, which was spectacularly symbolized in the Moscow Kremlin, was broken and the dominance of the state was asserted. While Peter professed to be Christian, his actions were increasingly driven by secular considerations. As Marc Raeff put it:

> The administration ceased to play a religious role . . . In the place of the most pious tsar we find the sovereign emperor, wearing a European-style military uniform, residing at the western extremity of his empire, and isolated from the spiritual and religious life of his people.[4]

In face of all these massive changes, the 'Old Believers' became the centre of the fight to keep the old Russian culture alive. To them, the Petrine reforms were an abnegation of the very nature of what was to them 'Holy Russia'. Their firm belief was that Moscow was the 'Third Rome' and the new capital was little more than a den of iniquity. The determination of the Old Believers to protect the culture gave rise to what Raeff termed the '"two nations", two cultural universes, between which there was little, if any, exchange'.[5] Raeff saw the process of westernization as having resulted in the erection of what he called a 'great wall' separating the political elite from the masses.

It is difficult to see how these great changes could possibly have been brought about were it not for the existence of St Petersburg, located well away from the old centre of power at the western extremity of the empire. There were indeed 'two nations', with two capitals. They may have been inhabiting the same territory but they were inhabiting different cultural universes. The new and the old capitals were geographical representations of this situation. The imperial vision of the old Russia was to liberate the Christian *terra irredenta* in the east, regain Constantinople from the Infidel and unite the whole of the Orthodox Christian world under Russian hegemony. The imperial vision of Peter's 'new' Russia was quite simply to convert a still medieval country into a modern European power.

The triumph of the new secular vision was also the triumph of St Petersburg and of the power, military and naval, scientific and commercial, which Peter was able to muster around him there. It was the triumph of the modern over the medieval but it also resulted in the opening up of a divide in Russia from that time on. The common complaint that Peter was foreign to Russia was voiced by disgruntled aristocrats who allegedly asserted that 'we don't have a sovereign any more but a substitute German'. The idea took hold that with the active encouragement of Peter, Germans were taking over the country. Whether this was true or not in Peter's time, it would certainly become more the case during the reigns of his immediate successors. Of course, Peter had first learned of the wonders achieved by foreigners from the Germans and later from the Dutch. This all amounted to much the same thing in the minds of the Russians, for whom 'Germans' and 'foreigners' became in many ways virtually interchangeable terms.

By the end of Peter's reign the new capital was still far from being the magnificent city it was to become later in the eighteenth century. Many of the buildings were of wood and most of them were either on the islands or on the St Petersburg (north) side. The growing city consisted of four distinct quarters, each separated from the others by water. The fortress was at the heart of it and adjacent to this was the St Petersburg side, which had some of the earliest buildings and was the original social hub. Thirdly there was Vasilievsky Island which by then centred on the *strelka* and still possessed some of the most splendid buildings. However, it had become obvious that future development should now be on the mainland and the south bank was the chosen place for this.

Here in 1705 was erected what to Peter must have been by far the most important building. This was the Admiralty which was central to the whole south bank development. In 1711 further improvements were

The Admiralty, St Petersburg. For Peter the Admirality would have been the true heart of his city; it is centrally located at the intersection of the major roads and avenues south of the river.

made to the building and later on in the century it was altered once more. From there radiated the major avenues leading to the south and along the banks of the Neva. Most important among them was a grand avenue, the Nevsky Prospect, which was planned to lead southeastwards to the Alexander Nevsky monastery. From 1710–11 a house was built for Peter slightly to the north of the Admiralty at the junction of the Neva and its tributary, the Fontanka. This was designed by Trezzini and was known as the Summer Palace. Around it were laid out magnificent gardens with fountains, lakes and conservatories. Most of Peter's architects for these projects, including Andreas Schlüter, Georg Johann Mattarnovy and Gottfried Schädel, were German, and nearby was the quarter known as the German Suburb. The German and Dutch input was decisive for the character of the new capital but a notable exception to this was that of Jean-Baptiste Alexandre Le Blond who arrived from Paris in 1716. It was he who laid out Peter's gardens, using Versailles as the model. He also drew up the plans for the Nevsky Prospect which later in the century was to become the most splendid grand boulevard of the city. In addition he planned the building and gardens for Peter's retreat at Peterhof on the south bank of the Neva just outside the city.

After the great emperor's death in 1725 most of his successors throughout the eighteenth century were women, and this succession of remarkable empresses continued the work of consolidating the new capital as the accepted centre of the empire and further embellishing it with buildings in the European architectural style. These were mostly on the south bank of the river which from then on became more and more the real centre of the city.

THE EIGHTEENTH-CENTURY SUCCESSORS
OF PETER THE GREAT

1725–7	Catherine I, second wife of Peter the Great
1727–30	Peter II, grandson of Peter the Great
1730–40	Anna Ivanovna, daughter of Ivan, early co-tsar of Peter the Great
1740–41	Ivan VI, great-nephew of Anna Ivanovna
1741–62	Elizabeth Petrovna, daughter of Peter the Great and Catherine I
1762	Peter III, grandson of Peter the Great
1763–96	Catherine II, 'the Great', wife of Peter III. A German Princess, Sophia Augusta, she became the empress by staging a coup and deposing her husband

The most impressive additions were made by Catherine the Great during whose reign the Russian Empire became more firmly European and more powerful than ever. It was said that when Catherine came to the throne her capital was built of wood and when she died it was built of stone.[6] This might have been something of an exaggeration, but a number of catastrophic fires had shown how unsafe the old wooden buildings were. Besides this, the empress required that her capital should have more buildings of greater splendour and this was another reason for brick and stone. Catherine was said to have been the second founder of St Petersburg. However, the building of the great imperial palace, the Winter Palace, in place of Peter's Summer Palace, had already been started as early as the reign of Anna and was continued under Elizabeth. Catherine greatly extended it and added the Hermitage which was later to become one of the great art galleries of Europe. During her reign the avenues were also built up and the quays, unstable from the outset, were strengthened and consolidated in stone. At that time the Commission of Stone Buildings which she set up did much to enhance the appearance of the city. The baroque architecture of Rastrelli's Winter Palace gave way during Catherine's reign to a more restrained classical style and the empress engaged new architects, notably Vallen de la Motte, Rinaldi, Cameron and Quarengi, to introduce and develop this style. It was as a result of the work of Catherine that St Petersburg

The Winter Palace, St Petersburg. In the 18th century this became the centre of power of the Russian Empire and remained so until the Revolution.

The Bronze Horseman, equestrian statue of Peter the Great by Etienne-Maurice Falconet. Commissioned by Catherine the Great to commemorate the 100th anniversary of the beginning of Peter's reign, it was unveiled with great ceremony in 1782.

attained its true classical splendour. Voltaire expressed the opinion that 'The united magnificence of all the cities of Europe could not equal St Petersburg.'

Catherine also made St Petersburg a far more desirable place for aristocrats and government officials to reside. No longer did they have to be cajoled into living there. By the end of the eighteenth century the capital had a vibrant social and cultural life and all the facilities necessary for luxurious living. The Russian upper classes came flocking to the capital both for the civilized life which was possible there and, more importantly, because without their presence in the capital they had little chance of promotion in government service. All this had echoes of Louis XIV's Versailles, which the aristocrats were encouraged to believe was the only place to live.

To link herself to Peter the Great and to further consolidate both her own legitimacy and that of St Petersburg itself, Catherine commissioned what has become one of the capital's most impressive symbols, the great bronze statue of Peter which was erected close to the Admiralty in 1782 to commemorate the hundredth anniversary of the coronation of the city's founder. The Bronze Horseman by Falconet show Peter in a dramatic pose. The Latin inscription on the great granite base refers to Peter as 'Imperator'. Catherine, a German princess before she became empress, was completely European in her attitudes and she was quick to assert that the Russian Empire was a European rather than an Asiatic power.

Yet, it was not until after her reign that the centre of the city really achieved its present architectural form. The Palace Square, with its triumphal arch and the General Staff Building, was not completed until 1820, during the reign of Alexander I, and the new Admiralty building, with its distinctive twisting steeple, was not completed until 1823. By then St Petersburg had became the most perfect example of a European classical city. It symbolized a Russian Empire which was very much part of Europe and its literature, art and music were integrated into the wider European cultural scene. The transformation of Russia, begun a century earlier by Peter the Great, was complete and by the end of the Napoleonic Wars the orientation of the country was firmly to the west.

Arnold Toynbee summed up the truly radical nature of the move of the capital to the Gulf of Finland. As a result, he asserted,

> Moscow was temporarily deprived of her prerogative as a result of her rulers' decision to open their doors to the West . . . Moscow was compelled, for more than two hundred years, to see her empire governed from a capital which was not only given a new name but was planted on virgin soil on a far-distant site . . . The transfer of the capital of the Russian empire by Peter the Great from Moscow in the heart of Holy Russia to Saint Petersburg on the banks of the Neva, within a stone's throw of the Baltic, is comparable to Nicator's choice in its cultural and geographical aspects.[7] In this case, as in that, the seat of government of a landlocked empire was planted at the corner of the empire's domain in order to provide the capital with easy access by the sea to the sources of an alien civilization which the imperial government was eager to introduce into its dominions. In its political aspect, however, Peter's act was much more audacious than Nicator's; for, in seeking to supplant Moscow by Saint Petersburg, Peter was ignoring the feelings of the Orthodox Christian ruling element in Muscovy with a brusqueness reminiscent of the revolutionary acts of Julius Caesar.[8]

The very existence of St Petersburg transformed Russia. From continental it had become maritime and from Eastern it had become Western. It was this which made Russia one of the acknowledged great powers of nineteenth-century Europe. In fact, during that century it transcended

Europe and became a global power. The other major nineteenth-century global power was Great Britain, and Russia became for a time Britain's main rival on the world scene.[9] Together they became the dominant powers of the age, strongly influencing events in both Europe and the rest of the world. It would have been very difficult to envisage such a situation a century earlier and it would certainly have been impossible without the move to St Petersburg and all that followed from this.

However, the existence of St Petersburg continued fundamentally to divide Russia. Moscow, the old capital, retained its position as the acknowledged heart of old Russia. Here was the centre of the Russian Orthodox Church and here the emperors continued to be crowned as tsars in the Uspensky Cathedral in the age-old manner. In this city the heart of traditional and unchanging Russia continued to beat. The old ways of life in the rural areas surrounding it, together with their traditional industries, the kustari, continued to flourish. This was all very different from the life of the capital. There the clothing was European, the preferred speech of the aristocracy was French, and a class of artists, writers and intellectuals had emerged who thought in an essentially European way.

Besides all this, the capital had become the site of much new industrial development. The industries set up there were very much like those of western Europe and as a result a class of industrial workers had come into being who were very different from the crafts people who worked in the kustari industries around Moscow. Those involved in the industrial life of the old capital were still closely associated with the land and remained essentially semi-urbanized peasants.

St Petersburg had no such large surrounding rural population and industrial workers moved there from other parts of Russia. They soon lost their association with the land and became, in Marxian terms, an industrial proletariat. This development was fraught with problems for the future. By the late nineteenth century new political ideas were in the air which advocated change to the way the autocratic country was run and the establishment of a democracy on the European model. Even more ominously for the existing system, there were new ideas about changing the nature of the economy so as to make it more equitable. The most significant of these ideas were those of the German Karl Marx who became ever more influential in the early twentieth century.

In 1904 revolution broke out in the capital and the autocracy was shaken to its foundations. St Petersburg, which Peter had deemed to be the safest place for his own revolution two centuries earlier, had now become the least safe place for his twentieth-century successors. Emperor Nicholas II conceded the establishment of a Duma (parliament) but it had little real power. The rumblings of revolution were in the air. Little more than a decade later the October Revolution took place. It was uncompromisingly Marxist and resulted in the overthrow of the Romanov dynasty and the transformation of the enormous Russian Empire into the Union of Soviet Socialist Republics. It is ironic that the last act to take place in the capital of Imperial Russia was the overthrow of that dynasty which had originally established it. It is equally ironic that after the fall of the regime the capital was forsaken by the revolutionaries and the centre of power was transferred back to the old pre-Petrine capital.

St Petersburg had come into existence shortly after Versailles and was, in many ways, modelled on the magnificence of Louis XIV's creation. Both had a crucial role in the radical transformation of the states of which they were the capitals. This resulted in considerable modernization and it is significant that both the French and Russian monarchies were subsequently overthrown by revolutions. Both revolutions owed much to the modernization which had prepared the ground for further change. While in each case modernization had centred on the purpose-built capitals, after the revolutions neither Versailles nor St Petersburg were able to regain the central role they had once possessed. Despite the glitter of Versailles, Paris was regarded as the 'natural' capital of France while, to many Russians, Moscow had always been the heart of the 'real' Russia. The post-revolutionary regimes later used these cities to fulfil their own particular purposes.

In the early twentieth century, around the same time that revolutionary activity was rocking the Russian Empire, its great global rival, the British Empire, was also in the process of change. This was considerably less revolutionary in character and, in the first instance at least, was intended to prolong its existence. In particular, a major change was being planned for India, that most strategically vital of British imperial possessions. This considerably altered the geopolitical character of British India and brought it closer to that of earlier empires in the subcontinent.

10

Ghosts of Glory:
Postscripts to Power

It has been observed how empires rise and fall; how power grows and shrinks. It is also quite normal for declining empires to be reluctant to acknowledge their diminished status. Rulers refuse to accept that they have become lesser beings than their great forebears and this often produces desperate attempts to resist the inevitable, to fight against history and to retain a status that is no longer possible. Their 'golden age' has either passed or is passing, but such a situation is rarely acknowledged. This stage in an empire's history is often accompanied by a spate of building to produce a tangible reminder of past glories and even to attempt to repeat them. The most impressive attempts to re-create past glories have been those which have had a transformational effect on capital cities. As a result of these, the capitals, or at least large parts of them, may be substantially altered and made grander than they ever were before. This has happened throughout history to many of the capitals of erstwhile great powers.

Portugal was the first European power to move onto the global scene. This it had done through the pioneering of sea routes and the protection of these by the construction of a large and powerful fleet. Following the discovery of the sea route to India by Vasco da Gama in 1498, Portugal became for a time the leading maritime power in Europe and accrued untold wealth. This took place during the reign of King Manuel I, 'the Fortunate' (1495–1521), a period which came to be thought of as being Portugal's golden age. This was reflected in the large number of magnificent buildings constructed in the highly ornamented Manueline style. The most important were religious buildings, many of which were in and around Lisbon itself. Notable among these were the Hieronymite monastery and the splendid Manueline Tower in Belém, the latter being a fitting symbol of the maritime power of Portugal. The numerous churches and monasteries, built with the country's new-found wealth, also proclaimed the Christian nature of the whole Portuguese enterprise and the closeness of the country to the papacy.

Portugal was to remain a significant maritime power throughout most of the sixteenth century until Philip II of Spain claimed the Portuguese crown in 1580. Spain then added the Portuguese possessions to its own, creating a global empire of formidable dimensions. Portugal became an important contributor to the power exercised by Philip II and for a time the Spanish monarch even made Lisbon his own capital. However, he soon retreated back to the Escorial, his newly built seat of power deep in the heart of the Spanish Meseta.

In 1640 Portugal regained its independence from a weakening Spain but by this time it had long lost its pre-eminence in world trade. In response to this, Portugal looked westwards to the New World and there began to develop Brazil, its one overseas possession in the western hemisphere. While this produced a new source of wealth for the country, little new building took place as a result of it. By the middle of the fol-lowing century the Brazilian trade was itself in decline and with it the fortunes of Portugal. New northern European powers, notably France and Great Britain, had arrived on the scene and were by then coming to dominate overseas expansion and world trade.

However, things were to change dramatically for Portugal in the middle of the eighteenth century as a result of a natural event which would have wide repercussions. In 1755 Lisbon was decimated by a massive earthquake followed by a tidal wave which together destroyed most of the centre of the city. For a time it looked as though the much weakened Portugal was on the verge of collapse. The destruction of one of Europe's great cities shook the eighteenth-century European world to its foundations. Voltaire, one of the foremost philosophers of the age, became pessimistic for humanity as a result of the destruction, which he lamented in his novel *Candide*. However, for the chief minister of King José I, Sebastião José de Carvalho e Melo, the Marquis of Pombal, the lamentable state of Lisbon seemed less a catastrophe than an opportunity.

Pombal was the son of a country squire from central Portugal. At first, he had little influence at court, but a propitious marriage introduced him to those who did. In 1738 he became ambassador to London and this had an effect on him similar to that which the British capital had had on Peter the Great half a century earlier. He was determined to use the British model to revive his flagging country. In 1750 he was appointed foreign minister but his great interests were in economic affairs and, in particular, reviving the trade which had given Portugal its wealth in earlier centuries. He also wished to strengthen the state against the influence of the Church and even toyed with the idea of establishing an independent church in Portugal on the model of the Gallican church in France.

Pombal was chosen by the king to deal with the reconstruction of the capital after the earthquake. The development of the urban plan was entrusted to Eugénio dos Santos, Carlos Mardel and other, mostly Portuguese, architects. The architectural style chosen, while strongly influenced by the French, has come to be generally known as Pombaline. The Baixa, the centre of the city between the hills of the Castle of São Jorge on one side and the Bairro Alto and Chiado on the other, had been completely devastated and so Pombal proceeded to rebuild it in grand style. On the quayside, where the royal palace had formerly been, he laid out a great square, the Praça do Comércio, which was surrounded on three sides by royal apartments and government offices. In the centre of this is a massive equestrian statue of José I and on the northern side of the square is a triumphal arch. Above this is the figure of Glory crowning Genius and Valour, and below it are representations of the Douro and the Tagus rivers, together with figures of the great Portuguese heroes Viriatus, Nun'Alvares Pereira and Vasco da Gama. A statue of Pombal himself was also incorporated into the arch.

The arch leads on to the fine tree-lined avenue of the Rua Augusta which connects the Praça do Comércio with the Praça de Dom Pedro IV. In the centre of this square is the statue of the monarch who later became Emperor Pedro I of Brazil. The whole of this area is laid out on a strictly geometrical pattern which accords with the stern sense of order that pervades the Pombaline style. This square in turn leads to the Praça dos Restauradores, named to commemorate the revolt of the Portuguese against Spanish rule in 1640 and the restoration of the country's independence. In the following century the magnificent tree-lined Avenida da Liberdade was laid out to the north of this with extensive gardens surrounding it. At the end of this avenue is a gigantic statue of Pombal himself, instigator of the whole massive project which he intended as a symbol of the revival of Portuguese power. The two great monuments to the Restoration and to Pombal at either end of the avenue are the twin foci of a geometrical urban landscape, intended as a magnificent demonstration of power. The building of what was virtually a new city in the midst of the ruins of the old could be seen, said Schneider, as

Statue of the Marquis of Pombal, Avenida da Liberdade, Lisbon. Pombal was responsible for the transformation of the centre of the city after the devastating earthquake which destroyed much of it.

an act of 'delusion and narrow-mindedness', but also, he conceded, as an act of 'grandiose defiance'.[1] However during this period the power of Portugal continued to wane and as building proceeded the new grandeur was already becoming an epitaph to past empire.

At the same time Pombal was also engaged in a host of other affairs of state. He attempted to assert the royal authority over the church and the independence of the Portuguese church from the Vatican. The Jesuit Order was outlawed in Portugal and in all Portuguese possessions overseas. Pombal did much to encourage non-religious education and he established state schools. He also encouraged the development of universities, in particular Coimbra which soon became acknowledged as one of the great universities of Europe. This was all part of Pombal's aim of taking Portugal from its medieval associations and steering the country northwards to share in the Enlightenment which was taking place in northern Europe. He was also attempting to rebuild Portuguese commercial power with the futile aim of making it match that of Britain.

In 1777 King José I, Pombal's patron, died and was succeeded by his daughter who reigned as Maria I until 1816. Maria was feeble-minded, and the government was run initially by her mother Marianna Victoria who dismissed Pombal, accusing him, among other things, of corruption. However, Marianna continued with the grand project of the new Lisbon, including the triumphal arch which was completed during her reign.

Despite this burst of architectural magnificence, the reality was that Portugal was now moving back into the position of being just a small country on the edge of Europe, much as it had been before the great voyages of discovery of the fifteenth century had precipitated it into the front rank. Before the end of the reign of Maria in 1816 Portugal had degenerated into a battleground between France and Britain and the restoration of Portuguese liberty in 1815 was brought about largely by Britain and her allies following the defeat of Napoleonic France. By then 'Lisboa Pombalina' had without doubt become one of the more magnificent capitals in Europe, but the power it sought to symbolize had largely faded away. The eminent Portuguese novelist José Saramago actually considered that Pombal's Lisbon represented 'a huge cultural break from which the city has not recovered'.[2] Even during the Manueline period the city had never enshrined such aspirations to imperial grandeur, aspirations being manifested and symbolized at just the time when the power behind them was fast disappearing. Richard Pattee saw Pombal having been much influenced by his time in London, capital of the most dynamic power of the age. This had been so with Peter the Great half a century earlier, who had dreamed of emulating Britain in his attempt to convert Russia into a modern world power. However, unlike Peter, who had been largely successful, it was impossible for such success to come to Pombal and his successors. He came from 'an empire of the past' and he was in no position to emulate an empire that was 'on the threshold of the future'.[3]

At the same time as Portuguese world power was vanishing, the power of its great neighbour and rival, Spain, was also on the wane. By the middle of the eighteenth century the northern nations were taking over the world and this was having much the same effect on Spain as it had on Portugal. Spain still possessed its large empire in Latin America but this was becoming less profitable and more restive in its desire for independence. Madrid did not have either an earthquake or a Pombal and there was no great project to build a new imperial city on top of the old. However, as the reality of power drifted away, the desire for the display of imperial grandeur became ever greater. This actually took place in Madrid before it did in Lisbon. In 1734 a fire largely destroyed the old royal palace which had originally been a Moorish stronghold, and this gave Philip v the opportunity to build a palace in the style of Versailles. Work began in 1748 and went on for the best part of twenty years. The principal architect was Giovanni Battista Sacchetti and the scale of the project was enormous, the palace having literally thousands of rooms. It was designed to impress and this it was bound to do on account of its sheer size.

The royal quarters were in the heart of the palace. The grand entrance hall with its statue of Carlos III as a Roman emperor led into the Hall of Columns which was intended to be the setting for grand events and ceremonies. This in turn opened to the Throne Room which contained two magnificent royal thrones in gold and scarlet. This chamber was adorned with paintings by the Venetian Giambattista Tiepolo, including an enormous painted ceiling entitled *The Apotheosis of Spain*. Such magnificence had never been aspired to by Philip II in the age during which Spain had really been a world power. Far from being built for grandeur, the stern Escorial was a statement of the severe aims of the Spanish monarchy at the time when there was a realistic chance of achieving them. On the other hand, Philip v's imitation Versailles was an example of a building that was in reality just another epitaph to empire. The diminishing wealth of the country was lavished on memories in the hopeless belief that this would help recreate the golden age of the fast-disappearing empire.

On the outside the grand south-facing facade of the palace looks out onto the huge Plaza de la Armería, into which the old Plaza Mayor with all its buildings could easily have fitted. To the south of this is the cathedral of Nuestra Señora de la Almudena. Despite the fact that this enormous building fits neatly into the whole complex, it was originally a smaller church. Work on the present building began in 1882 and the cathedral was finally consecrated in 1993. At the side of the royal palace are the Calle de Bailén and the Plaza de Oriente de Palacio which provide a suitable backdrop to the splendour of the palace.

As with Lisbon's transformation by Pombal, the magnificence of eighteenth-century Royal Madrid had little effect in reviving the declining fortunes of Spain. The battles for the attainment of mastery of the maritime world were by then being played out elsewhere and by others. At the end of the century the Napoleonic armies invaded and occupied Spain and for a time the country was, like Portugal, reduced to a battleground between France and Britain.

At the end of the Napoleonic Wars Madrid was left with the largest royal palace in Europe and Lisbon with one of its grandest squares and ceremonial avenues, but these were not matched by world significance either case. The transformation of Madrid by the Bourbon kings of Spain had not been on the scale of Pombal's transformation of Lisbon but the objectives of both had been essentially the same. By the end of the century in which they were built they had both become magnificent memorials to a vanished glory.

As has been seen, it was France which had initially taken over the European role of Spain and, after the Treaty of Westphalia in 1648, had become the dominant Continental power. France actually reached the apogee of this power at the end of the following century, led briefly to glory by Napoleon. His military achievements created an empire stretching from the Atlantic across Europe into Russia. However, there, as with other would-be conquerors, the ferocity of the Russian winters finally brought about his defeat. With the end of the Napoleonic Empire in 1815, France was never to attain such a powerful position again.

Napoleon himself had dreams of making his capital city reflect his glory and the glory of France and, in common with other imperial figures, he had ideas for grand architectural projects. However, Napoleon's reign was too short – he was emperor for just a decade – and his military preoccupations too urgent for much time to be given to such matters. It would be left to his successors to commemorate the military brilliance which had resulted in the creation of the largest

European empire since Charlemagne. For this purpose Paris had its own Pombal-in-waiting. This was Georges-Eugène Haussmann, who was appointed prefect of the Seine in 1853 and who was instrumental in that great transformation of the French capital that took place during the next two decades. This he did together with his master, Louis-Napoléon Bonaparte, the nephew of the first emperor, who was president of the Second Republic from 1848 until he proclaimed the Second Empire in 1852, taking the title Napoleon III. Together with Haussmann, he then embarked on the imperial transformation of Paris. The first Napoleon had expressed his determination to make Paris 'something fabulous, colossal and unprecedented' and his nephew, having rather more time, declared, 'Let us put all our efforts into embellishing this great city.'[4]

The centre of the whole grand project was the enormous processional way of the Champs-Elysées. The intention to create this grand avenue went back much earlier and had originally been envisaged by Colbert and laid out by Le Nôtre, who was responsible for the gardens at Versailles. However, it was not until after the Napoleonic wars that the impetus to complete it resumed. Further work proceeded during the reign of King Louis-Philippe and in the early 1830s the building of the great arch which was to dominate it was commenced. This Arc de Triomphe was intended to commemorate the victories of Napoleon and it was left to Napoleon III and his prefect Haussmann to complete the work. The Champs-Elysées was laid out and lined with trees and splendid new buildings rose on either side of it. The area around the Arc de Triomphe became the Place de l'Etoile, a round space from which twelve wide avenues radiated. The continuation from the Champs-Elysées on the other side of the arch was the Avenue de la Grande Armée, extending westwards towards the suburb of Neuilly. This commemorated the achievements of that army which had won so many great victories and conquered the greater part of Europe. Avenues leading from the Champs-Elysées present views of the striking Pont Alexandre III, constructed in the late nineteenth century to commemorate the Franco-Russian alliance, and, across the Seine, the Invalides, a magnificent hospital for wounded soldiers. It was here that the body of Napoleon I was re-interred after its ceremonial return from St Helena in 1843.

The Champs-Elysées extended eastwards for 1.5 km, from the Arc de Triomphe to the Place de la Concorde. From there the view continued eastwards through the Tuileries gardens to the smaller Arc du Carrousel, another arch commemorating the victories of Napoleon. This stood within the magnificent royal palace of the Louvre which, although largely dating from the seventeenth century, was incorporated successfully into the whole imperial scheme and soon became an integral part of it. Jan Morris clearly found this part of the scheme especially impressive when she wrote that, 'Retreating through the Tuileries from the gorgeous severity of the Louvre is like retiring backwards . . . down the interminable audience chamber of some royal presence'.[5]

Around this triumphal core Haussmann had instructions from his master to raze many of the poorer areas of the inner city and to replace them with a line of great avenues. These were the Grands Boulevards and in size and splendour they often rivalled the Champs-Elysées itself. Around them official buildings, new apartments and splendid shops replaced the slums. The intention was that these boulevards should be in a series of straight lines like the Champs-Elysées, one of the supposed reasons for this being the easier management of the mob should there be civil disturbance. The Revolution, although it had eventually brought Napoleon to power, had previously destroyed a dynasty, and his nephew wanted to ensure that this did not happen to his own dynasty. Nevertheless, Schneider sees this as being first and foremost about the display of power. Such boulevards, he wrote, 'imperiously and often brutally transecting a city, symbolize royal power – triumph of a masterful mind'.[6] Like so many emperors before him, Napoleon III aimed to use architecture as an instrument of political power, assisting him to retain his grip on France.

While the whole great project was above all intended to commemorate the triumphant achievements of the first emperor and to keep the memory of him alive in the minds of the French people, it was also to be the backdrop for a resumption of the whole imperial process by Napoleon III. The great emperor's nephew had his own schemes to assert once more the glory and grandeur of France. However, this was not to be. France was no longer the dominating power in Europe and, in this respect at least, the country had been in steady decline since the final defeat of Napoleon in 1815. Half a century later in 1871 the army of Napoleon III was defeated by the Prussians at Sedan. The Prussian army entered Paris and the victors were able to marvel at the magnificent axis of empire with its triumphal arches and grand palace. What had been intended as a new assertion of imperial might turned out to be yet another postscript to it. The proclamation of the King of Prussia as German Emperor took place in the Galerie des Glaces at the Palace of Versailles, that spectacular symbol of the rise of France under Louis

XIV. It is ironic that the advent of the Second Reich, which was to become the successor to France as the dominant Continental power, was proclaimed in the very heart of the palace built two centuries earlier to celebrate the arrival of France as a great power. Power had moved eastwards across the Rhine and in future wars France would need to call on the support of other countries, most importantly Britain and the United States. From that time on the Champs-Elysées and the great imperial monuments were left as a magnificent memorial to the Napoleonic age and to that period of imperial glory which had in fact been so brief.

Germany now assumed a dominating position in both Continental Europe and over the other German lands. This represented a historical change of some magnitude. Over the centuries it had been the Habsburg dynasty of Austria which had held the prime position, first as Holy Roman Emperors and subsequently as presidents of the German Confederation. For centuries Austria had also been the dominant power in east-central Europe, balancing France's position of dominance in the western part of the Continent. Austria had been defeated by Napoleon but this had also happened to Prussia. For the early part of the nineteenth century both were eclipsed by the overwhelming power of Britain and Russia and also by a resurrected France. By the middle of the nineteenth century, however, it was clear that the Austrian Empire was in terminal decline. The revolutionary events of 1848 had shaken the Habsburg monarchy to its foundations and considerable restiveness continued among the non-German peoples within the enormous empire. This was nowhere more so than in Hungary which in 1867 secured a large measure of control over its own affairs in the 'Compromise' that gave it its own parliament. In many ways the Hungarians now became imperial partners, and from then until its fall the empire was known as Austro-Hungarian. A year earlier Prussia had defeated Austria in the brief Six Weeks War and begun to assume the role of dominant power in Germany. Five years later this position was to be consolidated by the proclamation of the German Empire in Versailles, with the Prussian king as its new emperor. The power of Austria was from then on marginalized.

In 1848 the throne of the Empire had passed to the young Franz Josef who saw it as his duty to stem the decline and reassert the power of Austria both over its empire and in Europe generally. As part of his plan, Franz Josef embarked on one of the most impressive transformations of an imperial capital ever to take place. This entailed no less than the enveloping of the crowded old centre of Vienna, the *Altstadt*, with a new imperial city of unsurpassed grandeur. Amazingly this was to consist of only one great avenue, the Ringstrasse, but it was a massive one some 3 km in length. However, this was no Champs-Elysées or Avenida da Liberdade but was intended to encircle the old city completely. In undertaking his massive project, Franz Josef became his own Haussmann and his version of the latter's Grands Boulevards was designed to be the centrepiece of the whole project. While Franz Josef was certainly influenced by what Haussmann was doing in Paris, from the outset he made it clear that it was he who was in charge and would decide which particular public buildings were to be built along it. He used a number of architects who designed buildings in a variety of architectural styles. Nevertheless, it was always the emperor himself who was responsible for the final decisions.

The actual space designated for the project was the line of old walls surrounding Vienna. These, together with their accompanying dykes and earthworks, had to be demolished before the work could begin. What had been a circular barrier to keep enemies out of the city now became a circular line of communication linking together the centres of the major activities of the imperial capital. This line was in fact less a circle than a polygon consisting of five straight avenues joined together. The buildings around these avenues were then laid out on a gridiron plan. On the Ringstrasse itself, each had its own particular public buildings and architectural styles which imparted considerable variety to the whole project.

As befitted a capital noted for its great musical heritage, the first new building was the Opera House, built in the Renaissance Revival style and completed in 1869. This was followed by others including the Rathaus (city hall) built in a neo-Flemish style, the University in Tuscan Renaissance, the Börse (Stock Exchange) in neoclassical and the Reichsrat (parliament), also in classical style. Different architects were employed by the emperor for each building, important among them being Theophilus Hansen, a Danish architect whose work Franz Josef found particularly to his taste. This architect designed the music and fine arts academies, the Börse, a number of palaces and the Reichsrat. This latter building in the classical style recalls ancient Greece, and in front of it is a statue of Athena, protecting goddess of Athens. The junctions of the polygonal plan opened into squares laid out with gardens adorned with numerous statues, notable among which was the colossal statue of the eighteenth-century empress Maria Theresa. The Hofburg Palace of the emperor, although not actually on the Ring, was located in a square leading just off it and, like the Louvre in Paris, was close enough to have been incorporated successfully into the whole plan.

Although the Ringstrasse itself had a great variety of cultural, administrative and political buildings, they were all, in the words of de Waal, 'Prachtbauten' (buildings of splendour) and the whole project was 'breathcatchingly imperial in scale'.[7] One of the most significant things about the whole Ringstrasse project was that it had its back to the old city and looked outwards towards the wider world and, in particular, to Austria's empire. There the diverse peoples with their different nationalities, languages and religions would encounter the Kaiserlich-Königlich – imperial and royal – civilization. Being a ring it faced out in all directions towards all parts of the massive and unwieldy empire. In this way, with its art, architecture, literature and, above all, music it was imparting a civilization, which Franz Josef saw as being the most potent binding force, the cement, to hold the whole edifice together. As de Waal put it, 'The new street is not dominated by any one building; there is no crescendo towards a palace or cathedral; but there is this constant triumphant pull along from one great aspect of civilized life to another.'[8] He might also have added that neither was there a great arch such as that which dominates the Champs-Elysées and proclaims its most important purpose. Franz Josef's vision was altogether wider and more all-encompassing than that of Napoleon III. Rather than rely on military glory, which was in fact in short supply, he was using the arts in which Vienna had been supreme as the principal supports for his own imperial vision.

The fundamental purpose of all this diversity was to promote the empire and the imperial vision which lay behind it. 'The buildings along the Ring were designed to dazzle', said Barea in her survey of Viennese history, 'and to convey the message that the imperial city was again secure in regained power and glory'.[9] Yet the truth, she asserted, was that 'Vienna expanded and was embellished . . . while the empire contracted; its social and cultural life was growing while the foundations of its importance as a multinational state were assaulted and undermined'.[10] The truth was that all it signified was self-assertion and an illusion of permanence while the reality was that the massive multinational empire had already become the most fragile in Europe. By the end of the nineteenth century the clamour for greater autonomy and even independence by the subject nations had become impossible to ignore and not even the magnetic pull of the Ringstrasse, with its message of cultural imperialism, was strong enough to combat this.

The ultimate comment on the whole grand project was made by the young architect Adolf Loos. In an article entitled 'Die Potemkinsche Stadt', he compared the Ringstrasse to the Potemkin villages. These were facades of canvas and cardboard erected by Catherine the Great's minister, Alexander Potemkin, in the newly acquired Ukraine in an attempt to deceive the empress on her grand tour as to how much progress was being made by his administration in the new province. As with Potemkin's villages, Loos maintained, the Ringstrasse was all facade and behind it was wasteland.[11] Franz Josef's 1898 Golden Jubilee celebrations took place against this magnificent backdrop but it was as unreal in terms of representing the power of the Dual Monarchy as the Potemkin villages were in representing the economic progress of the Ukraine. It was, in fact, a magnificent stage set and its creators could but hope that nobody would notice it was all a fake.

Within a quarter of a century of the great celebrations of the Jubilee, in which the Ringstrasse was the stage, the empire was no more. The First World War began as a result of the assassination of Archduke Franz Ferdinand, heir to the Austrian throne, by nationalist opponents of Austrian rule in the Balkans. It ended four years later with the fall of that empire, which was then split up into a number of independent nation-states. Austria was left as a small country with a grandiose and over-large capital. Like the Champs-Elysées, the Avenida da Liberdade and Madrid's Palacio Real, the Ringstrasse was yet another postscript to a vanished empire.

But the story of the influence of Vienna as an imperial city, of which the Ringstrasse was the ultimate expression, was by no means over. In the years before the outbreak of war, a young Austrian painter and architectural student, Adolf Hitler, had lived in the city. During his time there he learned many things but the two to have the greatest influence on his subsequent career were architecture and anti-Semitism. The imperial architecture of the Ringstrasse greatly impressed the young man who saw it as an expression of the kind of power for which he yearned. Hitler wrote, 'From morning until late at night I ran from one object of interest to another, but it was always the buildings that held my primary interest. For hours I could stand in front of the Opera, for hours I could gaze at the Parliament; the whole Ringstrasse seemed to me like an enchantment out of *The Thousand and One Nights*.'[12] Hitler painted all the great buildings on the ring. To him they expressed 'eternal values' and taught him how space and buildings could be used in the assertion of power. In this, Franz Josef was his teacher.

When both the Austrian and German empires collapsed in the ruins of defeat in 1918, Hitler was left in despair. Soon he was joining with those who sought to bring Germany back to the greatness which they believed it deserved and of which it had been deprived by inefficient and treacherous leadership. This was the myth of the 'stab in the back' which underlay much of what subsequently took place. Hitler wanted above all to resurrect a Greater Germany which would include his home-land Austria within it. This necessitated putting many of the ideas he had learned in pre-war Vienna into practice. Central to these was the belief, which originally came from Franz Josef's grand scheme for Vienna, that the heart of any imperial plan must be its expression in buildings. During the turbulent decades that followed, this was something Hitler was never to forget.

The German historian Joachim Fest, discussing Vienna with his Austrian friends, observed that, 'Unlike Paris, Berlin, or Washington, the city didn't give itself airs with imperial majesty; even Heldenplatz (Heroes' Square) had, for those who really looked, an attractive domesticity . . . and through the combination of [Austrian charm and splendour] created a metropolis which was both grand and human in scale.'[13] Fest clearly saw a Vienna which was very different from the one that had enthused Hitler. Of course, all the great cities that evolved organically, and then had the grandeur of imperialism imposed upon them, display a variety of features which, unlike the purpose-built capitals, impress more with their variety than their uniformity.

All of those postscripts to power which have been looked at in this chapter were characteristic of the decline of states from their periods of great power. In this sense, they were all commemorations, reminders of what had once been. However, thanks to Hitler, Vienna proved to be rather different from this. The future German leader saw the Austrian capital as being a model for the kind of capital which he wished himself to create as the centre of a new German empire, rising from the ashes of both the old Austrian and German empires. The attempt to create this new empire resulted in massive destruction, loss of life and ultimate failure. But during it all Hitler maintained his desire to build a great capital which would symbolize both Germany's greatness and that of the Führer himself.

11

Apex or Decline? New Delhi and British Imperial Power

At the same time as Peter the Great was planning to move his capital to the Baltic, a new nation-state was emerging on the western margins of Europe. This was Great Britain which came into being as a result of the Act of Union between England and Scotland in 1707. Within a century this new nation-state, having become the greatest naval power in the world, was poised to achieve a global dominance greater than that of any previous country in world history.

By the nineteenth century the British Empire bestrode the world and, famously, large parts of the political map were coloured in bright pink, the favoured imperial colour. This enormous empire stretched into every continent and was proudly described as the empire upon which the sun never set. However, unlike Russia, where the move to a new capital had preceded the rise to world power, the centre of this vast political edifice remained in London, the old English capital. Many splendid buildings were later built in London, but it nevertheless remained essentially a multi-functional city which became the dominant political, financial and trading hub first of Britain and then of the whole British Empire. By the end of the nineteenth century, separate centres of government had been established in all the dependent territories but their role was, initially at least, largely administrative and very much subject to the overall authority of the home government in London. It was in India that a city was finally built that was more a statement of imperial power than any other city in the Empire.

The British association with India went back to the sixteenth century and by the following century ports or factories were established around the Indian coasts which were intended as bases for the growing trading relationship. Trade was in the hands of the East India Company and the most important base of operations was Calcutta in the delta of the

Ganges. When Britain attained a dominating position in the later eighteenth century Calcutta was the site chosen to be the capital. A Government House was built in the classical style, taking its inspiration from Kedleston Hall in Derbyshire, the seat of the Curzon family.[1] Calcutta's political role was further enhanced when Britain secured control over the greater part of the subcontinent in the early nineteenth century.

However, Calcutta with its hot and wet monsoon climate had never really been a very satisfactory place for Europeans. Tropical diseases were prevalent and in the early days the death rate in the city had been very high. To combat this, in 1863 the decision was taken to make the hill station of Simla the official summer capital. This lay in the foothills of the Himalayas north of the old Mughal capital of Delhi. Communication between Calcutta and Simla was poor and at times when it had removed to Simla the government of India was barely in touch with Calcutta, let alone with the massive subcontinent over which it ruled.

Until the middle of the nineteenth century the affairs of India were actually largely in the hands of the East India Company. Not only was it in charge of all trading operations throughout the subcontinent but it was also given a political role and even had soldiers from the British Army seconded into its service. The government representative in Calcutta was the governor general who, of necessity, had to work closely with the Company. However, following the Indian Mutiny in 1858, which shook the British establishment in India to its foundations, the company's dominating role was brought to an end and the government took direct charge of Indian affairs. At the head of the new government of India was the viceroy, the direct representative of the sovereign, who combined quasi-regal with quasi-prime-ministerial roles. The imperial seal was set on the new direct rule arrangements in 1877 when Queen Victoria was proclaimed Empress of India and the full inheritance of the defunct Mughal Empire was taken over by Britain.

However, Calcutta, the early British settlement, was still the capital and was to remain so until the beginning of the twentieth century when it was decided to move to the old Mughal capital of Delhi. The decision was actually made in 1905 just at the end of the period of office of Lord Curzon, one of the most remarkable viceroys. This period is generally regarded as having been the apex of British imperial power, not just in India but throughout the world. The decision to make the move therefore came at a time when signs of the forthcoming decline were as yet barely perceptible. Curzon, a great believer in empire, was actually very much against moving the capital away from Calcutta, but in spite of the objections of this highly influential statesman, the move began shortly afterwards.

The reasons for this momentous decision were various. Delhi had, of course, been the Mughal capital, and before that the seat of the Sultanate of Delhi, and it was widely thought of in India as being the real capital of the country. Calcutta, on the other hand, was a foreign city built on the edge of the subcontinent to meet the needs of a foreign power. The fact that a few decades earlier Queen Victoria had been proclaimed Empress of India put the British sovereign directly in the line of succession to the earlier rulers. It seemed natural that the representative of the empress would be in their capital and so the move would be a late but much needed symbol of British imperial rule.

Of greater practical significance was the huge geopolitical change which began to take place in the Indian subcontinent after 1867. This was a decade before the proclamation of the queen as empress and was brought about by the opening of the Suez Canal in that year. This event made communications with Britain much faster and easier. The sea route was now through the Red and Arabian seas and then directly to the west coast of India. This made a west coast port such as Bombay a far more logical terminus for the voyage than Calcutta, which was on the east coast. This all produced the beginnings of a massive geopolitical reorientation of the Indian subcontinent from east to west. With ships now docking in Bombay, Delhi was also more accessible than Calcutta, the train journey to the former being much shorter and easier than to the latter. In addition the British were already using the Simla hill station which was also far more accessible from Delhi. As a result, everything was now pointing to Delhi as the preferred seat of government.

There were also more purely political factors involved. British imperial policy was an evolving one and had entailed giving greater power to the overseas possessions. Canada was the first to secure a form of home rule as early as 1868. This policy of limited devolution was then continued with other dependent territories. By the early twentieth century it was widely considered that more political power should be given to the Indians and this process was soon to be expedited following the election of a Liberal government in 1906. The transfer of more power to India was something the British increasingly felt it wise to do. The Indian Mutiny had come as a great shock and had reminded the British of their tenuous hold over this massive country. They remained fearful that it might all happen again and it was always necessary to keep Indian sensibilities in mind. By the end of the nineteenth century these were already coming to be expressed more volubly. In 1885 the first meeting of the Indian National Congress took place. Interestingly, this organization was actually the inspiration of a British official, A. O. Hume, and it soon became the vehicle for the expression of the feelings of the Indians and their desire to have more power in their own hands. The combination of a Liberal government and Indian aspirations was a powerful motive for a policy of greater power-sharing.

There were thus powerful historical and political motives for the move of the capital to Delhi but there was also an underlying strategic one deriving from the fact that the British now ruled over a gigantic world empire. In many ways India had become the most vital link, controlling and protecting the imperial routeways crossing the Indian Ocean and connecting the west to the east of the vast chain of imperial possessions. Thus the move of the capital of what was in many ways the keystone of the arch of British power was also motivated by reasons connected with the retention, not the relinquishment, of British world power. 'India', wrote the French political geographer Goblet in 1935, 'is the imperial geographical centre of the British Empire . . . Here rules Britannia, who holds the trident of Poseidon.' At the same time, he added, 'Her rule is subject to evolution, just as all in this very varied world is subject to evolution.'[2] Both continuity and change were being catered for in the choice of Delhi as the new capital.

The move now made by the British at the beginning of the twentieth century was in geopolitical terms in most ways the opposite of the move which Peter the Great had made two centuries earlier. By transferring his capital from Moscow to St Petersburg he had moved from land to sea. That move was made in pursuit of modernization, which was linked closely to maritime power, and away from an old capital which, in Peter's mind at least, had all the wrong associations. In the case of Delhi, the move was away from the sea and back to the old capital in the centre of the land. This capital had all the associations of imperial power dating back over many centuries. It represented more than anything the fact that Britain had moved from being a dynamic commercial nation to an imperial power in the more traditional sense.

It would seem from this that in the early twentieth century the British intention was to embrace the Indian past and its political arrangements rather than to carry on with the creation of something new, western and distinctive. This reflected deeper differences in the imperial attitudes of Britain and Russia, which were still in the early twentieth century the two major world powers. The Russians, powerful on land, had wished to complement this power by achieving power at sea. The British, supremely powerful at sea, wished now to increase their power on land. The pursuit of global power was seen to require far more than the establishment of a network of trading stations. India was a massive landmass which also needed to be defended on its landward side and to achieve this territorial thinking was essential.

These were all factors of which the viceroy Lord Curzon had been well aware, but his advocacy of a dynamic and forward frontier policy was something the London government found difficult to swallow.[3] Nevertheless, Delhi was far more strategically suitable for this purpose as a result of its location much closer to the vulnerable northern frontiers. For the Mughals and their predecessors who had conquered India from the land, the continental connection, together with the security of the northern frontiers, had been of prime importance. Historically Delhi had been the natural capital for the invaders from the land who had always remained highly conscious of the direction from which new dangers to the subcontinent were most likely to come.

In 1912 the viceroy moved to the newly built Viceregal Lodge just north of the old city. This was close to the Ridge which was where the British army had been concentrated during the Mutiny. The old fortifications dating from that turbulent time now looked down on the new seat of power below. It was not far from the fort, the old centre of Mughal power, where the last emperor had surrendered to the British. However, this move was meant to be only a temporary one and was not exactly where the new capital was intended to be.

Two architects were chosen to build the new capital, namely Edwin Lutyens and Herbert Baker. Both had been prominent figures in the move away from the old mid-Victorian Gothick to the new late and post-Victorian architecture. This was intended to combine a greater attention to efficient house design with an Edwardian neoclassical style. The centre of the new capital was to be the palace of the viceroy flanked by two adjacent government buildings. While Baker was to be the principal architect for this Imperial Secretariat, Lutyens was put in charge of the viceroy's palace, which was designated as the centrepiece of the new capital. There was considerable discussion on the actual architectural style of the new capital and this reflected the two very different ideas underlying it. The Liberal imperialists now in power considered that the architecture should include traditional Indian, especially Mughal, features while the Conservative imperialists wished it to be primarily a magnificent assertion of the British Raj. The former included Baker, who wished to make a subtle combination of styles. Lord Hardinge, the new viceroy appointed by the Liberal government, was basically of the same view but he favoured Revival Gothick with Indian features. This was a style close to the traditional British architecture to be found in many other cities throughout India. It was referred to by Jan Morris as being 'still in its Mongrel phase – Saracenic Gothic, High Victorian Pathan'.[4] Others, including Lutyens himself, wanted the whole project to be essentially British and he was in favour of adapting a form of the new British neoclassical style. This was the beginning of the many arguments which were to strain relations between the two principal architects to breaking point.

It was King George V himself who inaugurated the whole great project in 1911. The king-emperor, together with the queen-empress, were in attendance at the magnificent Coronation Durbar held in Delhi that year and in his speech the monarch praised the splendour of Delhi as the historic capital, stressing the need that all new buildings should be sympathetic to its existing architecture. He immediately laid the foundation stone of the new capital. The original location chosen in the north of Delhi did not please either Hardinge or Lutyens and within a short time the foundation stone had been moved secretly at night to Raisina Hill in the south.

The plan was for the viceroy's palace to be on the highest point and for the Secretariat to consist of two huge buildings on either side of it. A frontal view of the whole complex would therefore not obscure the palace itself. It was intended that a wide avenue would run eastwards from this complex of buildings, terminating in a triumphal arch much in the manner of the Champs-Elysées. On the northern side was to be the new Indian parliament building which would have large numbers of houses for government officials in its vicinity. The church behind the palace was to be constructed in the same architectural style, linking in with the imperial buildings. This was a demonstration of the close relationship between Church – the Church of England – and state in the whole imperial enterprise.

The whole of this vast project was set back by the First World War and building did not resume until after 1918. India had made a considerable contribution to the war effort and suffered numerous casualties. This had a marked effect on the way the project was conducted from this time on. Meanwhile, the government of India was still being carried

Photograph from the air of New Delhi in the 1930s. At this time the imperial buildings stood in splendid isolation with little evidence of the infilling which was soon to link them to the old city.

on from the other side of Delhi and from Simla during the summer months. It took another ten years before the central core of buildings on Raisina Hill was completed and the full move of the government did not to take place until 1928. At that time the grand imperial buildings were set apart on their own, so demonstrating the separation of this 'New Delhi' from the 'Old Delhi' some distance away.

The centrepiece on Raisina Hill was Lutyens's Palace of the Viceroy which was bigger even than Versailles. Despite the architect's dislike and even contempt for Indian architecture, concessions had to be made to it and many Indian features were incorporated. At the front was a flight of steps leading to the huge pillared entrance. This led through to the circular Durbar Hall which held the thrones of the viceroy and the vicereine. This hall was designed for the great ceremonies of state. Behind it were large rooms, including the State Drawing Room, the State Dining Room and the Ballroom. The ground floor also had a State Library and accommodation for guests. The first floor contained the private accommodation of the viceroy and his family, together with office space for the large personal secretariat of the viceroy. The exterior view of the palace was the most impressive of all.

In the centre, above the Durbar Hall, was a great shallow copper dome raised on a cylindrical plinth. There have been some suggestions

The Palace of the Viceroy, now the Presidential Palace, New Delhi.

that this has Byzantine features and others that it has the features of a Buddhist stupa. It may be that Lutyens, who is known to have enjoyed architectural puzzles, deliberately left this for others to work out for themselves. On either side of this centrepiece were a series of smaller features which balanced the great dome itself.

Behind the palace were the gardens, at the centre of which was the Mughal Garden. Lutyens had always considered that house and garden should complement one another and that an impressive garden was essential to show off the house. The famous garden designer Gertrude Jekyll had long cooperated closely with Lutyens in designing the gardens for his houses in England but it seems improbable that she would have contributed directly to this one. However, signs of her influence were certainly present, perhaps indirectly through Lutyens himself. The vicereine, Lady Hardinge, was closely involved in the project and the Mughal Garden accorded well with the viceregal desire to incorporate Indian features into the palace.

The two Secretariat buildings by Baker were essentially architecturally a prelude to the palace when approached from the avenue but in reality they were where the serious business of governing the vast subcontinent actually took place. Baker incorporated many Mughal features into them and they too each had their own smaller cupolas. These two domes balanced on either side of the great dome itself, imparting a wonderful architectural unity to the whole. All was plan and balance and all had a mathematical accuracy of design. The policy of Indianization meant that by the 1930s increasing numbers of the government officials were themselves Indian and the new capital steadily gained a more Indian character which was in many ways at variance with the basically European architecture.

The great avenue leading eastwards was completed at around the same time as the government buildings. It was named the Kingsway after George v and behind the arch was a statue of the king-emperor himself. The intention of the Kingsway was to provide the most impressive

The Memorial Arch, New Delhi, at the eastern end of the Kingsway, now the Rajpath. Near it is the empty cupola (which can be seen through the arch, beyond) which formerly housed the statue of George v, the only king-emperor actually to visit India. This statue was removed when the country became independent but nothing was put in its place.

view of the palace and especially of its crowning glory, the magnificent dome, and also to be the way along which ceremonial parades would display the might and splendour of the British Raj. The arch itself was renamed the War Memorial Arch and was dedicated to India's war dead in the First World War. This was another way of incorporating India and Indians more closely into the whole imperial project.

While there was a great deal of input from a number of sources, Lutyens was certainly the mastermind behind the whole gigantic project. As William Dalrymple put it, from the shape of the doorknobs to the suitability of the flowers in the flowerbeds, Lutyens was closely involved in every detail.[5] When the project was revealed in all its magnificent contradictions it was through the perspective of Lutyens's architectural ideas that the whole had to be viewed and its success or otherwise judged.

What conclusions can be reached about the real nature of the New Delhi which was in place by the 1930s and how it fits into the general pattern of cities built for imperial power? Did it represent the apex of British power or the beginning of its decline? The fact was that it was undoubtedly both of these things. In 1905, when the project was first conceived, Britain was still at the apex of that world power which had been commemorated in splendid style just eight years earlier in the magnificent pageant for the Diamond Jubilee of Queen Victoria. In 1905, on the surface at least, the Empire appeared still to be as solid as a rock. 'There seemed no doubt in most British minds', wrote Jan Morris, 'that the empire in India was more or less eternal.'[6]

William Dalrymple placed New Delhi in the wider imperial context. He wrote that it was the 'impression of the might and power of the Imperial State that the architects aimed above all to convey'. However, Dalrymple also made more disturbing comparisons when he pointed out its similarity to the buildings of the dictatorships that had arisen in Europe in the wake of the First World War. 'In its monstrous, almost megalomaniac scale, in its perfect symmetry and arrogant presumption, there was a distant but distinct echo of something Fascist or even Nazi about the great acropolis of Imperial Delhi . . . all belonged to comparable worlds.'[7] Certainly the British Empire, born into the age of maritime imperialism, lived on into the age of the dictatorships which also aspired to their own versions of empire.

It is certainly true that, despite concessions to the fact that this was India and that the British were virtually the self-proclaimed successors to the Mughals, New Delhi was essentially intended as an assertion of British power. Above all, it was particularly designed to be an assertion in stone of the magnificence of its Indian arm, the Raj, the so-called 'richest jewel in the British Crown'. As Baker put it, the new capital was not to be Indian, English or Roman but imperial. This 'eighth Delhi' was intended above all to be a British Delhi, just as the many earlier Delhis had taken the names of their imperial masters down the ages.

However, by 1928, when the full move of the government took place, the world was a very different place from what it had been a quarter of a century earlier. Although after the First World War the British Empire was larger than ever and its power appeared, on the surface at least, even greater, the reality was that Britain had been greatly weakened by the war. This was partly due to the enduring economic problems resulting from it and also the growth of strong national movements in what had always been referred to as the 'colonies'. Their peoples felt that they had come to the aid of the mother country in her hour of need and that they now deserved some acknowledgement of this. In addition, by 1928 the concept of the 'Commonwealth' had come into being and Britain, as well as retaining her position as the major imperial power, was now at the heart of an essentially new organization, the British Commonwealth of Nations. In India the arch at the end of the Kingsway no longer asserted imperial triumph only but was the Indian War Memorial. The new Assembly Building close to the viceroy's residence acknowledged that the will of the Indian people as expressed by its representatives had to be taken into account. The Indian Congress Party, which had by then been in existence for over half a century, had never been more influential in the affairs of state.

Yet India still remained more closely tied to Britain than the new self-governing dominions of the Commonwealth. The Raj was still very much in place, even though it was by the 1930s recognized that fundamental changes in the relationship would soon have to be made. Writing in 1937, Percival Spear caught the sense of change at the end of his book on Delhi:

> The importance of Delhi is founded on more than the presence of a court or an army; it rests upon its great public buildings which cannot be lightly abandoned, its easy communication with all parts of the country, its geographical position which all historical experience has confirmed, and finally upon the accumulated sentiment of seven centuries, and the mounting aspirations of the new nationalism. Delhi is the natural centre of the Indian Dominion, as Calcutta was of the old British Empire.[8]

By 1937 the British Indian Empire certainly no longer seemed eternal to many people, but an association with Britain as a dominion in the new post-imperial Commonwealth was certainly considered feasible. It was what Goblet, writing at around the same time, considered to be a trans-formation of British power designed to ensure its permanence in the new era. The emerging Commonwealth was certainly still Anglocentric and was intended to place British world power on a firmer footing in the new and more assertive world.

However, perhaps the reality was that the approaching end of empire, together with the nineteenth-century form of imperialism and all that it entailed, had also underlain the creation of New Delhi from the outset. The fact that the whole project was begun while a Liberal government was in office was the most powerful factor of the time.

The Liberals had never really been imperialist in the sense in which the Conservatives had been since the time of Disraeli. The post-Gladstonian Liberal imperialists of the later nineteenth century were an adaptation to the all-pervasive imperial idea of the time which could not be ignored or easily opposed. From the outset the viceroy Lord Hardinge shared the Liberal sentiments and saw the future as being one of closer Anglo-Indian cooperation rather than the uncompromising old imperial dominance. Thus while the imperial vision was certainly present, the vision of an eventual dominion of India was there too.

Jan Morris considered that the Viceregal Palace was probably the last of the great royal palaces of history. The Raj did not long survive the move to New Delhi. In 1947, after less than twenty years, India at last achieved independence. What had been the British Indian Empire reigned over by the king-emperor in London was divided into four separate dominions of the Crown. The biggest of these was India itself and, as Spear had predicted only ten years earlier, New Delhi became the capital of this new dominion. The viceroy was replaced by a governor-general and the last viceroy, Lord Mountbatten, was invited by the government of the new dominion to be the first to hold this office. In 1963 India broke the direct link with the British Crown and became the first republic within the Commonwealth. The first prime minister of the new India, Pandit Nehru, had formerly been scornful of the Raj's new capital, referring to it as 'a visible symbol of British power, with all its ostentation and wasteful extravagance'.[9] Yet despite such condemnation, New Delhi became the capital of the Dominion and subsequently the Republic of India. In this way it was decided that the new state would continue a historic tradition going back even beyond the Sultanate to Prithviraj. By then well into its eighth century, power in India continued to be symbolized by the stones of this city much as it had during earlier times.

12

Architects of Empire: Hitler, Speer and the Germania Project

In 1933, just twenty years after the end of the Vienna period in his life, Adolf Hitler became the chancellor of Germany. He immediately embarked on the rapid transformation of the country together with his own role in it.

After service in the war during which he had been awarded the Iron Cross, Hitler had begun his political career by joining an extreme nationalist party in Munich. This was the German Workers' Party and it rapidly gained support from those disillusioned with the humiliating state in which Germany then found itself. Discovering a natural ability to captivate an audience, he worked his way up and by 1921 had become leader of the party. Its name was changed to the National Socialist German Workers' Party (NSDAP), later known as the Nazi Party. During the economic troubles of the 1920s the Nazis, promising to solve all Germany's problems, gained ever more support.

The Nazis hated the Weimar Republic, which they saw as having been established by the left after what they considered the traitorous 'stab in the back' inflicted on the army in 1918. Germany had then been forced to accept the humiliating peace of Versailles. The subsequent internationalism of the leaders of the Weimar Republic was anathema to the Nazis who saw the future as being Germany's resurrection to great power status. The German middle and governing classes feared the Communists more than the Nationalists and in January 1933, in a futile attempt to tame the violence which had become endemic in the political scene, President Hindenburg called on Hitler to form a government. By doing this the president unwittingly paved the way for the most aggressive, extreme and ruthless regime in modern European history. In 1934, following the death of President Hindenburg, Hitler became head of state and the so-called Weimar Republic, established in the wake of the country's defeat in the First World War, was brought to an end. In its place came another empire, the Third Reich, and Hitler took the title of Führer – leader – of this neo-imperial creation.

In its early years the Nazi Party had been strongest in Bavaria and the decision to move its headquarters to Berlin was taken in order to get a foothold in the capital. Berlin was certainly not a popular city with the Nazis. 'Red Berlin' was by this time a huge industrial city with a large working class which favoured the Communists and Socialists rather than the parties of the right. The Communists looked towards Moscow and saw their best interests in the unity of the workers of the world rather than in the nationalism advocated by the Nazis. Josef Goebbels was put in charge of the Berlin operation and the result was that the city soon became the epicentre of the confrontation between right and left in German politics. Street marches often made this confrontation violent and bloody, adding to the tensions existing in the republic.

Despite this animosity, Berlin was the capital bequeathed to Germany by its history and Hitler expressed the opinion that it was 'not away from Berlin but towards Berlin' that the main thrust of National Socialism had to take place.[1] The decision to keep the turbulent and unsympathetic city as the capital was taken for a number of reasons. It had, of course, been the capital of the Second Reich so there was considerable precedent. It was also the Prussian capital and, besides having great admiration for Prussian military prowess, Hitler had a particular admiration for the Prussian king, Frederick the Great. In future years he was often to compare himself with 'the Great King' and towards the end he convinced himself that their lives had much in common. There was also a wider consideration involving Hitler's racist ideology. He saw the Germans as the most powerful nation among the Aryans of northern Europe and, in common with other racists of the period, he believed them to be a superior people destined eventually to secure domination not only over Europe but over the whole world. Although he himself was an Austrian and his main experience of Germany had been in Bavaria, he saw the north of Germany as being the natural centre of this Aryan world. However, like the Austrians, the Germans had been diluted and corrupted by the huge influx of foreigners, in particular the Slavs and Jews. Hitler asserted that 'the Berlin of Frederick the Great has been turned into a pigsty by the Jews.'[2] It was essential that the capital be cleansed and made truly German once more. 'When I come to Berlin', he said, 'it will be like Christ entering the Temple and driving out the money changers.'[3]

Yet Hitler did not consider Berlin as it was to be worthy of the role of the imperial city of his new Reich. It had few grand buildings and the only great avenue was the Unter den Linden with its triumphal arch, the Brandenburger Tor, at its western end. He considered these to be highly inadequate symbols of power when compared to the Champs-Elysées in Paris and the Ringstrasse in Vienna. He expressed his determination that his Reich was to be 'neither a boarder nor a lodger in the royal chamber of bygone days'.[4] The main problem was, according to Hitler, that his predecessors had no idea how to build a great imperial capital. To him everything in the old Berlin was shoddy and second rate and the whole city was little more than an ugly industrial sprawl. He expressed the opinion that Berlin may have been a big city but it was not a real metropolis. It was so unlike Paris, which he grudgingly admitted was 'the most beautiful city in the world'.[5] At first Hitler toyed with the idea of moving the capital away from Berlin to a completely new site, with the Mecklenburg region mentioned as a possibility. This scheme seems to have been abandoned, not for political but for geological reasons.[6] However, Hitler expressed the opinion that if the imperial capital had to be Berlin, it would need to be radically transformed. 'I am too proud to move into former palaces', he asserted, and this must have been all the more so since he did not think much of those in Berlin anyway.[7]

The beginning of the transformation of the city got under way rapidly. Berlin had been chosen to host the 1936 Olympic Games and Hitler saw this as being a great opportunity to use the city to display his new Third Reich to the world. The Olympic stadium and the other buildings on the Olympic site were built as much with political as with athletic purposes in mind. With the swastika flags flying and the great flame burning in the stadium, Goebbels, now propaganda minister, was able to use the whole event as a great celebration of Aryan might, something which the filmmaker Leni Riefenstahl caught so effectively in 1934 at Nuremberg in *Triumph of the Will*. The display of the Third Reich in architecture and pageantry had begun.

In the following year came the celebrations of the 700th anniversary of the foundation of Berlin, a date which the Nazis seem themselves to have invented. These centred on a great pageant of the city's history and included exhibitions, parades and outdoor events which attracted large numbers of people. The whole jamboree seems to have increased the enthusiasm of Berliners for their new regime, something Goebbels had all along been hoping for.[8] The Germanic origins of Berlin were stressed and besides being the historic capital, the importance of the city in

German science, culture and literature was everywhere emphasized. In the Nazi press, Berlin was referred to as 'the centre of the Reich', 'the much loved capital' and, most significantly, 'the most powerful city in the world'.[9] One article in *Berliner Illustrirte Zeitung* asserted grandly that 'Berlin is the Reich and the Reich is Berlin', proclaiming that the city had now been transformed and the shame of Weimar wiped out.

This may have been so, but for Hitler it had not been transformed enough by any means. The intended transformation was on a far more radical scale than the Berliners of the time could possibly have envisaged. Following the 700th anniversary celebrations, Hitler began to formulate in detail his plans for the city.

In the earlier plans for the rebuilding of the capital, and also for other grand buildings in other German cities, a number of architects had been involved. Pre-eminent among them was Paul Ludwig Troost who was greatly admired by Hitler and whose restrained, severe neoclassical style became virtually the official architecture of the Third Reich. The Berlin of the 1920s and early 1930s had certainly not found favour with Hitler and besides its alleged lack of imperial splendour there was another feature which he found even more insidious. Berlin had become the major European centre of contemporary art and architecture. It was the era of the Bauhaus which had become the driving force in the modernist movement. In the 1920s architects such as Mies van der Rohe and Walter Gropius were beginning to transform Berlin and other German cities but they were doing it in a very different manner from that envisaged by the Nazis. This situation was similar to that of Vienna in the early years of the twentieth century when the artistic and architectural avant garde of the time existed alongside the solid imperialist architecture of Franz Josef's Ringstrasse. Needless to say, it was the latter, and what it represented politically, that had fascinated Hitler during his period in Vienna. Hitler now proposed to transpose his version of Franz Josef's grand monuments to his own new imperial city. Berlin was to be transformed and his own idea of the Ringstrasse project was to be imposed on it. After the premature death of Troost in 1934 the young architect Albert Speer was put in charge of bringing this about. What Hitler and Speer planned for Berlin was far more radical than anything the Austrian capital had ever experienced. The Nazis made sure that any Vienna-type coexistence of the old and the new would not be allowed to take place.

Speer had greatly impressed the Führer with his ideas on the way in which Nazi architecture should evolve. Speer had been given the task of designing the stadium in Nuremberg in which Nazi party rallies were to be held. The design of the enormous podium intended for Hitler and his entourage greatly appealed to the Führer who believed that the architecture of power had to be gigantic in size in order to impress. He came to regard Speer as an architect of genius with whom he felt he could work easily. Consequently, he was appointed Inspector General in charge of all the major building projects in the Reich. However, it was always Hitler's intention that he should himself be directly involved in all these projects. In this respect he was more like Franz Josef than Napoleon III, but what actually took place was a close partnership between the Führer and his architect. Overwhelmingly the most important project with which Speer had to deal was the transformation of Berlin into the kind of imperial city which Hitler wanted as the monumental centre of his Third Reich.

So radical was the envisaged transformation that the city was not even to be called Berlin any more. The new name chosen for it was Germania. This, Hitler believed, would indicate both the city's newness and its inclusiveness. It would no longer be just another version of the Prussian capital or the capital of the Second Reich. Perhaps most importantly of all to the Nazis, by changing its name the stain of Weimar, so much associated with Berlin, would finally be removed. It would in effect be a new city where the old Berlin had been, built on top of, and in place of, the old city. One of the few things left would be the fact that it was situated in the same geographical location and so at the heart of what was destined to be the Greater German Reich. Hitler asserted that: 'The name Germania for the capital of the Reich in its new representative form would be very appropriate, for it would give every member of the German community, however far away from the capital he may be, a feeling of unity and closer membership.'[10]

The first major building in Berlin for which Speer was responsible was the new Reich Chancellery. This was at the junction of the Wilhelmstrasse and Voss Strasse at the heart of what had been the diplomatic quarter of the old German Empire. Despite the limited space available, Hitler and Speer were determined that the building should be designed above all to symbolize power. It was to be a practical demonstration of the expression of political power through architecture which Hitler regarded as being the principal tool for consolidating his grip on power. It was, for Hitler, a form of legitimization and would symbolize in stone the endurance of the 'Thousand Year Reich'.

The whole Chancellery was aligned on an east to west axis following the line of Voss Strasse. The entrance on Wilhelm Strasse was

Plan of the Regierungsviertel, the Government Quarter, of the Third Reich in Berlin. Centring on the Wilhelmstrasse, this was the heart of Nazi power. The Reich Chancellery at the junction with Voss Strasse was surrounded by the most important ministries.

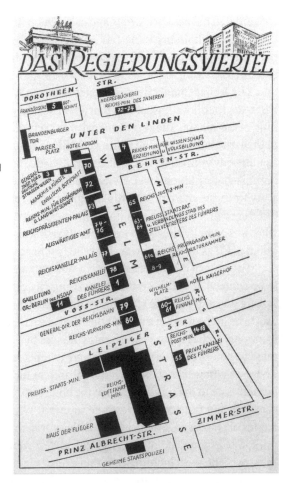

marked by two massive pillars topped by a gigantic eagle clutching the swastika emblem. This led to a huge red marble hall, the walls of which were covered in mosaics depicting Germanic legends. It was the commencement of what Sudjic referred to as 'The long march to the Leader's desk'.[11] The hall led to another grand reception hall intended for diplomatic gatherings and yet another hall, the walls of which were covered with tapestries depicting the victories of Alexander the Great. This led finally to Hitler's massive study or work room. On reaching the gigantic door the visitor had still not completed the long march, since the sheer size of the study meant that it was a considerable walk to get to Hitler's desk where the Führer would be waiting. The long march was along what Sudjic termed 'a triumphal axis', culminating in the presence of the Führer. The whole was intended to intimidate all

who entered its massive portals and as a demonstration of the power of
the Third Reich. In his Table Talk Hitler is recorded as having asserted
that 'when one enters the Reich Chancellery one should have the feeling
that one is visiting the "master of the world"'.[12]

The Reich Chancellery, completed in 1938, was but a taster for
what was to follow. It was then that Speer set about the full-scale planning of Germania. The two principal architects of the new empire, one
of them the Führer himself, were determined to turn their backs on the
existing city with all its associations and inadequacies. This again was
reminiscent of Franz Josef's Vienna in which the Ringstrasse looked
away from the old city towards the great empire surrounding it. The
difference in Berlin was that it was intended to pay very little regard to
what was actually already in existence. If anything was in the way of the
grand plan, as much of it was, it would just have to be removed.

The scale of the projected new city was truly awesome. Its centre was
to be somewhat to the west of the existing city centre and its principal
feature was a grand axis stretching from north to south for 7 km. This
was to be in the form of a grand boulevard at each end of which were not
triumphal arches like on the Champs-Elysées but, more practically, two
massive new railway termini which were to replace all the existing ones.
There was, however, to be a triumphal arch of formidable proportions
located close to the southern end of the boulevard. In designing it, Hitler
certainly had the Arc de Triomphe in mind. While the latter had the
names of Napoleon's victories, on Hitler's arch the names of all the 1.7
million German dead of the First World War were to be carved. With
the size of the great buildings of other capitals in mind, especially Paris,
Hitler decided that his arch was to be twice the height of the Arc de
Triomphe. While he conceded that Paris was magnificent he intended
that Germania would be even more so.

Northwards from the arch were to be some three miles of avenue
leading to the central square of the city in which the most important
official buildings were to be situated. The largest and most impressive
of them was to be the Great Hall, with a capacity of 150,000. This huge
building was to be capped by a massive dome far larger than that of St
Peter's in Rome. At some 300 m in height this was intended to be by
far the largest structure in the new capital. Opposite this on the south
of the square was to be Hitler's palace, a massive building which Hitler
would use in addition to the Reich Chancellery. The western side was
intended for the new headquarters of the high command of the
Wehrmacht and the eastern side was reserved for the old Reichstag.

Model of Germania showing the Arch of Triumph and the Great Hall.

This was one of the few old buildings to be incorporated into the centre of the new city and it would have been dwarfed in size by most of the other buildings. Perhaps its incorporation was intended to give a nod in the direction of the imperial past, but it may also have been a demonstration of how relatively insignificant that past had been compared to the massive and monumental present.

The great central square was at the intersection with the new city's other principal axis which extended from west to east. This was to incorporate the existing Unter den Linden and the Brandenburger Tor and from there follow the boulevard westwards past the Tiergarten to link with the western suburbs. Another monument to be incorporated on this axis was the Siegessäule. This was the victory column erected by Bismarck to commemorate the Prussian victories over Denmark, Austria and France between 1866 and 1871 which paved the way for the creation of the German Empire. This part of German history was acceptable within the new German historical memory which the Nazis were in the process of creating. Other grand new buildings on the north–south axis were to include an Admiralty, a Rathaus and Reichsmarschall Göring's massive palace, which apparently was going to rival that of Hitler in sheer size and splendour. This axis was clearly intended to be the main ceremonial way through the city and it was actually unveiled in 1938 with a great parade.

By the beginning of the Second World War work was well under way on the new city and this continued into the war years. The SS was heavily involved in the project, and forced labour was used to quarry the stone and to build the massive foundations needed for the new buildings. However, in 1942 all work finally came to a stop. The Russian campaign was not going well and following the defeat at Stalingrad in January 1943 the Third Reich had other, far more pressing military pre-occupations. The RAF first bombed Berlin in 1941 and after the American entry into the war later that year the bombing became more intense and the resulting destruction more widespread. At first Hitler had been cavalier about the bombing of his capital, musing that the RAF was helping to destroy the old Berlin which is what he wanted to do anyway. As the bombing became more regular and the destruction ever greater there were no more jokes about this.

In February 1945 Hitler left his headquarters in East Prussia, from which he had been conducting the Russian campaign, and moved back to Berlin. His home and HQ for the final months of his life was to be the Reich Chancellery, but this time it was not the grand halls of power above ground but the bunker well below them. A large system of underground bunkers had been built below the gardens of the building in the 1930s and now in these final months they became the centre of power of the Third Reich. The Chancellery built for the purpose of intimidation was now being itself intimidated by constant Allied bombing. It was soon reduced to rubble and Hitler, rarely appearing above ground, issued ever more unrealistic orders for the conduct of the war from his concrete dungeon. It was there that Hitler committed suicide on 29 April 1945. The great dream of a world empire died with him in his Chancellery.

Little evidence of the Germania project now remains in Berlin. A few notable but curious survivors are Speer's lamp posts intended to light the great routeways, which are still to be found lining part of the surviving east–west axis. The massive foundations for the planned buildings can still be identified in some places. The Olympic stadium and swimming pool that housed the 1936 Games are still in use and may well be the only real survivors in Berlin of that dark period in German history. Immediately after hostilities ceased, the ruins of the Reich Chancellery, the centre of power during the period of triumphant conquests and the place where the Third Reich came to its dismal end, were visited by Allied leaders who wished to see for themselves what Churchill had called Hitler's 'lair'. The Chancellery was in the designated Soviet zone of Berlin and was almost adjacent to the wall which after 1961 separated the Soviet from the western zones of the capital. The Soviets demolished the Chancellery building and filled in the bunker in which the Third Reich had come to an end. They wished to erase all evidence of the regime which had done so much harm to them and to the rest of Europe. Today in the reunited capital of the German Federal Republic this former centre of power of the Third Reich remains an empty space. In contrast to its desolation, a few hundred yards to the north of it is the Reichstag, which has been rebuilt and greatly extended. The centre of German democracy, much despised by the Nazis, has had a new lease of life while the centre of the worst dictatorship in its history has been obliterated. While the Reichstag is vibrant with the activity of running a rich and peaceful state, the bunker is now, as Jan Morris put it, but 'the grave of a lost empire'.[13]

Architecture was Hitler's great passion and he fused this with his desire to raise Germany up from its humiliation at Versailles to become the greatest power in the world. He saw architecture as the expression of this power and as a kind of legitimization of it. 'If I continually put architectural problems in the foreground', he said, 'that is because they lie nearest my heart.'[14] He pronounced that his preferred role was 'master builder of the Third Reich'. The buildings were intended as a 'stage set' for his grand design and their twin function was to 'to inspire his followers and oppress his enemies'.[15]

The particular architecture favoured by Hitler was classical, which clearly he believed to be the most appropriate style for the display of power. This was the architecture in which Troost had excelled and, while the actual styles adopted were sometimes allowed to deviate from this, Troost's work remained the Führer's ideal. He sometimes used the term 'Greek-Nordic' architecture and so linked the classical world with his own. In fact he was appropriating classical architecture for that

Teutonic empire which he was engaged in building. In this context it is significant that at the entrance to his study were tapestries of the victories of Alexander the Great. Greece and Rome were thus fused architecturally in his mind into the overall classical designs. He expressed the desire that his capital should be a new ancient Rome and his architects were expected to do their best to provide it.

From early on in his life architecture and politics had been linked in Hitler's mind. His political dreams were to be expressed in what he built. Speer suggested that Hitler considered himself first and foremost an artist, a passion which he later channelled into architecture. Frederic Spotts went further and asserted that it was not possible to understand Hitler and what he did unless one realized that for him the artistic impulse transcended everything else.[16] Dana Thomas saw the whole iconography of Nazism as having arisen from his Vienna period: 'The Nazi flag and uniforms, the soaring eagles, the neoclassical outdoor theatres where he staged his riveting rallies – all these grew out of his drawings and watercolours of Vienna monuments and edifices.'[17] She also turned the conventional view on its head by asserting that 'politics became the tool of his artistic expression'. If this was so, he certainly used art in a most violent way and it eventually destroyed all that had been created.

Hitler once reflected that he had considered ordering the destruction of Paris because it was so beautiful. This beauty had aroused his jealousy and he wished his own city to surpass it as the most beautiful in the world. However, the plans for Germania, wrote Richie, 'are memorable not for their beauty but for their cold forbidding giantism'. Their main purpose was to overawe and intimidate all who saw them. While the beauty of Paris transcended its display of military grandeur, Germania was in the end nothing but 'a reflection of the dark misanthropic heart of Nazism'.[18]

Most of what remained by 1945 of the real and planned capital of the Third Reich has long disappeared into the foundations of a new and very different Berlin. Since those dark times, Berlin has once more displayed that capacity for change and transformation which characterizes most of the world's great capital cities.

13

Cyrus with Golden Caviar: Persepolis Revisited

Since the destruction of Berlin in 1945 and the end of the Germania project, there have been no further attempts to build new cities designed exclusively for the display of imperial power. A number of new capital cities have been built but they have been mostly intended as administrative centres, far from having any realistic aspirations to display great power. The post-imperial great powers after the Second World War eschewed such projects and they returned their seats of power to earlier capitals. Moscow, Beijing and Delhi were inherited by the new post-imperial governments of the Soviet Union, China and India respectively. Geopolitically, at least, the legitimacy provided by the former imperial capitals appeared to be more powerful than the promotion in stone of the ideas and ideologies which these republics now espoused.

Since the Second World War there has been only one attempt to revive a fallen empire and, significantly, this was the ancient empire of Persia. This first great empire of the ancient world had astonishingly survived in one form or another for most of the next 2,500 years but by the twentieth century it had become quite insignificant on the world scene. It was a dinosaur from the past still living among those great powers which had come into existence long after it had lost its own great power status. In the attempt to revive this empire, its purpose-built capital, Persepolis, the first of the imperial cities to be examined in this book, had one final part to play. By the twentieth century the world had undergone many changes since the city had been the ceremonial capital of the world superpower of its time. However, in the late twentieth century the ruins of the old imperial city were brought briefly back to life for the purpose of commemorating, and even resurrecting, the Persian Empire of antiquity.

The first Persian Empire, the Achaemenid, was for some 200 years the world's greatest power. It dominated much of the eastern Mediterranean and the Middle East until its defeat by Alexander of Macedon in the fourth century BC. Persepolis fell to the new conqueror in 331 BC and Alexander wreaked destruction on the city. He had chosen Babylon to be the capital of his new empire but he died before his dreams could be fulfilled. Following the subsequent Hellenistic period, during which Alexander's successors ruled, the Persian Empire was revived under the Sassanian dynasty which ruled until its defeat by the Arabs in the middle of the seventh century, after which it became for a time part of their Islamic Empire. By the ninth century Persia had regained its independence, remaining in this position until the twentieth. It did so under a number of Islamic dynasties, all of which claimed their legitimacy through their relationship to the earlier ones.

The last of these dynasties was the Pahlavi in the twentieth century. Reza Khan, who was crowned shah in 1926, was actually a Persian general who had staged a coup in the previous year, replacing the much weakened Qajar dynasty with his own. By this time Persia had come strongly under the influence of the great powers of the time, especially Britain, the Soviet Union and the United States. Their interest in the country was to a certain extent strategic but more importantly it was in Persian oil, which was in great demand with the coming of the age of the internal combustion engine.

Reza Shah wished to associate his new dynasty with the pre-Islamic Persian past and especially the great age of the Achaemenids. However, at the same time he saw that if Persia was to regain any of its lost glory there had to be modernization. In order to achieve this he undertook a radical programme of westernization which included the secularization of the legal system, the establishment of secular state schools, a state bank and a national university in the capital, Tehran. The wearing of western dress was made obligatory. In 1938 the name of the country was officially changed from Persia to Iran. This was a name derived from the Aryan peoples who had moved during the first millennium BC from the centre into the Asian peripheries and had become rulers there. The Persians were members of this racial group, a fact used to add to the illustrious heritage which the shah was attempting to present to his people and to the world. This root and branch modernization and secularization was very similar to that happening at the same time in adjacent Turkey under Mustafa Kemal 'Atatürk'. Reza Shah greatly admired the Turkish leader and followed the Turkish model whenever he could.

However, one significant way in which the shah differed from Atatürk was that in the Second World War he favoured the German side. This resulted in his forced abdication as a result of pressure from the British and Russians in favour of his young son Mohammad Reza, who had shown himself more inclined towards them. The young heir accepted his new role, realizing the necessity of remaining firmly on the side of the allied powers if he wanted to avoid the fate of his father. In 1943 the first conference of the 'Big Three' – the Soviet Union, Britain and the United States – took place and Tehran was chosen for this. The first draft of the new post-war world order thus came into existence in the Iranian capital. While the shah was officially the host for this momentous event, his role was really that of a spectator and this made it abundantly clear to the young monarch how insignificant his country had become in the modern world. It was this which sowed the seeds in his mind of the idea of returning his country to its former status as a great power.

While in the years following the end of the war Iran remained under the influence of the great powers, a strong nationalist movement arose which succeeded in moving the country into a more independent position. This included taking greater charge of its own oil production, a move which initially did much harm to the country's economy and resulted in considerable destabilization. In the 1950s the shah softened the Iranian stance and in this way presided over a period of considerable economic success. At the same time he continued to dream of reviving the glories of ancient Persia and its Aryan past and saw further economic development as an important step towards achieving this end. In the 1960s he founded the National Resurrection Party, dedicated specifically to the revival of the greatness of his country. At the same time he continued to maintain a close relationship with the west during the years of the Cold War and this ensured that he continued to receive the military aid which helped build up powerful armed forces.

By the 1960s the idea of the revival of past greatness seems to have completely taken over the shah's mind and the needs of the economy were increasingly neglected. The shah stressed the continuity of Persian history and even attempted to trace a tenuous relationship between the Pahlavi and the Achaemenid dynasties. As the centrepiece of this upsurge of national pride it was decided to hold a great celebration of the 2,500th anniversary of the foundation of the Persian Empire by Cyrus the Great: 1971, the date chosen for this, was quite an arbitrary one but it was accepted and preparations went ahead. The intention of the shah was to demonstrate to the Iranian people and to the world at large the heritage of their country and the role which his dynasty was playing in its preservation.

In Tehran great preparations were made including the placing of bas-reliefs with ancient Persian themes in prominent sites across the city. Most important was the construction of an enormous tower incorporating an archway intended to be symbolic of the whole event. This was the Shahyade ('Souvenir of the Shah') Tower. Inside was an extensive display of precious artefacts illustrating the history of Iran. The whole vast structure was incorporated into a massive archway and was located at the end of a grand avenue leading from the centre of the city. In this spectacular position it was intended to be the unmissable symbol of the empire and an impressive culmination for great events in the capital.

However, the *pièce de résistance* of the events was planned to take place not in the modern capital but in Persepolis, the ancient capital itself. Although lost in the sand by the nineteenth century, its name had remained as an evocative symbol of power. Christopher Marlowe's Tamburlaine, the leader who came to symbolize fearsome eastern power, recalls its glory when he asserts that his ultimate wish was to take this city as Alexander had done over a millennium before:

Is it not passing brave to be a king,
And ride in triumph through Persepolis?
Tamburlaine the Great, Part One, Act II, Scene V

There was also to be a role for Pasargadae, which was where the impressive tomb of Cyrus the Great still stood in lonely isolation in the plain north of Persepolis.

It cannot be denied that the great ceremonial celebrations which took place in Persepolis in the summer of 1971 were spectacular. Large numbers of heads of state, with the monarchs being given pride of place, were invited, together with ambassadors and other high officials and huge tents were put up to accommodate the guests for the lavish banquet which was to be the centre of the event. A history of it all gives some flavour of the extent to which the shah went in providing luxurious food and drink for his guests:

In the sparkling light of huge crystal chandeliers, hung from a ceiling of pure silk, six hundred guests drawn from royalty and the world's executive power sat down together for a five hour banquet of the century . . . Chef Max Blouet of Maxim's de Paris had created . . . such minor triumphs as quail eggs stuffed with the golden caviar of the Caspian Sea, saddle of lamb with truffles [and] roast peacock stuffed with foie gras capped by its own brilliant plumage . . . There were some 25,000 bottles of wine.[1]

The only thing in the banquet which had actually come from Iran was the golden caviar from the Caspian. It is significant that the French President Pompidou stated that he was unable to attend. A number of other heads of state, including Queen Elizabeth II, also made their apologies.

In his address at the tomb of Cyrus, the shah concluded with the exhortation, 'Sleep, O Cyrus, for we are awake.' Throughout the proceedings, the emphasis was always more on Cyrus than on Darius, who had actually built Persepolis, and the shah announced that the Iranian calendar was to be changed with Year One being the date of the accession of Cyrus. The Cylinder of Cyrus on which were itemized many of the deeds of the great monarch, became one of the emblems of the whole extravagant celebration.[2]

After the banquet was over, the ruins of Persepolis became the backdrop for great processions of Iranian soldiers dressed in the uniforms of ancient Medes and Persians. The link between the remote past and the present day was stressed and the continuity of Iranian history was the underlying theme. The feeling was engendered that day 'that the departed shades of the former lords of Asia were hovering unseen over the stage of their former glory'.[3] However, to Axworthy it was all *folie de grandeur* on a sublime scale.[4] Certainly it was also Hollywood at its most extravagant.

By this time the shah had become totally intoxicated by the whole project and what it represented and was far more concerned with linking his dynasty to the glorious past than with the welfare of his people. None of this pomp and display was to save the Pahlavi dynasty. Rather than covering it in borrowed glory, as had been intended, it actually increased the dissatisfaction of the Iranian people with their monarch. The summer of festivities emptied the exchequer, weakened further the economy and put the shah's relationship with his people under ever greater strain.

Meanwhile, Iran was showing little sign of regaining any of the former glory for which the shah yearned. The international position of the country failed to improve and it became ever clearer throughout the 1970s that in reality it was becoming ever more dependent on the Americans. The result of this was increased restiveness among the population and this led to a resurgence of Islam which had played little part in the shah's great schemes. The Ayatollah Khomeini, a respected Islamic cleric from the holy city of Qom, became the undisputed leader of the new Islamic movement. It was he rather than the shah who became the leader whom the Iranian people saw as being able to deal with their humiliating situation and resolve their problems.

In 1979 the dynasty, self-proclaimed heir to two and a half millennia of power, was toppled and the shah was forced to go into inglorious exile. He was replaced by an Islamic Republic with the Ayatollah Khomeini as its first supreme leader. Islam, marginalized by the shah, returned to centre stage and the secular state which the Pahlavis had attempted to establish was swept away and replaced by a theocracy. The symbols of power created by the shah were either destroyed or put to new uses. The Shahyade Tower in Tehran was renamed the Azadi (Freedom) Tower and was converted into a symbol of the Islamic revolution. What was left of the grandeur of the shah was from then on used to commemorate the new, and very different, masters of the country.

The Pahlavis had sought to bring back the pre-Islamic past but after 1979 Persepolis returned again to being the ruin it had been for most of the time since Alexander's conquest. At first largely ignored by the new regime, it soon became frequented by tourists, who like others before them marvelled at the long-gone power and splendour of Darius and his successors. The tents erected in 1971 gradually fell away and disappeared into the sand. The signs of the great celebrations themselves soon became part of that past which the shah had attempted to resurrect.

This effort to restore a long-vanished empire was in many ways the last vainglorious gasp of the traditional imperialism deriving from ancient empires and their dynasties. In the years after the Second World War new political forms had been superseding most of the empires. These accorded more closely with the desires of their peoples and were better adapted to contemporary world conditions. In the 1970s, while the last shah was looking back to a dynastic past, the world was changing fast. Ironically, this change had been foreseen in the Tehran Conference of 1943 which took place in the shah's capital but in which he had been but a spectator. The neo-imperialism of the post-imperial great powers certainly represented a form of continuity with the past but these powers were employing twentieth-century ideologies rather than ancient dynasties as their justification. In the case of Turkey, to which the last shah's father had looked for guidance, nationalism was the creed used to underpin the state and no attempt was made to resurrect the old Ottoman Empire. This had been consigned to history by Atatürk and under him the country followed quite a different, and far more realistic, path than that of its neighbour. Atatürk looked outwards towards modern Europe while the Shah's Iran had looked inwards to a Middle Eastern world which was long gone. It also looked back nostalgically to a form of imperialism which had little part to play in the new global system. New forms of power were emerging which in the following decades were to render traditional ones outdated and increasingly irrelevant.

There was also a much bigger change in wider geopolitical arrangements taking place as a result of new global perspectives. In many aspects of life, the world was by then being viewed as an entity and problems and issues were seen as being most effectively addressed in the context of the terrestrial whole. The changes were beginning to have the effect of making economic power ever less linked to political power and so less dependent on it. Out of all this a new form of global power was coming into being which was necessitating the reappraisal of existing political arrangements.

The Azadi Tower, Tehran. Originally this was built as a centrepiece for the Shah's great commemoration of the establishment of the Persian Empire by Cyrus the Great. Following the Islamic Revolution it was adopted as one of the symbols of the new Iran.

204 POWER IN STONE

The symbolism arising from this new scenario was still in its infancy but it was to be very different from that of the past. The invocation to 'look on my works' was soon to be replaced by very different physical manifestations of the emerging global order.

14

'Cities and Thrones and Powers'

Cities and Thrones and Powers
Stand in Time's eye,
Almost as long as flowers,
Which daily die . . .

Like Shelley's 'Ozymandias', Kipling's poem 'Cities and Thrones and Powers' is about the transitory nature of power.[1] Power which at one time appears to be so absolute and permanent is inevitably destined to decline and disappear. The poem also catches the fact that the principal repository of such power is the city and that when new power emerges this will also seek to display itself in a similar manner.

In the two millennia between Persepolis and Germania a large number of cities were created for the specific purpose of proclaiming power through stone. They were usually the work of powerful rulers seeking to use these cities to endow their regimes with the grandeur, legitimacy and endurance intended as visible proofs of their attainments. Such cities have had a variety of forms and characteristics but certain of these frequently recur.

The most favoured architecture has certainly been of the classical type. The control and ordered severity to be found in this style has found echoes throughout the ages in the constant desire to give an aura of permanence to imperial endeavours. Dalrymple saw the architectural vocabulary of power as consisting of 'great expanses of marble, a stripped-down classicism, a fondness for long colonnades and a love of Imperial heraldic devices'.[2] Both Persepolis and the unfinished Germania were in this classical form. Consciously or unconsciously, Hitler used the ancient world as his model and he found the severe neoclassical style of Troost ideal for giving architectural expression to this. In Europe the notion of 'Translatio Imperii' implies the idea of the renewal of the Roman Empire, so often considered to be the original or prototype empire, and this then imparts a legitimacy to the new or aspiring power. 'Hitler wanted Ancient Rome and Speer did his best to provide it.'[3] While this has, of course, been mainly the case with European and

Middle Eastern empires, the capitals outside this cultural tradition have often developed styles which bear a remarkable similarity. While the architectural traditions are in each case very different, the same kind of severity and power is conveyed by the great walls of the Red Fort and the Forbidden City.

Mathematics, especially geometry, and cosmology have underlain the planning of many such cities and determined their precise locations. This was especially to be found in China where feng shui, geomancy, was used to ascertain with precision where everything should be and how it was to relate to everything else. Numbers and colours, also usually relating to the cosmic, were used in creating the correct ambience for the wielding of power and determining the exact centre from which this power needed to emanate. The same sort of ideas also underlay the configuration of other capitals. From the Hall of Supreme Harmony in the Forbidden City to the Bedchamber of Louis XIV in Versailles, mathematical principles were used to determine the precise location for the most effective exercise of supreme power. The Chinese emperor was the Son of Heaven and Louis XIV was the Sun King, and similar attributes were bestowed on monarchs elsewhere and at other times. Whether the ultimate source of power was Heaven, the sun or God, the supreme source of worldly power was deemed to be in direct contact with it and to derive his own power and authority from it.

Although it was not available everywhere, stone was usually the preferred building material. This was most conveniently the local stone and so proximity to good workable building stone was often another factor influencing and even determining location. Among the most favoured stones have been the young red sandstone of northern India, the darker sandstones of the Guadarrama mountains of Spain and the limestone of Fars in Persia. Always especially prized has been marble which was used for the features of the most sacred and important sites. The walls of the divans of the Mughal emperors were faced in marble while in Fatehpur Sikri the most sacred site, the tomb of the saint, is in brilliant white marble. This white also denotes purity, another feature of power that at its strongest is, or appears to be, uncorrupted and devoted exclusively to the well-being of the state.

A further common characteristic is that from Darius's Persepolis to Hitler's Germania the powerful ruler often embarks on the building of a new capital city which will enshrine the nature of his own regime. Such rulers do not wish to be under the shadow of forebears, however illustrious they may have been. They wish to stamp their own particular character on their capitals, which will probably for this reason be given very different architectural styles from earlier ones. In this way, the capital is an assertion of what the regime intends to be and to do. The 'seven cities' of Delhi were built by different regimes, each of which attempted to stamp its own particular character on the city it built. The lavish architecture of Siri was totally different from what has been called the 'stark cyclopean grandeur' of Tughluqabad and the regimes which built them acted accordingly.

While the ruler's direct relationship to ultimate celestial power is a powerful factor in determining the nature of his city, religion in the wider sense has also played an important role. The ancient Persians were Zoroastrians and Persepolis was surrounded by temples containing the eternal flame sacred to that religion. The stone tablets of the Great Kings maintain how it was invariably the god Ahuramazda who commanded or sanctioned certain courses of action. Later empires have sought similar legitimization through their own particular religions. The whole concept of the 'Three Romes' was both political and religious and in all three Christianity became virtually a partner of the state. In Byzantium the relationship between the basileus and the patriarch was a close one and this was passed on to Kievan and Muscovite Russia. At first sight the Kremlin looks more like a large group of churches than the heart of a powerful state and while it was by no means a theocracy, the territorial aims and acquisitions of Holy Russia were invariably accorded religious justification. This close relationship of state and Church is reflected in the close proximity of their buildings. Palaces lead into cathedrals with the tombs of the tsars in a manner which blurs any distinction between them.

During the twentieth century this role of religion was taken over by ideology and the ideologies of racism, nationalism and communism underpinned the quasi-imperial pretensions of both Nazi Germany and Communist Russia. The great hall at the centre of the Germania project looked very much like a cathedral and the heart of the communist state was itself surrounded by churches.

The image of the autocratic ruler has frequently been incorporated into his capital. The image of himself which Ramesses II wanted to be seen was found in the many statues embellishing his kingdom. The face with the frown and the 'sneer of cold command' was of the pharaoh who was to be feared and respected by all. Many of the achievements the pharaoh claimed for himself, such as his heroic deeds in battle, do not appear actually to have taken place. Likewise Trajan's column in Rome, which displays the military prowess of that most warlike of emperors, and the icons in Constantinople of the Holy Basileus with Christ were images of rulers as they wished their subjects to perceive them.

However, it was in many ways not so much the ruler himself as the created image, and the myths and commands associated with it, that his subjects were expected to fear and obey. If anyone still doubts my power, 'Look on my buildings', was the command of Timur. In this way the imperial city with its images of power itself became in many ways more representative of power than the emperor. Timur appears to have been a plainly dressed, even unimpressive, figure sitting in the midst of his architectural and artistic splendour. Similarly, the sense of power emanating from the grandeur of the 'Sublime Porte' was incomparably greater than that of the usually quite inadequate sultans, most of whom were rarely seen. The same could be said of the sense of power emanating from the great Red Fort in Delhi, the heart of Mughal power from the time of Shah Jehan. When the British arrived in 1803 the Great Mughal presented a pathetic figure, contrasting starkly with the splendour of his palace. This often applied most to the weaker successors of a great ruler who were not of the same calibre as their illustrious forebear. It applied markedly to the successors of both Sultan Süleyman the Magnificent and Aurangzeb. It also applied in a rather different way to the successors of Louis XIV. They proved so incapable of ruling the great state which had been bequeathed to them that later in the century of the Sun King's death his grandson was beheaded on the guillotine.

While in the long term the great capital city proclaims the enduring character of the empire, its more immediate function is to overawe, even intimidate, those who see it. It is redolent of a power which they would be unwise to challenge and both Persepolis and Germania proclaimed this to the full. In Persepolis it was first encountered on the great stairway leading to the Throne Room above it. Bas-reliefs of the Persian guards and the subject peoples climbing up bearing tribute covered the walls of this stairway. Together with the statues of the Great King and Ahuramazda above, this is one of the earliest and finest examples of the display of 'power in stone' and the effect it was clearly intended to produce. The height factor was very often used to force all who approached the seat of power to look up while the bearer of the supreme power looked down on them.

In modern times, one of the most strident examples of intimidation was Hitler's Reich Chancellery with what Sudjic called 'the long march to the Leader's desk'. The whole edifice was intended to display in an uncompromising manner the power of the Third Reich and its Führer. That this tactic was certainly a successful one is clear from the many encounters between Hitler and lesser rulers who had virtually given in to the demands made on them before even reaching the Leader's desk. 'New buildings are put up to strengthen our authority', proclaimed Hitler. At first they certainly did this, until they were bombed out of existence by a combined air power greater than anything that Hitler was able to muster.

The same intimidation as the Great Stairway and the Reich Chancellery would certainly also have been found on entering the grand portals of the Forbidden City or on approaching the Divans of the Mughal Emperors. If not intimidation, at least awe is still experienced when proceeding along the ceremonial ways leading to centres of power such as Versailles and the Palace of the Viceroy, now the Presidential Palace, in Delhi.

The great power which was implied and displayed by these magnificent capital cities was basically intended to be seen, initially at least, from outside. The real power was exercised well away from the display. In the Red Fort, while the Diwan-i-Am was the stage for the display of power, the inner Diwan-i-Khas was where the power really lay. In the Forbidden City it was the 'great within', while the great red walls of the Kremlin swathed a centre of power which allowed little intrusion from outside.

The display of power was thus essentially extramural while its exercise was strictly intramural. The great empires were never known for their consensual government. Democracy, as understood in Ancient Greece, was something quite alien to them. The direction of power was down rather than up; it was imposed from above and the size and grandeur of its buildings was intended to be a clear demonstration, for those who might have wished to challenge it, that this was so.

The initial acquisition of control, and then its consolidation and extension, has invariably necessitated the use of force, and this can be costly in terms of both lives and resources. Consequently another function of the imperial capital has always been to instil in the conquered peoples the inevitability of their being within the sphere of this power and the impossibility of escaping from it. In the most successful empires the subject peoples will then be persuaded to exchange their role from that of free peoples to that of willing subjects. In this way internal peace is brought about by means of consent rather than by constant reliance on repression. The surplus resources of the state can then be used for other purposes such as the extension of territory or the further embellishment of the capital. If and when consent ceases to be given, even the splendour of the capital will not be sufficient to save the ruler or his dynasty. New 'Cities and Thrones and Powers' will then become the inheritors of the fallen empire and new imperial states will attempt to create their own systems of control which inevitably require their own displays of power.

The stanza of Kipling's poem quoted at the beginning of this chapter concludes:

> But as new buds put forth
> To glad new men,
> Out of the spent and unconsidered Earth
> The Cities rise again.

At the present new buds are certainly putting forth with some vigour but it is yet to be seen what precisely will grow from them. However, whatever this may be it is certain that cities will continue to play a central role, as they have done in the past, both as the holders of power and as the symbols of it.

15

After Empire: Post-imperial Symbols of Power

Germania was the last serious attempt to create a city specifically designed to symbolize the rise of a new imperial state, while the shah's vainglorius return to Persepolis was the last endeavour to revive a long-vanished empire. Both were doomed to failure in the twentieth-century world in which the traditional forms of imperialism were rapidly being consigned to history. The post-imperial powers, which played an increasingly important role in international affairs after the Second World War, may have sought to legitimize themselves by the return to old imperial capitals, but their ideological justification had little to do with past empires. Although they were in so many ways the inheritors of empire, they rejected everything these empires had represented and proclaimed the beginning of a new era in history. Purpose-built capital cities, such as Brasilia, and earlier on Canberra in Australia, came into being, but they were basically intended as the administrative capitals of federal states rather than displays of imperial power. Smaller states, such as Nigeria, also built federal capitals designed largely to hold together diverse and frequently antagonistic populations.

However, there was one intriguing, and unexpected, exception to this general pattern of functional capitals. The Soviet Union had been the first of the post-imperial powers and it was also the first to come to an end. When this massive federation collapsed in 1991, fourteen new sovereign states sprung into being in its place. Five of these were in Central Asia while the others were in European Russia. Some of them had never existed before as independent states while others, such as Armenia, had long and distinguished histories before being conquered and incorporated into the Russian Empire. The Soviet Union had also brought a number of other states around its perimeter into its sphere of influence and it was here that the first signs of the most unexpected development took place.

The most significant part of the old Soviet sphere of influence was Eastern Europe, with its six so-called 'satellite' states. As the Soviet grip weakened in the later twentieth century these states became less inclined to follow slavishly the Soviet line and began to embark on paths of their own. The most assertive of them was Romania, which by the last quarter of the twentieth century had largely disengaged itself from the Soviet sphere and was following a highly independent course. This took place under President Nicolae Ceaușescu who was in effect the dictator of the country for the quarter of a century between 1965 and 1989. He instituted a policy of strict controls and centralization in many ways harsher even than the Soviet Union during the time of Stalin. Independent elements within the state were removed and all opposition was hunted down and crushed. The aim of the dictatorship was to obliterate all evidence of the pre-communist Romania, including its religion and historic buildings, and to produce a mechanistic communist state which in many ways resembled Fritz Lang's *Metropolis*.[1] The Romanian capital, Bucharest, was turned into the centre of this fearsome operation and intimidating symbols of power arose in place of the older buildings.

The principal symbol of the dictatorship was the enormous House of the Republic, the construction of which necessitated razing to the ground large areas of the old city. This destruction was given the functional name of 'systematization' and its objective was to build a new communist city almost literally on top of the old one. In this respect it very much resembled the Germania project in Nazi Germany and was driven by the same megalomaniac dreams of power. When finished the massive House of the Republic was the largest building in Europe and was intended to house the national parliament, a convention centre and a museum. It was above all designed to be the presidential palace, the official residence of Ceaușescu himself. The architecture of the building was a severe form of neoclassical, always the favoured style of the power-hungry, and it was reached by a series of high steps which bore the visitor upwards to the great halls of power.

One of the few earlier official structures in Bucharest not only to survive but to be converted by the regime for its own use was the Triumphal Arch. Built in the 1930s in the style of the Arc de Triomphe, what had been intended as a national symbol became a symbol of what Ceaușescu wanted his nation to be.

In front of the House of the Republic was a massive square intended for great parades and mass expressions of solidarity with the leadership. Such rallies of popular support took place frequently and from the balcony of the presidential residence Ceauşescu received the adulation of the masses and stimulated them to ever greater efforts. In 1989, as things were changing rapidly throughout the whole communist world, the masses failed in their adulation and the dictatorship was ousted. It is ironic that it was when the dictator was on the balcony of the great palace, haranguing the crowds, that the revolt began in the square below, soon seeing the end of the dictatorship and the summary execution of its leader.

Deep in the heart of Asia within the Soviet sphere something very similar had taken place rather earlier. Following the fall of the Qing dynasty, Mongolia, long part of the Qing empire, detached itself from China. Sukh Bator, who emerged as leader after a complicated civil war, was a communist and chose to ally his country with the new Soviet Union. As a consequence, in 1924 the People's Republic of Mongolia came into being as the world's second communist state. In the 1930s its dictator, Choibalsan, modelled himself closely on Stalin and in many ways behaved in much the way Ceauşescu was later to do. He unleashed a reign of terror on his country and brought about a fearful transformation. Most of the country's Buddhist temples were destroyed and the lamas slaughtered. Virtually all evidence of Buddhism, long the religion of the country, was eradicated. Even more, evidence of Mongolian pre-communist history removed and knowledge of their nation's past was denied to generations of Mongolians. All opposition to this policy was dealt with in the most brutal manner. Large parts of the capital Ulaanbataar were razed to the ground, in the same way as at Bucharest, and a massive square replaced them modelled on Red Square in Moscow.[2] On one side of this an impressive congress hall was built, in front of which was the massive tomb of the founder of the state, Sukh Bator. The whole complex was a colossal display of power and had a function almost identical to that of the squares in Moscow and Bucharest.

With the fall of the Soviet Union the communist regime in Mongolia also came to an end and was replaced by a government more in tune with the needs and desires of the people. Soon Sukh Bator had been replaced in the popular Mongolian affections by a return to Genghis Khan and a statue of the great leader was soon erected in the centre of the city. Significantly, Genghis Khan had been a great empire builder and the revival of knowledge of the country's history gave birth to the idea of reuniting the whole Mongolian people. Large numbers of Mongols and similar peoples lived in adjacent Russia and China, and for a time reunification became a very real – if totally unrealistic – objective.[3]

Perhaps the most megalomaniac development of all took palace in North Korea on the far eastern side of the communist world. There the communist dictator Kim Il-Sung embarked on the creation of a communist state resembling what took place in Choibalsan's Mongolia and Ceauşescu's Romania. However, the Korean dictator did not share the fate of his Romanian counterpart. After his death in 1994 his son Kim Jong-Il succeeded and so began the only process of dynastic succession in the communist world. Sabre-rattling and aggressive, this increasingly isolated state drew its power from intimidating its people and threatening its neighbours, in particular South Korea.[4] With the fall of the Soviet Union and the collapse of world communism, North Korea became even more aggressive in its stance and ever more harsh in its treatment of its own people.

By the end of the twentieth century the capital, Pyongyang, was filled with the symbols of power. After the manner of Bucharest, large parts of the old city were demolished to make way for spectacular new buildings. The Kumsusan Palace of the Sun was the centre of the power of the state and the official residence of Kim Il-Sung. The palace was built in the 'socialist-classical' style and looked out onto the huge Kim Il-Sung Square designed for military parades and popular assemblies. After the leader's death the palace became a mausoleum with the embalmed body of Kim as its centrepiece. Around his tomb are statues of grieving people. Enforced mass grief became one of the rituals associated with the death of the leader and this was extended even to the statues. During the period in which Kim Jong-Il was in power the policy of aggressiveness continued and North Korea, a country in which the majority of the people lived in considerable poverty, devoted its resources to becoming a nuclear power. Following his death in 2011, the embalmed body of Kim Jong-Il soon joined that of his father in the mausoleum. It is the largest mausoleum in the communist world and is an obligatory place of pilgrimage for all North Koreans.

Other massive structures in the capital are the Arch of Triumph, built in honour of the first Kim, and the Arch of Reunification demonstrating in stone one of the principal objectives of the foreign policy of the North Korean state. The massive Juche Tower overlooks Kim Il-Sung Square and is intended to be a statement in stone of Juche, the official ideology of the North Korean state.[5]

In 2011 the grandson of Kim Il-Sung, Kim Jong-Un, became dictator and this harsh and extraordinary state continued to behave in much the same way as before. On attaining power the young ruler first embarked on the by now virtually obligatory policy of aggressiveness towards the country's neighbours and also towards the United States, long considered to be the country's greatest enemy. While the world had changed radically this state, in many ways a relic of the Cold War, continued to harbour its own strange illusions of power and mission.

As has been observed, these three incongruous and bizarre states clung around the edges of the Soviet Union, which had been founded on the principles of egalitarian communism and a hatred for most things western including inequalities, class systems and hereditary monarchies. These peripheral states, while at first claiming to be upholders of these principles, proceeded over the years to move towards unequal and even quasi-monarchical systems. This was enshrined in their chosen symbolism, much of which could be classed as a bizarre kind of neo-imperialism.

The fall of the Soviet Union in 1991 soon produced more states which were in many ways similar to these. They were especially to be seen in former Soviet Central Asia and were born out of the old Soviet republics. Very soon they had reverted to being dictatorships even harsher than the ones they had replaced, the only real differences being that they replaced communism with nationalism and had a strong tendency to develop hereditary quasi-monarchical systems.

In Uzbekistan, Islam Karimov, who had been the leader of the Communist Party of Uzbekistan, became the first president of the new Republic of Uzbekistan. It was soon clear that he was determined to entrench himself in power and the presidential elections which continuously gave him huge majorities became ever more suspect. Uzbek nationalism replaced communism as the official ideology of the state and the Islamic religion, after a brief post-communist resurgence, was increasingly repressed. Corruption became rife and the Karimov family and its cronies came to occupy the choicest positions both in the state and the economy. The Karimov regime inherited the grand Uzbek capital Tashkent from the preceding regime. This had certainly been the most splendid city in the whole of the old Soviet Central Asia and had been intended as a showpiece for the triumph of communism in Asia. Under the Karimov regime this city was soon adapted from a display of the glory of the Soviets and of communism to the glory of Uzbekistan and its history. The old pre-communist city of Tashkent had been largely razed to the ground during the communist period and very little of it remained. The official buildings grouped around the grand central square collectively made a suitable backdrop, inherited from the communists, for the display of the newly rediscovered splendours of Uzbekistan. In the centre of the square, an equestrian statue of Timur Lenk, based on the Bronze Horseman in St Petersburg, became its most striking feature. This was intended to link contemporary Uzbekistan with its greatest historical hero and with the Timurid dynasty that followed.

The mausoleum of Timur in Samarkand and the great statue of his grandson, Ulugh Beg, nearby also became new places of pilgrimage. Significantly Timur, like Genghis Khan, had been a great empire builder, and as a result the idea of being the heirs to an illustrious empire, this time an Asiatic one, rather than a European import, was soon implanted in the minds of the Uzbek people. One striking building on the edge of the square in the traditional Timurid architectural style was actually built in 1970 to house the Museum of Lenin.[6] After 1991 all evidence of Lenin was removed and the building was reincarnated as the museum of Uzbek history. An enormous mural in the entrance gallery displays the great heroes of Uzbek history and, as would be expected, Timur looms large. However, leading the cavalcade of Uzbek heroes is Karimov, positioned as the great contemporary hero firmly carrying on the great traditions of the Uzbek nation.[7] A whole hagiography has now been developed around Karimov as heir to Timur who, interestingly, himself claimed to be heir to Genghis Khan. In Tashkent, built originally for the display of communism in Central Asia, Asian architecture was used to link communism with the culture of the region. Now this same architecture has been converted to symbolize the Central Asian, and in particular the Uzbek, identity, a change accomplished with considerable ease.

Neighbouring Kazakhstan is by far the largest of the five Central Asian post-Soviet republics. The chairman of the Council of Ministers of the Kazak SSR had been Nursultan Nazarbaev and in 1990 he was selected to be the first president of the new republic. The capital of the Kazak SSR was Almaty (formerly Alma Ata), situated on the edge of the magnificent snow-capped mountains in the south. Despite this backdrop, the city was far less impressive than Tashkent and was not built on the grand scale of the Uzbek capital. Tashkent, as has been observed, was designed for a far wider role. However, Kazakhstan is well endowed with reserves of gas and oil and this soon enabled the

The National Museum of Uzbekistan, Tashkent. This originally housed the Lenin Museum but after the fall of the Soviet Union its Timurid architecture made it a good symbol for the new independent state.

new country to engage in a number of major projects. The biggest of these was the building of a completely new capital city, Astana. This became the official capital in 1997 and is in a more central location in relation to the country as a whole. It was on the site of the old town of Akmola, large parts of which were demolished to make way for the new city.[8]

Originally intended as an administrative city after the manner of Brasilia, it also had the objective of unifying this large and diverse country and of helping to secure its place in the world. The Palace of Peace and Accord, the architect for which was Norman Foster, was originally intended for this purpose and treaties laying the foundations for pan-Asiatic cooperation were signed there. The nearby Glass Pyramid contains a display of the various faiths to be found in the country and to which tolerance is extended. Like the rest of this part of Central Asia, Kazakhstan had before the Soviet period been mainly a Muslim country but the suppression of religion under the Soviets gave place to a more enlightened approach.

Towards the end of the century things began to change. In 1999 Nazarbaev was re-elected president and from then on his new Fatherland political party dominated the Kazakh parliament. There was a crackdown on the opposition and Islamists and their activities were highly curtailed. At further elections Nazarbaev continued to be re-elected by implausibly large margins. As the power of the president became more entrenched, the capital became more ambitious and grandiose. The early internationalism has been replaced by a greater emphasis on nationalism and this came to be reflected in the capital. Today Astana has a number of highly impressive buildings designed to reflect the glory of Kazakhstan and the power of the president. The splendid Orda Presidential Palace is in a prominent position. Kazakhstan cannot claim a historic figure of the stature of either Genghis Khan or Timur but important former leaders have been used to emphasize past glories. The Bayterek Tower supports a sphere and a statue of Kenesary Khan, a nationalist who had fought against the Russians. To commemorate the seventieth birthday of Nazarbaev in 2010 an enormous tent was erected covering a large part of the centre of the city. This was given the name of the Khan Shatyr after another Kazak national hero.

Kazakhs have a long history as conquerors and the twenty-first-century additions to the capital are very much intended to demonstrate that contemporary Kazakhstan is in this great tradition. As with other Central Asian countries such as Mongolia and Uzbekistan, nationalism has replaced communism as the official state ideology and this has been reflected in the increasing splendour of the new capital. The historical Central Asian imperialism has found new, and quite unexpected, outlets.

Thus around the peripheries of the old Soviet Union, and since 1991 within the corpse of the fallen communist giant itself, are evidences of the desire for the kind of grandeur associated with the great regimes of the past. Virtually all vestiges of communism have been jettisoned with little compunction and there was a rapid reversion to the kind of power associated with earlier regimes. Often this has been symbolized in extreme forms. However, as with the shah in the 1970s, these dreams of recreating past glory are completely unrealistic. They are examples of attempts to revive an old form of power quite inappropriate to today's world. Most strange of all has been their particular association not with capitalist states but with the great communist state dedicated to the creation of a new and more egalitarian world. It seems that the dream of this new world has been rapidly transformed into a nightmare version of the old world at its most intemperate. With its fall, egalitarian communism gave birth to very unegalitarian dictatorship. The opposite of the original ideal has prevailed and this change has been very much symbolized in the capital cities.

In the capitalist world a very different situation has prevailed and this has been reflected in its symbols. The historic capitals examined in this book have usually been centres of absolute power. Virtually every aspect of state power has been contained within their walls. At their most absolute, such capitals attained complete control over vast territories. With the rise of democracy in the western world a very different political situation came to prevail. This entailed a devolution of power away from the centre which inevitably had a profound effect on the capitals themselves. Elements of power became more localized and many aspects of activity were detached from direct state control. These have included cultural, religious, educational and social activities and, perhaps most significantly, economic power. As economies have grown more complex, and industry has developed more widely, usually in response to the geographical potential of different regions, the devolution of economic power has become ever more necessary to allow for its proper functioning. At the heart of this has been control over finance, which by the seventeenth century had become the most essential requirement for the generation of new economic development. This has resulted in the rise of financial centres which have been to a large extent inde-pendent, and often quite geographically separate, from the centres of political power.

In states with long democratic histories something of this sort has been a feature for a very long time. In the case of London the separation of Westminster, with its royal and subsequently parliamentary power, and the City with its business and financial power has been a feature over many centuries. In effect there have been two cities which are con-tiguous but have developed quite different and separate functions within the state. The Civil War of the seventeenth century, although generally presented as Crown versus Parliament – in other words something taking place within Westminster itself – was rooted also in the confrontation between these two centres of power within the capital.

As the move towards forms of devolution developed further, so the emergence of an alternative centre of power became a concomitant and this alternative centre was often geographically separate. This was very much in evidence in the United States, which gained its independence in the late eighteenth century. Here the separation was to be seen early on between the two cities of Washington and New York, respectively the centres of political and financial power. Following the country's independence from Britain, it was decided to build the new capital, to be called Washington after the first president, and the site was chosen because of its central location in relation to the original thirteen states of the union. However, from the outset, the powers of the federal government were highly limited both by those which remained vested in the individual states and by a system of government based on checks and balances which gave the president only a limited say over the country's internal affairs.

By the nineteenth century New York was growing into the country's most important alternative centre of power and gathering a great deal of cultural, educational, business and commercial activity. Most importantly, it was becoming the national financial centre, a role it maintained and enhanced during the twentieth century. Located at the mouth of the Hudson river and having good communications with the interior of the country via the Hudson-Mohawk gap, the city has grown up on a number of adjacent islands and peninsulas which from the outset made internal communications difficult. Furthermore, there were constraints on suitable building land and as the city grew this became ever more problematic. The city centred on Manhattan Island, the southern part of which soon developed into the main financial quarter. The urgent requirement for more accommodation was solved in a way that was at the time entirely new. It was the idea of building ever higher, and with the development of new architectural techniques and engineering possibilities the first 'skyscrapers' came into existence in the late nineteenth century.

By the early twentieth century these were being built on a huge scale and the competition among them resulted in their going up ever higher. This all rapidly transformed the Manhattan skyline into something that had never existed before. In 1931 came the most splendid of all the skyscrapers, the Empire State Building, which was higher than anything previously built in the world.[9] Faced using oolitic limestone, it was certainly a clear demonstration of the new power in stone, a power that was present in New York more than any other city at that time.

The name of this magnificent building, Empire State, comes from an old nickname for New York. Many explanations have been given for this, including its pre-eminence among the states of the union. Another is that it proclaims 'the imperial power of liberty' which invokes the symbolism of the Statue of Liberty and its effect on the migrants who arrived in the New World hoping for a better life. In their Portrait of New York, written in 1939, Riesenberg and Alland asserted that, 'We will discover and uncover this new Imperial City of Today, celebrating its peak of arrogance.'[10] If New York were deemed 'imperial' it was certainly at the time a significant and novel use of the term. Yet it accords with the pre-eminence of this city among all the others in the United States. A telling assertion around this time made by a member of the Federal Writers Project was that, because of its monopoly of finance and business, New York had been for years virtually the capital of the United States. This same writer went on to dismiss Washington as being 'merely the loud-speaker through which New York announced itself'.[11] There can hardly have been a more powerful proclamation than this of the new form of power in the land.

The very different architecture of the two cities was a clear demon-stration of a profound functional difference between them. By the middle of the twentieth century New York's buildings were not only able to strike the newcomer with something akin to awe, but they also become the principal symbols of the new form of autonomous power deriving from business and finance. This symbolism had at first been inadvertent, imposed on the city by the necessities of the limited space available for further growth. However, it was soon transformed into something iconic of a rival power which was quite separate and different from that of the capital itself.

During the later twentieth century in other democratic states a similar devolution of power has also taken place and the New York type of symbolism has come to be widely copied. In the German Federal Republic, a high degree of devolution has always been the norm and from the beginning Berlin has been entrusted with only a limited range of powers. Frankfurt became the financial capital and its high-rise modern buildings are symbolic of their function.[12] During the twenty-first century, one of the most spectacular such developments has taken place in China. In the 1980s the country moved away from the hardline communism of Mao to embrace a free-market economy under Deng Xiaoping. He transformed the country by introducing the so-called 'socialist market economy' and embraced capitalism pragmatically in a way which would have been quite inconceivable during the time of Mao. The principal financial centre of the new China has been Shanghai. This old port city, with its powerful international trading links dating back to the nineteenth century, was well equipped to lead the trans-formational change in China. This produced a massive building programme resulting in the old skyline of the 'Bund' being replaced by a new skyline of high-rise buildings. Some of these boast the most fanciful and astonishing architectural designs and collectively they make a powerful statement of the arrival of China as a powerful player on the world economic scene. They are also symbolic of the tremendous transformation which has taken place in China since the Mao era.

While the development of an alternative centre of power within a single state, together with the architectural symbolism associated with it, has been a most significant development, there has been another even more spectacular one. This is the rise of new centres of financial and economic activity outside the territories of the large states. These constitute new forms of city-states, and many of those which have flourished since the Second World War are the remnants of old maritime empires, notably the British. Both Hong Kong and Singapore are city-states that emerged out of the end of the British Empire.[13] Originally intended as the bases of imperial naval, political and economic power in their regions, they have since evolved into important business and financial centres and the rapid building of skyscrapers has produced what has become the characteristic new skyline of such places. Like New York, constraints of space have been an important factor in both of them, so to build upwards, beside being symbolic, has been a natural thing to do.

The biggest concentration of city-states of this sort is now in the Persian Gulf and here some of the most spectacular architectural projects have been undertaken. While during the twentieth century oil became the most important resource in the Gulf, business and finance are now of paramount importance. Qatar and Bahrain are among the most important and both have achieved important roles in the business world.

The United Arab Emirates is a grouping of seven sovereign city-states of a similar type.[14] One of its member states, Dubai, has since the 1980s been transformed into the largest business hub in the Middle East. The city also has some of the most spectacular new architecture and the first skyscraper in the Middle East, significantly called the Dubai World Trade Centre, was opened here in 1979. This was followed by a host of similar buildings, notable among which have been the Emirates Tower and the Al Kazim Twin Towers. There are other new buildings on an artificial island just offshore. Most spectacular of all, in 2010 the Burj Khalifa skyscraper was completed. At 828 m, this became the tallest building in the world just as the Empire State Building had 80 years earlier. With numerous Arab architectural features, it is in many ways the ultimate expression of the symbolism not only of the power of business and finance but of the Middle East region itself.

While clearly not completely replacing the old power, this new form of power has since the late twentieth century moved into the position of being the most important element in the running of the global business and financial world. The success of many nations increasingly depends more on the policies embarked on in these great financial centres than on anything their own governments can do. The latter have often proved powerless to challenge the agility of business in locating and relocating in accordance with what is perceived to be their own interests rather than those of the states in which they happen to be at any particular time. The unmistakable symbols of this new power are its buildings, in much the same way as with old power in the past. Political intimidation may have given place to forms of financial intimidation but symbolism remains an essential ingredient of the whole process. The desire to build ever higher has led to considerable architectural competition among rival centres, both in the Gulf and elsewhere, so asserting in stone the power that has become a major force in the twenty-first-century world.

As has been seen, the last attempt to revive an ancient empire died just across the Gulf in the sands of southern Iran in the 1970s. At the time the shah's futile imperial charade was taking place in his empire's ancient capital, on the other side of the Gulf the Dubai World Trade Centre was already taking shape. Within a few decades of the end of the shah's quasi-imperial rule, the Burj Khalifa skyscraper was stridently proclaiming the significance of a very different form of power. This and the many other spectacular buildings rising in the adjacent city-states look out across the Gulf towards the centre of the empire which ruled the world over two millennia ago. Just as Persepolis was built to be the symbol of that ancient *imperium*, so the new buildings are symbols a new *imperium*, which has become a major force in shaping the world of the twenty-first century.

In this new world the attempts to perpetuate old power have continued but they have proved absurdly unrealistic in their aspirations. Money and resources have been squandered on creating the illusion of some kind of quasi-great power but the translation of such illusions into any kind of reality has proved impossible. Of course, the great new symbols of financial power have also entailed the expenditure of great wealth. In the competition to assert power, ever-more fantastic architecture has been employed in buildings, the practical uses of which have often been far from clear. The intentions behind the excesses of Pyongyang's Kumsusan Palace of the Sun and the Burj Khalifa do not appear to have been that different. Both were seeking to convey the idea of power in stone and both entered into the realms of fantasy in order to achieve it.

Since the financial crisis which began in 2008, many of the buildings intended for the display of the new power have in many ways proved to be white elephants. They have drained resources in much the same way as did those of the past and the consequences have been not dissimilar. The financial as well as political results of the irresponsible squandering of wealth in the twenty-first century have proved in many ways quite as serious as the follies of Shah Jehan and Louis XIV in the seventeenth. The new form of power has yet to establish itself as a credible alternative to the old before it can seriously be seen as its legitimate heir, let alone a desirable development for mankind as a whole.

There are many possible paths which such a desirable course might follow but one which would detach itself most absolutely from the old could well be a contemporary version of Aristotle's 'good life', which the philosopher saw as being the one facilitated by the Greek *polis*.[15] To attain this, the possession of financial wealth is an essential prerequisite and the holders and providers of such wealth inevitably become crucially important. However, the *polis* achieved what it did not just because of its wealth but because of the political restraints placed on it; it was successful in Aristotelian terms above all because of the liberties it engendered and the use to which these were put. Unless this is done, and the wealth generated used for the wider good, its creators are on course to become the new emperors and tsars of the world rather than its liberators.

To liberate wealth for the wider benefit of humanity will certainly be a hard task necessitating the clarification of ideas about what such benefits may be expected to bring. If this process requires symbols, they are certainly not likely to be found in ever-larger palaces or ever-higher skyscrapers. Perhaps they can most appropriately be identified in less spectacular projects such as Bournville in Birmingham or New Lanark in Scotland. In them the ideals of philanthropic business people such as the Cadbury family and Robert Owen were put into practice to produce environments where the lives of human beings could be happier and more fulfilled. It may be that this is what 'the imperial power of liberty' really means.

APPENDIX
The Terminology of Empire and Imperialism

The terminology of empire and imperialism generally used in English is mainly of Latin origin and is derived from the Roman Empire. Although other similar states have used their own terminology to describe the various aspects of power, the Latin ones have nevertheless usually been accepted. In this list these terms and their meanings are explained.

Res Publica
Public good, republic. The Roman Republic came into being with the end of the monarchy in 510 BC.

Italia
Italy south of the Rubicon river. This was deemed to be the homeland of the Romans, and military commanders were not permitted to enter it or, in other words, to 'cross the Rubicon' at the head of their armies. The crossing of the Rubicon by Julius Caesar at the head of his army in 49 BC challenged the authority of the Senate and precipitated civil war. This marked the beginning of the end of the Roman Republic and the institution of Imperial rule.

Imperium
Originally the authority or power granted by the Roman Senate for the government of a province. Normally this was restricted to a particular province outside which the Imperium granted would lapse.

Imperium Proconsulare
Authority given by an official of the state for the performance of some specific task.

Imperium Populi Romani
Authority given by the Senate on behalf of the Roman people.

Imperium Maius
Unlimited authority given to Octavian in 27 BC which effectively marked the beginning of the Roman Empire.

Imperator
The name given to the holder of such authority.

Fasces
The bundle of rods with an axe which was the symbol of the authority given to the bearer.

Princeps
Title given to the emperor which gave him all the forms of authority rolled into one. Some later emperors even extended this to *Optimus Princeps*, which meant authority transcending all others.

Augustus
The name taken by the first emperor and subsequently used by later emperors to denote their office.

Caesar
Name frequently given to junior emperors and heirs to the Imperial throne.

Pax Romana
The peace and order provided throughout the Roman Empire.

Imperium Orbis Terrarum
Roman power and control over the whole world. The world as understood by the Romans was the Roman Empire. It was only during the reign of Hadrian that the idea of setting limits on the size of the empire came into being. The lands outside it were inhabited by barbarians and therefore deemed to be of little account.

REFERENCES

Prologue: Symbols of Power

1 F. Braudel, *The Mediterranean in the Ancient World* (London, 2001), p. 83.
   Braudel points out that Morenz considered the divinity of the pharaoh to
   have been the central 'political theory' of ancient Egypt (S. Morenz, *Egyptian
   Religion* (London 1973)).
2 N. MacGregor, *A History of the World in 100 Objects* (London, 2010), pp. 125–9.
3 This is really poetic licence on the part of Shelley since the statue actually
   conveys the impression of a benign ruler. More probably it was its colossal
   size and royal headgear which would have conveyed the impression of
   power to those who saw it.
4 See chapter Fifteen.
5 L. Mumford, *The City in History* (London, 1975).
6 This classification was implicit in the works of Halford Mackinder. The
   political geographer identified the main distinction as being between land
   empires and sea empires but he also pointed to the considerable political
   importance of the marginal areas located between the two. Mackinder's
   theory is set out in his article, 'The Geographical Pivot of History',
   Geographical Journal, XXIII/4 (1904), and he later elaborated this in his
   book, *Democratic Ideals and Reality: A Study in the Politics of Reconstruction*
   (London, 1919).
7 J. Marozzi, *Tamerlane: Sword of Islam, Conqueror of the World* (London, 2004),
   p. 33.

1 Persepolis and the Persian Empire

1 R. N. Sharp, *The Inscriptions in Old Persian Cuneiform of the Achaemenian
   Emperors*, Central Council of the Celebrations of the 25th Century of the
   Foundation of the Iranian Empire (Tehran, 1971).
2 H. Loveday, 'Ferdusi and the Shahnameh', in *The Odyssey Illustrated Guide to
   Iran* (Hong Kong, 1997), p. 38.
3 J. Gloag, *The Architectural Interpretation of History* (London, 1975), p. 58.

4 Sharp, *Inscriptions in Old Persian Cuneiform*, p. 87.

5 W. H. Forbis, *Fall of the Peacock Throne* (New York and London, 1980).

6 Sharp, *Inscriptions in Old Persian Cuneiform*, p. 87.

7 J. Hicks, *The Persians* (New York, 1975), p. 28.

8 G. Parker, *Sovereign City* (London, 2004), pp. 47–56.

9 Ibid., pp. 52–4.

2 'Three Romes': City-state, Imperium and Christian Capital

1 The Apollinarians were a heretical sect, founded in the middle of the fourth century by Apollinaris of Laodicea, which denied that Christ had a human soul. This heresy was condemned by the Council of Chalcedon in 451. Filofei must have believed that this was the cause of the fall of Rome but in reality it had little to do with it. The end of the western Roman Empire is generally considered to have taken place a quarter of a century later in 476 when the last emperor, Romulus Augustulus, was deposed by a barbarian chieftain.

2 A. Voyce, *Moscow and the Roots of Russian Culture* (Newton Abbot, 1972), p. 16.

3 V. Cornish, *The Great Capitals* (London, 1923). Vaughan Cornish put forward the theory of the 'forward capital' which was close to the most dynamic or endangered frontier. Such a capital was well located for the direction of military activity in the frontier areas. If the frontier was an expanding one, and as a result territory was gained, such a capital would sometimes be moved forward to keep as close as possible to the new theatre of operations.

4 G. Parker, *Sovereign City* (London, 2004), pp. 64–5.

5 E. Gibbon, *The Decline and Fall of the Roman Empire* [1776–88] (London, 1995), vol. III, p. 1062.

6 See Appendix on the terminology of empire.

7 Eusabius of Caesaria, *Life of Constantine*, from M. J. Cohen and J. Major, *History in Quotations* (London, 1904), p. 90.

8 E. Ludwig, *The Mediterranean: Saga of a Sea* (London, 1943), p. 202.

9 J. Gloag, *The Architectural Interpretation of History* (London, 1975), p. 127.

10 R. Browning, *The Byzantine Empire* (London, 1980), p. 29.

11 T. Hunczak, ed., *Russian Imperialism from Ivan the Great to the Revolution* (New Brunswick, NJ, 1974), pp. 106–7.

12 The Russian for Red Square is *Krasnaya Ploshad*, which also means 'Beautiful Square'. In Russian, red is equated with beauty and this may have contributed to the amount of red in the centre of Moscow, most notably the great outer walls of the Kremlin. In the twentieth century this fitted in well with red being the chosen colour of revolution.

3 Constantinople and the New Lords of the Golden Horn

1 George Trapezuntios to Mehmed the Conqueror, 1466, quoted in
  P. Mansel, *Constantinople: City of the World's Desire* (London, 1995), p. 1.
2 P. Mansel, *Constantinople: City of the World's Desire, 1453–1924* (London, 2006), p. 21.
3 Ibid., p. 35.

4 From Karakorum to Shakhrisabz: Centres of Power of the Imperial Nomads

1 The Tartars were a tribe who lived near to the Mongols in their central Asian homelands. They were among the first to be defeated and brought into the growing Mongol Empire. The early Russian accounts of the Mongol invasions confused these people with the Mongols and from then on the Russians called them Tatars. The Mongol occupation of the Russian lands is known in Russian history as the period of 'the Tatar Yoke'.
2 V. Yan, *Jenghiz-Khan*, trans. L. E. Britton (London, 1943), p. 254.
3 O. Steeds, 'The Hidden Grave of History's Greatest Warrior', *Newsweek* (10 December 2012). The homeland of the Mongol people is the Onon-Kerulen region of eastern Mongolia and it is generally believed that Genghis Khan was buried there. This was generally thought of as being 'sacred space' by the Mongol people and many of the kuriltais, the great gatherings of the Mongol nobility, took place there. See chapter Six note 2.
4 P. Ratchnevsky, *Genghis Khan: His Life and Legacy*, trans. T. N. Haining (Oxford, 1991), pp. 96–8.
5 O. and E. Lattimore, *Silks, Spices and Empire: Asia Seen through the Eyes of its Discoverers* (London, 1975), p. 78.
6 Ibid., p. 79.
7 *The Travels of Marco Polo the Venetian*, ed. John Masefield (London, 1911), p. 169.
8 Ibid.
9 O. and E. Lattimore, *Silks, Spices and Empire*, p. 89.
10 Samuel Purchas's travel book, *Purchas His Pilgrimage* (1613), purports to be a history of the world in sea voyages and travel. Allegedly Coleridge was reading this book when he fell into a drug-induced sleep. Purchas paints a vivid picture of the palace of 'Kubla Khan', with its splendid natural surroundings. Much of Purchas's writing was based on the work of Hakluyt and the accounts of early travellers.
11 He is known by various names but Timur or Temur appears to be the most accurate transliteration. The suffix Lenk, meaning 'lame', refers to the disability from which he suffered as a result of an injury sustained in an early battle. In his play, Christopher Marlowe altered his name to 'Tamburlaine' and this was a name by which he subsequently came to be widely known. The generally accepted spelling of his name today is 'Tamerlane'.

12 J. Ure, *The Trail of Tamerlane* (London, 1980), p. 170.

13 Ibid., p. 189.

14 A. S. Beveridge, trans., *Memoirs of Babur* (London, 1922).

15 J. Marozzi, *Tamerlane: Sword of Islam, Conqueror of the World* (London, 2005), p. 227.

16 Ibid., p. 201.

17 G. Moorhouse, *Apples in the Snow: A Journey to Samarkand* (London, 1991), p. 161.

18 Marozzi, *Tamerlane*, p. 39.

5 Power over East Asia: The Forbidden City and the Middle Kingdom

1 V. Cornish, *The Great Capitals* (London, 1923).

2 O. Sirén, *The Imperial Palaces of Peking*, quoted in A. Cotterell, *The Imperial Capitals of China* (London, 2007), p. 226.

3 F. Dorn, *The Forbidden City* (New York, 1970,) p. 14.

4 O. Sitwell, *Escape with Me* (1939), quoted in *The Travellers' Dictionary of Quotation*, ed. P. Yapp (London, 1983), p. 89.

5 Dun J. Li, *The Ageless Chinese: A History* (New York, 1965), p. 301.

6 Cotterell, *Imperial Capitals of China*, p. 25.

7 Quoted in A. Peyrefitte, *The Collision of Two Civilisations: The British Expedition to China, 1792–94*, trans. J. Rothschild (London, 1993), p. 192.

8 Ibid., pp. 303–4.

9 O. E. Clubb, *Twentieth Century China* (New York and London, 1965), p. 43.

6 Power over South Asia: The 'Seven Cities' of Delhi and the *Saptusindhu* Capital Region

1 P. Spear, *Delhi* (Oxford, 1945), p. 1.

2 The geopolitical term 'core region' means the historical centre or heart of a state or nation. In most cases the state will have been formed by expansion from this region. It is there that the capital city is normally located, together with other important features such as the principal centre of the national church, universities and cultural monuments. Its location is the result of a variety of factors, important among which are centrality and ease of communication. It can be thought of as being the brain in the body of the state. It may also be the economic centre of the state, although in modern times this has in most countries become less the case. It may also be seen as being the home of a nation or people and so will be vested with a special place in their affections. Over time it gains a rather mystic aura, and the term 'sacred space' has been used to describe this. In many cases, such as in the Persepolis region, it gives way to other regions but it will for long continue to retain its special and 'sacred' hold.

3 Spear, *Delhi*, pp. 26–9.

4 Ibid., p. 12.

5 Ibid., p. 28.

6 O.K.H. Spate and A.T.A. Learmonth, *India and Pakistan*, 3rd edn (London, 1967), p. 5.

7 Spear, *Delhi*, p. 33.

8 Ibid.

9 A. S. Beveridge, trans., *Memoirs of Babur* (London, 1922).

10 J. Fergusson, *History of Indian and Eastern Architecture* (London, 1910). James Fergusson was a Victorian architectural historian who spent much time travelling around the subcontinent. He rated Indian, and especially Mughal, architecture very highly. In addition to his comments on Fatehpur Sikri, he was of the opinion that, 'The palace at Delhi is . . . the most magnificent palace in the East, perhaps the world.' By the 'palace' he meant, of course, the Red Fort, and he condemned the British administration of the time for not doing more to preserve it and other Indian historical buildings.

11 Lovat Fraser, *At Delhi* (1903), in L. Nicholson, *The Red Fort, Delhi* (London, 1989), p. 80.

12 Nicholson, *The Red Fort*.

13 F. Bernier, *Travels in the Mogul Empire*, ed. A. Constable and V. A. Smith (Oxford, 1934), pp. 60–70.

14 J. Keay, *A History of India* (London, 2000), p. 334.

15 Spear, *Delhi*, p. 61.

16 Palam is a village a short distance away from Delhi. The couplet signifies that by the time of Shah Alam the territory of the Great Mughals, once the rulers of the greater part of the subcontinent, had shrunk to little more than the area around the capital itself.

7 Global Power: Philip II and the Escorial

1 G. Parker, *Sovereign City* (London, 2004), p. 158.

2 Ibid., p. 159.

3 A. F. Calvert, *An Historical and Descriptive Account of the Spanish Royal Palace, Monastery and Mausoleum* (London, 1911), pp. 27–8.

4 Ibid., p. 54.

5 J. H. Elliott, *Imperial Spain, 1469–1716* (London, 1990), p. 253.

6 F. Braudel, *The Mediterranean and the Mediterranean World in the Age of Philip II* (London, 1972), p. 687.

7 H. Belloc, *Places* (1942), quoted in *The Travellers' Dictionary of Quotation*, ed. P. Yapp (London, 1983), p. 766.

8 Elliott, *Imperial Spain*, p. 249.

8 Grandeur: Louis XIV and Versailles

1 H.A.L. Fisher, *History of Europe* (London, 1977), p. 628. The Count of Olivares was the chief minister of Philip IV of Spain in the middle of the

seventeenth century. Together with his sovereign he attempted to revive the greatness his country had achieved in the previous century but was unsuccessful even in holding the Iberian peninsula together. In 1640 Portugal regained its independence and Catalonia continued to retain a strong sense of independent identity. Fisher attributes this lack of success to the fact that, unlike France, Spain lacked a really effective geographical centre of power which could be used to pull the country together.

2 D. Seward, *The Bourbon Kings of France* (London, 1976), p. 80.

3 A. Panicucci, *The Life and Times of Louis XIV*, trans. A. Mondatori (London, 1965), p. 36.

4 N. Pevsner, *An Outline of European Architecture* (London, 1978).

5 M. Ashley, *Louis XIV and the Grandeur of France* (1946), quoted in A.E.J. Morris, *History of Urban Form Before the Industrial Revolution* (London, 1996), p. 212.

6 Seward, *Bourbon Kings of France*, p. 71.

9 St Petersburg and the Imperial Vision of Peter the Great

1 L. Hughes, *Russia in the Age of Peter the Great* (New Haven and London, 1998), p. 210.

2 Ibid., p. 40.

3 Ibid., p. 212.

4 M. Raeff, *Understanding Imperial Russia*, trans. A. Goldhammer (New York, 1984), p. 47.

5 Ibid., p. 76.

6 J. H. Bater, 'The Further Development of the City: The Important Role of the Masonry Commission', in *St Petersburg: Industrialisation and Change* (Montreal, 1976). Extract published in L. Kelly, *St Petersburg* (London, 1981), p. 31.

7 Seleucus founded the Hellenistic Seleucid Empire in 305 BC. He took the title of Nicator and built his first capital just to the north of Babylon, giving it the name Seleucia-on-Tigris. Even before his new capital had been finished he transferred his seat of government to Antioch-on-Orontes, close to the Mediterranean. Toynbee considered this to have been a big mistake since it took the capital away from the richest part of the empire and its natural core region. A. Toynbee, *Cities on the Move* (London, 1970). See chapter Six note 2 on core regions.

8 A. Toynbee, *A Study of History* (Oxford, 1954), vol. VII, p. 195.

9 The political and historical geographer Halford Mackinder proposed a theory of history based on the idea that the greatest conflict throughout history has been that between the maritime and the continental powers. He examined the long conflict between the Greeks and the Persians which he considered to be an early example of this. By the nineteenth and early twentieth centuries the great global conflict was between the British and the Russian empires and this he considered to be the contemporary version

of the age-old maritime–continental conflict which had dominated history. See G. Parker, *Western Geopolitical Thought in the 20th Century* (London, 1985), chapter Three.

10 Ghosts of Glory: Postscripts to Power

1 W. Schneider, *Babylon is Everywhere: The City as Man's Fate*, trans. I. Sammet and J. Oldenburg (London, 1960), p. 211.
2 J. Saramago, *Journey to Portugal*, trans. A. Hopkinson and N. Caistor (London, 2000), p. 334.
3 R. Pattee, *Portugal and the Portuguese World* (Milwaukee, 1957), p. 147.
4 J. Kotkin, *The City: A Global History* (London, 2005), p. 74.
5 J. Morris, *A Writer's World* (London, 2003), p. 68.
6 Schneider, *Babylon is Everywhere*, p. 221.
7 E. de Waal, *The Hare with Amber Eyes: A Hidden Inheritance* (London, 2011), p. 113.
8 Ibid., p. 249.
9 I. Barea, *Vienna: Legend and Reality* (London, 1992), p. 241.
10 Ibid., p. 44.
11 A. Loos (1898), in Barea, *Vienna*, p. 257.
12 Quoted in de Waal, *Hare with Amber Eyes*, chapter Twelve, 'Die Potemkinische Stadt', pp. 116–17.
13 J. Fest, *Not Me: Memoirs of a German Childhood*, trans. M. Chalmers (London, 2012), p. 162.

11 Apex or Decline? New Delhi and British Imperial Power

1 The residence of the governor general and later the viceroy in Calcutta was built in 1799 during the period when Richard Wellesley was governor general and his brother Arthur Wellesley, later the Duke of Wellington, was the head of the Indian armed forces. It is in the style of an eighteenth-century English stately home and the one chosen as the model was Kedleston Hall in Derbyshire. This was the home of the Curzon family and Lord Curzon, one of the more remarkable of the viceroys, was a later occupant of the Calcutta residence. He must have been very much at home there and this may have been a contributory factor to his opposition to the move of the capital to Delhi, although the old capital would have been more suitable for the implementation of his foreign policy. See note 3.
2 Y. M. Goblet, *The Twilight of Treaties* (London, 1936), p. 101.
3 Lord Curzon, statesman and eminent geographer, was the viceroy of India from 1899 to 1905. He believed that secure frontiers were of paramount importance to the security of any state and formed the opinion that the security of the British Indian Empire could best be ensured by creating a line of friendly buffer states around its borders. This was one of the main

reasons for his active support of the Younghusband Mission to Tibet in 1904. The main object of this was to bring that country into the British sphere of influence, thereby denying it to the Russians whom he was convinced had their eye on India. The mission to Tibet was a complete failure and Curzon's aggressive frontier policy was not supported by the British Liberal government which came to power in 1906. It was reversed by subsequent viceregal administrations. See N. Curzon, *Frontiers*, The Romanes Lecture (Oxford, 1907).

4 J. Morris with S. Winchester, *Stones of Empire: The Buildings of the Raj* (Oxford, 1986), p. 80.
5 W. Dalrymple, 'The Rubble of the Raj', *The Times* (13 November 2004), Arts, pp. 18–19.
6 Morris and Winchester, *Stones of Empire*, p. 80.
7 W. Dalrymple, *City of Djinns* (London, 1993), p. 82.
8 P. Spear, *Delhi* (Oxford, 1945), p. 100.
9 Dalrymple, 'Rubble of the Raj'.

12 Architects of Empire: Hitler, Speer and the Germania Project

1 Quoted in T. Friedrich, *Hitler's Berlin: Abused City* (New Haven and London, 2012), p. 21.
2 Ibid., p. 26.
3 Ibid., p. 21.
4 *Hitler's Table Talk*, 1941–44, ed. M. Borman, introd. H. Trevor-Roper (Oxford, 1988), p. 45.
5 Quoted in A. Richie, *Faust's Metropolis: A History of Berlin* (London, 1998), pp. 470–71.
6 *Hitler's Table Talk*, p. 710.
7 Quoted in Richie, *Faust's Metropolis*, p. 471.
8 Ibid., p. 466.
9 Ibid., p. 467.
10 *Hitler's Table Talk*, p. 523.
11 D. Sudjic, *The Edifice Complex: How the Rich and Powerful – and their Architects – Shape the World* (London, 2006), p. 12.
12 *Hitler's Table Talk*, p. 81.
13 J. Morris, *A Writer's World: Travels, 1950–2000* (London, 2003), p. 66.
14 Quoted in E. S. Hochman, *Architects of Fortune, Mies van der Rohe and the Third Reich* (New York, 1989), p. 189.
15 Sudjic, *The Edifice Complex*, p. 30.
16 F. Spotts, *Hitler and the Power of Aesthetics* (London, 2002).
17 D. Thomas, 'From Art to Hate', *Newsweek* (2 December 2002).
18 Richie, *Faust's Metropolis*, p. 468.

13 Cyrus with Golden Caviar: Persepolis Revisited

1 J. Lowe et al., *Celebration at Persepolis* (Geneva, 1971), extract in P. Clawson and M. Rubin, *Eternal Iran* (London, 2005), p. 78.
2 The Cyrus cylinder was actually excavated in Babylonia and brought to Persepolis. It contains the proclamations of Cyrus written in cuneiform and covering a variety of subjects relating to the proper governance of an empire. It confirms that the founder of the Persian Empire had been a wise ruler and that the early success of the empire was in large part attributable to his actions. This was of great value to the shah as it depicted the ancient Persian Empire in the most positive way.
3 P. Kriwaczek, *In Search of Zarathustra* (London, 2002), p. 171.
4 M. Axworthy, *Iran, Empire of the Mind* (London, 2008), p. 256.

14 'Cities and Thrones and Powers'

1 Rudyard Kipling, 'Cities and Thrones and Powers', *Puck of Pook's Hill* (London, 1906).
2 W. Dalrymple, *City of Djinns* (London, 1993), p. 82.
3 D. Sudjic, *The Edifice Complex: How the Rich and Powerful – and their Architects – Shape the World* (London, 2006), p. 21.

15 After Empire: Post-imperial Symbols of Power

1 *Metropolis* was a film directed by Fritz Lang in 1926. It presents a modern nightmare vision of a highly stratified society. In a fantastic futuristic city the workers toiling below ground have bleak and mechanistic lives while a small elite above enjoy lives of ease and pleasure. Eventually this was all destroyed by human refusal to accept such a tyrannical situation. Ceauşescu's Romanian dictatorship was brought to an end in much the same way and for similar reasons.
2 Ulaanbataar replaced Karakorum as the capital of Mongolia in the nineteenth century. Its location reflected Russian penetration southwards along the most direct route from Siberia into northern China. It became an important centre for Russian trade and resulted in a steady increase in Russian influence. This eventually led to Mongolia moving from the Chinese into the Russian sphere.
3 Large numbers of Mongolians live in Inner Mongolia, which remained part of China when the Mongolian People's Republic – Outer Mongolia – attained its independence. In line with the policy of the relatively liberal treatment of minorities – so long as they did not engage in anti-Chinese activities – Inner Mongolia was allowed by the Chinese to keep its own language, culture and history. As a result, Inner Mongolia enjoyed a far more liberal regime than that which existed in the Mongolian People's

Republic itself under Choibalsan and his successors. When the communist government came to an end in the Mongolian People's Republic the Inner Mongolians' knowledge of their history and culture greatly assisted the Republic in regaining its own national identity.

4 North Korea, officially the Democratic People's Republic of Korea, was formed from the Soviet zone after the partition of the country in 1945. Professing communism, it was from the outset aggressive, one of its main policy objectives being the reunification of the country as a communist state. In 1950 it launched a full-scale invasion of South Korea and so began the Korean War. North Korea was supported unofficially by the communist world while the South was in general supported by the West under the guise of the United Nations. The war went on for three years and ended in stalemate. An armistice was signed and the 38th Parallel border between the two Koreas was re-established.

5 From early in its history, Juche became the official political philosophy of North Korea. Invented by Kim Il-Sung, it is based on a combination of communism, nationalism and self-reliance.

6 The Museum of Lenin in Tashkent was opened in 1970 as part of the great celebrations that took place throughout the Soviet Union in that year to commemorate the 100th anniversary of the birth of Lenin. The Uzbek capital was one of the main centres of the celebrations which were intended to demonstrate the way in which Marxist-Leninist communism had triumphed in Soviet Central Asia.

7 Karimov is not himself an Uzbek, any more than Stalin was a Russian or Hitler a German. This did not stop any of these dictators from hailing the greatness of their adopted countries and of themselves as incarnating this greatness.

8 Akmolinsk was founded in 1830 as a Russian *ostrog*. Its origins were therefore similar to those of Moscow. The meaning of the name chosen for the new capital is uncertain. One suggestion is that it comes from the Kazak 'White Mountain'. However, it is more likely to be derived from the old Persian *astane*, meaning 'royal porte'. This suggests an interesting resemblance to the 'Porte' which was a symbol of the power of the Ottoman Empire.

9 This massive skyscraper is 381 m high and has 102 floors. It is built in the art deco style favoured at the time and rapidly became an American cultural icon.

10 F. Riesenberg and A. Alland, *Portrait of New York* (New York, 1939).

11 G. Moorhouse, *Imperial City: The Rise and Rise of New York* (London, 1988).

12 While a number of large cities in Germany fulfil the function of regional capitals, Frankfurt has moved into the position of being the country's major economic hub. As well as being the headquarters of the Bundesbank, the city also has the Federal Audit Office and the country's principal airport. It is also the location of the German Library and the National Archives and is the country's most important publishing centre.

13 Hong Kong was actually a British Crown Colony but by the late twentieth century it had attained a high level of self-government. In 1997 it reverted to Chinese rule and, despite becoming part of China, the Chinese government has prudently allowed it to retain much of its independence, especially in the conduct of business and financial affairs.

14 G. Parker, 'The Globalization of the City-state', in *Sovereign City* (London, 2004), pp. 213–24.

15 Parker, 'The Ancient Greek *Polis*', ibid., pp. 28–46.

BIBLIOGRAPHY

Axworthy, M., Iran, Empire of the Mind (London, 2008)

Barea, I., Vienna: Legend and Reality (London, 1992)

Bernier, F., Travels in the Mogul Empire [1670], ed. A. Constable and V. A. Smith (Oxford, 1934)

Beveridge, A. S., trans., Memoirs of Babur (London, 1922)

Braudel, F., The Mediterranean in the Ancient World (London, 2001)

——, The Mediterranean and the Mediterranean World in the Age of Philip II, 2 vols (London, 1972)

Browning, R., The Byzantine Empire (London, 1980)

Calvert, A. F., An Historical and Descriptive Account of the Spanish Royal Palace, Monastery and Mausoleum (London, 1911)

Clawson, P., and M. Rubin, Eternal Iran (London, 2005)

Cornish, V., The Great Capitals (London, 1923)

Cotterell, A., The Imperial Capitals of China (London, 2007)

Curzon, N., Frontiers, The Romanes Lecture (Oxford, 1907)

Dalrymple, W., City of Djinns (London, 1993)

——, 'The Rubble of the Raj', The Times (13 November 2004), Arts, pp. 18–19

Dorn, F., The Forbidden City (New York, 1970)

Elliott, J. H., Imperial Spain, 1469–1716 (London, 1990)

Farr, M., Berlin! Berlin! Its Culture and its Times (London, 1992)

Fergusson, J., History of Indian and Eastern Architecture (London, 1910)

Fest, J., Not Me: Memoirs of a German Childhood, trans. M. Chalmers (London, 2012)

Fisher, H.A.L., A History of Europe (London, 1977)

Forbis, W. H., Fall of the Peacock Throne (New York and London, 1980)

Friedrich, T., Hitler's Berlin: Abused City (New Haven and London, 2012)

Gibbon, E., The Decline and Fall of the Roman Empire, vol. III [1781] (London, 1995)

Gillingham, P., 'The Macartney Embassy to China, 1792–94', History Today, XLIII (November 1993), pp. 23–34

Gloag, J., The Architectural Interpretation of History (London, 1975)

Goblet, Y. M., The Twilight of Treaties (London, 1936)

Hibbert, C., Cities and Civilisations (London, 1987)

Hicks, J., *The Persians* (New York, 1975)

Hitler's Table Talk, 1941–44, ed. M. Borman, intro. H. Trevor-Roper (Oxford, 1988)

Hochman, E. S., *Architects of Fortune, Mies van der Rohe and the Third Reich* (New York, 1989)

Hughes, L., *Russia in the Age of Peter the Great* (New Haven and London, 1998)

Hunczak, T., ed., *Russian Imperialism from Ivan the Great to the Revolution* (New Brunswick, NJ, 1974)

Keay, J., *A History of India* (London, 2000)

Kelly, L., *St Petersburg* (London, 1981)

Kotkin, J., *The City: A Global History* (London, 2005)

Kriwaczek, P., *In Search of Zarathustra* (London, 2002)

Lattimore, O., and E. Lattimore, *Silks, Spices and Empire: Asia Seen through the Eyes of its Discoverers* (London, 1975)

Loveday, H., 'Ferdusi and the Shahnameh', in *The Odyssey Illustrated Guide to Iran* (Hong Kong, 1997)

Ludwig, E., *The Mediterranean: Saga of a Sea* (London, 1943)

MacGregor, N., *A History of the World in 100 Objects* (London, 2010)

Mackinder, H., 'The Geographical Pivot of History', *Geographical Journal*, XXIII/4 (1904), pp. 421–37

——, *Democratic Ideals and Reality: A Study in the Politics of Reconstruction* (London, 1919)

Mango, C., *Byzantium: The Empire of the New Rome* (London, 1980)

Mansel, P., *Constantinople: City of the World's Desire, 1453–1924* (London, 2006)

The Travels of Marco Polo the Venetian, ed. John Masefield (London, 1911)

Marozzi, J., *Tamerlane: Sword of Islam, Conqueror of the World* (London, 2005)

Moorhouse, G., *Apples in the Snow: A Journey to Samarkand* (London, 1991)

——, *Imperial City: The Rise and Rise of New York* (London, 1988)

Morenz, S., *Egyptian Religion* (London, 1973)

Morris, A.E.J., *History of Urban Form before the Industrial Revolution* (London, 1996)

Morris, J., *A Writer's World: Travels, 1950–2000* (London, 2003)

Morris, J., with S. Winchester, *Stones of Empire: The Buildings of the Raj* (Oxford, 1986)

Mumford, L., *The City in History* (London, 1975)

Nicholson, L., *The Red Fort, Delhi* (London, 1989)

Parker, G., *Sovereign City* (London, 2004)

——, *Western Geopolitical Thought in the 20th Century* (London, 1985)

Panicucci, A., *The Life and Times of Louis XIV*, trans. C. J. Richards (London, 1965)

Pattee, R., *Portugal and the Portuguese World* (Milwaukee, 1957)

Pevsner, N., *An Outline of European Architecture* (London, 1978)

Peyrefitte, A., *The Collision of Two Civilisations: The British Expedition to China, 1792–94*, trans. J. Rothschild (London, 1993)

Raeff, M., *Understanding Imperial Russia*, trans. A. Goldhammer (New York, 1984)

Ratchnevsky, P., *Genghis Khan: His Life and Legacy*, trans. T. N. Haining (Oxford, 1991)

Richie, A., Faust's Metropolis: A History of Berlin (London, 1998)

Riesenberg, F., and A. Alland, Portrait of New York (New York, 1939)

Rürup, R., Topography of Terror, trans. W. T. Angress (Berlin, 2001)

Saramago, J., Journey to Portugal, trans. A. Hopkinson and N. Caistor (London, 2000)

Schneider, W., Babylon is Everywhere: The City as Man's Fate, trans. I. Sammet and J. Oldenburg (London, 1960)

Seward, D., The Bourbon Kings of France (London, 1976)

Sharp, R. N., The Inscriptions in Old Persian Cuneiform of the Achaemenian Emperors, Central Council of the Celebrations of the 25th Century of the Foundation of the Iranian Empire (Tehran, 1971)

Spear, P., Delhi (Oxford, 1945)

Spotts, F., Hitler and the Power of Aesthetics (London, 2002)

Steeds, O., 'The Hidden Grave of History's Greatest Warrior', Newsweek (10 December 2012)

Sudjic, D., The Edifice Complex: How the Rich and Powerful – and their Architects – Shape the World (London, 2006)

Toynbee, A., Cities on the Move (London, 1970)

——, A Study of History (Oxford, 1954)

Ure, J., The Trail of Tamerlane (London, 1980)

Voyce, A., Moscow and the Roots of Russian Culture (Newton Abbot, 1972)

de Waal, E., The Hare with Amber Eyes: A Hidden Inheritance (London, 2011)

Yan, V., Jenghiz-Khan, trans. L. E. Britton (London, 1943)

ACKNOWLEDGEMENTS

I wish to record my thanks to those who have helped me directly and indirectly in the writing of this book. My thanks to the Government of India for the award of the Aneurin Bevan Fellowship which has enabled me to travel widely in that country. Also to the British Council for awards which have enabled me to travel in other parts of Asia. The University of Birmingham has always been cooperative in supporting my research in a number of European and Asian countries.

My thanks to Ben Hayes, Commissioning Editor at Reaktion Books, who has devoted much time to this book and whose readily given advice has resulted in many improvements. Also to the editor Aimee Selby who has seen the book through the production stages and has been meticulous in ensuring that everything was in good order.

Most of all I wish to record my indebtedness to Brenda, my wife. From the outset she has been an active participant in the writing of this book and her help and advice throughout has been invaluable. She has done important research on a number of particular subjects and has also compiled the index. She contributed greatly in the shaping of the book and has been my partner throughout the whole project.

PHOTO ACKNOWLEDGEMENTS

The author and publishers wish to express their thanks to the below sources of illustrative material and/or permission to reproduce it.

Copyright © the author: pp. 20, 22, 23, 25, 26, 36, 38 43, 45, 55, 63, 76, 78, 79, 88, 90, 101, 105, 108, 109, 115, 125, 148, 152, 154, 155, 162, 180, 181, 203, 217; © The Trustees of the British Museum, London: p. 10; from *Indian Railways Handbook* (1935): p. 179; from *Mongolian Architecture* (Ulaanbaatar, 1988): p. 65; copyright Musée National des Châteaux de Versailles et de Trianon, Paris: p. 135.

INDEX